"*Words without Walls* will motivate new readers to rea__ ___ _____ __w writers to write. The stories here are human and painful; the telling itself is direct, intimate, and sharp. I can almost imagine the conversations this book was created to enliven, and the new stories and poems that will be born."

—JUDITH TANNENBAUM, author of *Disguised as a Poem: My Years Teaching Poetry at San Quentin*

"*Words without Walls* is filled with the descendant voices of García Lorca and Jean Genet, of Voltaire and Akhmatova. These writers know that incarcerated voices, marginalized voices, and exiled voices are sacred guides to resisting everything that makes us less human than we are capable of being."

—DARRELL BOURQUE, author of *Megan's Guitar and Other Poems from Acadie*

"If, as William Blake says, 'Prisons are built with bricks of law,' then this searing, delving, heartbreaking, and healing collection, composed in diverse conditions and shared in a thousand lightless places, is potently unlawful. Featuring an array of America's most admired writers along with new voices speaking out bravely, this book sings with a power no walls can quell: the power of witness. *Words without Walls* is a unique and necessary tool—both balm and weapon—for those of us teaching, reading, writing, and listening in the world beyond the academic pale."

—PHILIP BRADY, editor at Etruscan Press

"In the six years I ran a prison workshop, I would have welcomed a broad collection of work like this. These brilliantly selected pieces would have helped the inmates I worked with more easily see themselves as part of a community of people whose voicelessness can be the cruelest aspect of incarceration. *Words without Walls* offers a range of writers across genres, holding a lens to human consequence and the incredible capacity of people to endure—and even rise again."

—STEPHEN PETT

"Words in spaces of forced confinement and places of recovery, which often squelch our humanity, become connective fibers, not only to the world removed but most importantly to the self who fights against intense hurdles to bring those words, their truth, to the surface. *Words without Walls* is an amazing collection, a powerful tool to inspire and empower all people to let their voices be heard."

—KYES STEVENS, founder and director, Alabama Prison Arts and Education Project

WORDS
WITHOUT
WALLS

WORDS
WITHOUT
WALLS

WRITERS ON ADDICTION,
VIOLENCE, AND INCARCERATION

EDITED BY
Sheryl St. Germain
and Sarah Shotland

TRINITY UNIVERSITY PRESS ⊘ San Antonio

PUBLISHED BY TRINITY UNIVERSITY PRESS
San Antonio, Texas 78212

Cover design by Anne Boston
Book design by BookMatters, Berkeley, California
Cover art: ©iStock.com/Viorika Prikhodko Photography, ©iStock.com/
Purdue9394

Trinity University Press strives to produce its books using methods and
materials in an environmentally sensitive manner. We favor working
with manufacturers that practice sustainable management of all natural
resources, produce paper using recycled stock, and manage forests with
the best possible practices for people, biodiversity, and sustainability. The
press is a member of the Green Press Initiative, a nonprofit program dedicated to supporting publishers in their efforts to reduce their impacts on
endangered forests, climate change, and forest-dependent communities.

The paper used in this publication meets the minimum requirements of
the American National Standard for Information Sciences—Permanence
of Paper for Printed Library Materials, ANSI 39.48-1992.

CIP data on file at the Library of Congress

ISBN 978-1-59534-255-3 paperback
ISBN 978-1-59534-256-0 ebook

19 18 17 16 15 | 5 4 3 2 1

. . . for the first time, I had something to lose—my chance to read, to write, a way to live with dignity and meaning.

—Jimmy Santiago Baca

CONTENTS

Fiction

Drama

EDITORS' INTRODUCTION

Alternative spaces: a shorthand phrase for jails, prisons, rehab centers, shelters, community centers in urban areas, spaces where any of us might land to wait out a trial, serve a sentence, recover from an abusive situation, or work through withdrawal. In other words, places where we learn to restart our lives, places where the heart and mind often find themselves more open and vulnerable, and where writing can help give shape to the chaotic and unspeakable.

We are familiar with these spaces because we enter them each week to lead creative writing workshops for a program known as Words Without Walls, after which this anthology is named. Words Without Walls, housed at Chatham University in Pittsburgh, trains MFA students to go into jails, prisons, and rehabilitation facilities to teach creative writing. The program also sponsors a weekly community workshop for those released or out of rehab who wish to continue writing.

The poems, stories, essays, and scripts in this anthology, written by some of America's finest creative writers, are pieces the teachers from Words Without Walls have used successfully over the years to inspire and model writing for their students. Here are brave poems that make the heart race, passionate stories, essays, and scripts that speak directly of some of the most difficult human experiences—pieces that dare to say the thing that most scares us. These are not crossword poems or puzzle stories but rather essential pieces that inspire the reader to reach deep and explore his or her own dark places.

It has often been noted that the United States spends far more money on incarceration than it does on education. Budget cuts in education have caused creative programs of all kinds to fall by the wayside, and many people have never had the opportunity for exposure to or engagement in the contemporary arts. Those whose lives are affected by these factors number in the millions. And yet few publications such as this one are curated for them.

Our goal in creating this anthology has been to gather voices that speak intimately, with a sense of urgency and immediacy, to those who read and write outside the walls of the traditional classroom. We have compiled these poems, essays, stories, and scripts to connect with educators and students who come together in largely anonymous rooms to discuss and create writings that speak to vital yet often unvoiced aspects of our lives. The rooms are found in a variety of spaces—they are almost endless—but include jails and prisons, rehabilitation centers, halfway houses, hospitals, transitional housing facilities, and shelters. This collection also has a place in the innovative college classroom, especially those whose undergraduate students might be considered at risk or whose graduate students might wish to teach creative writing in alternative spaces. Our hope is that *Words without Walls* will serve as a resource for writers who work and teach in these spaces and as a tool for the students they teach.

For the past six years we have worked in these spaces through a creative outreach program also called Words Without Walls. Housed in the MFA program at Chatham University in Pittsburgh, Words Without Walls trains MFA students to teach creative writing to inmates in the Allegheny County Jail (ACJ), the State Correctional Institution in Pittsburgh, and Sojourner House, an in-patient rehabilitation center for mothers and their children. We've also, throughout our careers, taught creative writing at a state women's prison, a veterans' hospital, a transitional housing facility for homeless veterans, shelters for victims of domestic violence, drop-out recovery centers, and after-school programs for at-risk youth.

We have seen in these spaces the strength of language to connect people, to guide them to reflect on the past and reimagine the future, to confront difficult and complicated truths, and to provide momentary respites from pain and regret. It's not an exaggeration to say that the power gained in these spaces through the practice of creative writing has been transformational for both student and teacher. Mia Tuzlic, one of our students from the ACJ and Sojourner House, whose affecting essay about overdosing is included in the anthology, tells us that it was through writing that her "knotted life slowly started to untangle itself." "Today," she writes, "I have a voice, and people actually would like to hear my story."

We have witnessed firsthand how reading a powerful piece of writing can inspire bravery and insight in our students' own work, both on the page and in their daily lives. We have seen in the jails and prisons and rehab centers of North America the same intense desire to write and share one's writing that we find, for example, in the Russian poet Irina Ratushinskaya, who scratched her poems on bars of soap in a Gulag shower to help her remember them, or in the Turkish poet Nazim Hikmet, who smuggled bits of poetry out of jail in the clothing of friends who came to visit.

This anthology brings together the most successful pieces of writing we've used in our nontraditional classrooms, and it also includes a few exceptional pieces of writing from our students in ACJ and Sojourner House. When selecting pieces to include, we looked, first of all, for immediacy—writing that captures the reader quickly because of its content or style. We looked for pieces able to craft a sense of intimacy on the page—pieces that demonstrate the power of words to cut through circumstance and hit the gut. We've generally chosen brief works, due to the nature of the nontraditional space and reader. Shorter works, or excerpts of longer works, allow for more time to discuss and explore. We've discovered our students' lives are actually quite busy, despite what can appear to outsiders as endless time. They are often engaged in complicated legal cases, intensive therapy, repairing relationships, and finding employment or housing. For these reasons, much of our reading is done within the classroom itself.

We also chose what we considered to be masterful pieces—from both established and emerging writers—because our students are quick to catch the sentence that doesn't ring true, the line that obscures rather than illuminates, the ending that leaves a reader wanting. Perhaps even more than in the traditional classroom, these spaces and students demand writing that nourishes and challenges the imagination and spirit. We chose contemporary writing because we wanted pieces that spoke to present-day experiences, and we wanted models of voices students might try on in their own writing. We chose pieces that felt essential, stories and poems written to be shared, as Pablo Neruda wrote of poetry, "by all our vast, incredible, extraordinary family of humanity."

In addition to organizing the anthology by genre, we've also included a thematic table of contents, focusing on themes we found to be most relevant to our students' lives. Choosing works that speak to their circumstances opens the door for discussions of craft and style but also allows for meaningful discussion of content and personal situations. Our students, while from diverse backgrounds, often share experiences that include addiction, incarceration, and familial violence. Exposing them to writers such as Dorothy Allison and Greg Bottoms, for example, who write about families for whom violence is a way of life, or Natalie Kenvin and Toi Derricotte, whose pieces speak of violence against women, gives our populations robust mentors as well as permission to write about these difficult issues themselves.

It was also important to us that we include writings by those who have spent time in prison themselves or wrote powerfully about their own experiences with drug and alcohol abuse. Jimmy Santiago Baca, Dwayne Betts, Ken Lamberton, and Etheridge Knight, among others, write poems and essays about time spent incarcerated. Eric Boyd, one of our ACJ alums, writes about the day he was released from jail; Stephon Hayes, another alum, about what he sees outside his jail window every day; and Terra Lynn evokes the experience of being put in solitary confinement.

In 2011 almost half of all prisoners in federal facilities were there for drug-related offenses. We include pieces here of many, including James Brown, Nick Flynn, and Ann Marlowe, who explore their own addiction and alcoholism. Others, such as Natalie Diaz, Scott Russell Sanders, and Christine Stroud, write of drug use by family and friends.

With 5 percent of the world population, the United States now has about 25 percent of the world's prison population. While stereotypes about those who are institutionalized remain, the truth is that as numbers continue to grow, the stereotypes ring less and less true. Women are now the fastest growing segment of the prison population. Drug treatment centers have been flooded with younger patients, many of whom are seeking help from prescription drugs rather than street drugs. Mandatory minimum sentencing means that more and more are incarcerated for nonviolent drug offenses. The wars we've engaged in have flooded the Veterans Affairs system with those transitioning into new lives.

We hope this volume can begin to bridge the gap between the traditional literary world and the millions of people whose voices and stories go unheard in the halls of academia.

While the themes we address above speak specifically to nontraditional spaces, we also wanted to include works inspired by more universal themes, for example, home and family, love, sex, or body image, the kind of material with which we all have a lifetime of experience. Because this will be a dark period in the lives of many who will make use of this anthology, we thought it important that they have access to writing that evokes the power of kindness and gratitude, as the works of Naomi Shihab Nye and Derek Walcott do, as well as writing infused with a vibrant sense of humor, such as the poetry of Tim Seibles.

Because those who find themselves incarcerated or in recovery represent a vast group of people, we have sought out a diverse group of writers from varied geographies, cultures, and classes. Bonnie Jo Campbell, for example, gives voice to the hidden grit of the Midwest, while Jessica Kinnison sings a southern story, and Sapphire brings alive blocks of Harlem. Ken Lamberton writes from the perspective of white middle-class America; John Wideman comes from a poor black community in Pittsburgh; Natalie Diaz's poems reflect her Mojave heritage; Jimmy Santiago Baca, Chicano and Apache.

In his essay "The Caging of America," Adam Gopnik writes: "For most privileged, professional people, the experience of confinement is a mere brush, encountered after a kid's arrest, say. For a great many poor people in America, particularly poor black men, prison is a destination that braids through an ordinary life, much as high school and college do for rich white ones. More than half of all black men without a high-school diploma go to prison at some time in their lives." Upward of 75 percent of those we teach in the ACJ are black, and we have sought to include a large percentage of moving and masterful writers of color for this reason.

As educators and artists whose day jobs involve teaching in the academy, we often find ourselves in spaces that inherently value the work we produce. We may be met with audiences who have had the privilege of art history classes or exposure to literature and philosophy. But the professionalization of literature and the teaching of creative writing in the university has too often veered toward elitism; the academy, especially literature departments, have often shied away from audiences who might demand more from art or literature than theory or existence for its own sake. The following comments about art by Alain de Botton, from *Art as Therapy*, apply equally to creative writing:

> What if art has a purpose that can be defined and discussed in plain terms? Art can be a tool, and we need to focus more clearly on what kind of tool it is—and what good it can do for us. Like other tools, art has the power to extend our capacities beyond those that nature has originally endowed us with . . . art is a therapeutic medium that can help guide, exhort and console its viewers, enabling them to become better versions of themselves.

We have both experienced the potent effect creative expression has on the personal lives of our students. We often say to each other—and to whoever else will listen—that our time at the jail or the prison or Sojourner House is the best time of our week. If it seems odd that we enjoy being in jail or prison or rehab centers, it is, in part, because these spaces ask us to bring more of ourselves to the present moment. They ask us to reveal more, not to hide behind the elevated language of the academy but instead to say it straight—to make clear the reasons we were drawn to writing in the first place. Why, for example, as young people, we were drawn to the peaceful solitude of a book. How journaling led to story making or how shaping a disturbing experience into a poem moved us toward healing and provided a safe space for reflection and more nuanced questioning.

Too often in MFA programs, we encourage graduate students to think solely about publication or accolades, recognition or teaching careers in academia. We hope that an anthology such as this one will encourage writers coming out of the academy to reach out to those who might never enter the university but who have important songs to sing and potent stories to tell.

Wole Soyinka wrote forty years ago, in solitary confinement, that "creation is admission of great loneliness." We find that, in these communal spaces, our loneliness is lessened, our vulnerability exposed, our honesty tested, and when we reveal ourselves, our students, too, share the whispering corners of their minds.

In his classic book *Pedagogy of the Oppressed*, Paulo Freire writes that education should be about the practice of freedom, and we hope that this volume contributes to that theory of educational practice: That poetry and prose can serve as tools of freedom. Freedom from endless regret or replaying of the past, freedom from physical confinement, freedom from habit, freedom from the monochromatic narratives we may have been taught about our own lives. We acknowledge that creative writing does not solve every problem, especially not the practical problems so many of our students face: finding employment, chemical dependency, familial violence, and a personal history of broken relationships. But we believe that words can open a dialogue with the self and the greater community. Words can begin to heal the pain of the past by illuminating the darker corners of silence. Words can begin the process of acknowledging truth—seeing it plain and straight in the lines of a notebook. Words can shape a letter to a child, conjure a lost friend, re-member and redefine the self. Words are tools to dig, to shatter, to bear witness, to plant, to build.

We hope this anthology is a useful tool, one that will be passed through cell blocks and hospital corridors, one that can find its way into the hands of readers hungry for voices that echo their experiences, that remind them of their pasts and invite them to dream new futures. Many pieces included here are graphic and dark, but by virtue of their being written down, spoken, and shared, they are inherently hopeful. They are pieces that remind us, educators and students alike, that we turn to the written word when our spoken voices have been silenced, when we are too afraid to say the thing aloud and instead must first feel it come through our hand and see it on the page. They remind us that when we share our truth, we become part of something bigger than ourselves. We become part of a chorus of voices searching for words that will move us toward understanding, some measure of intimacy and connection in what sometimes feels like an isolated world. We hope the pieces included here will inspire writers, wherever they are, to write the words vital to their own lives.

NONFICTION

Coming into Language

JIMMY SANTIAGO BACA

On weekend graveyard shifts at St. Joseph's Hospital I worked the emergency room, mopping up pools of blood and carting plastic bags stuffed with arms, legs, and hands to the outdoor incinerator. I enjoyed the quiet, away from the screams of shotgunned, knifed, and mangled kids writhing on gurneys outside the operating rooms. Ambulance sirens shrieked and squad car lights reddened the cool nights, flashing against the hospital walls: gray—red, gray—red. On slow nights I would lock the door of the administration office, search the reference library for a book on female anatomy and, with my feet propped on the desk, leaf through the illustrations, smoking my cigarette. I was seventeen.

One night my eye was caught by a familiar-looking word on the spine of a book. The title was *450 Years of Chicano History in Pictures*. On the cover were black-and-white photos: Padre Hidalgo exhorting Mexican peasants to revolt against the Spanish dictators; Anglo vigilantes hanging two Mexicans from a tree; a young Mexican woman with rifle and ammunition belts crisscrossing her breast; César Chávez and field workers marching for fair wages; Chicano railroad workers laying creosote ties; Chicanas laboring at machines in textile factories; Chicanas picketing and hoisting boycott signs.

From the time I was seven, teachers had been punishing me for not knowing my lessons by making me stick my nose in a circle chalked on the blackboard. Ashamed of not understanding and fearful of asking questions, I dropped out of school in the ninth grade. At seventeen I still didn't know how to read, but those pictures confirmed my identity. I stole the book that night, stashing it for safety under the slop-sink until I got off work. Back at my boarding house, I showed the book to friends. All of us were amazed; this book told us we were alive. We, too, had defended ourselves with our fists against hostile Anglos, gasping for breath in fights with the policemen who outnumbered us. The book reflected back to us our struggle in a way that made us proud.

Most of my life I felt like a target in the crosshairs of a hunter's rifle. When strangers and outsiders questioned me I felt the hang-rope tighten around my neck and the trapdoor creak beneath my feet. There was nothing so humiliating as being unable to express myself, and my inarticulateness increased my sense of jeopardy, of being endangered. I felt intimidated and vulnerable, ridiculed and scorned. Behind a mask of humility, I seethed with mute rebellion.

Before I was eighteen, I was arrested on suspicion of murder after refusing to explain a deep cut on my forearm. With shocking speed I found myself handcuffed to a chain gang of inmates and bused to a holding facility to await trial. There I met men, prisoners, who read aloud to each other the works of Neruda, Paz, Sabines, Nemerov, and Hemingway. Never had I felt such freedom as in that dormitory. Listening to the words of these writers, I felt that invisible threat from without lessen—my sense of teetering on a rotting plank over swamp water where famished alligators clapped their horny snouts for my blood. While I listened to the words of the poets, the alligators slumbered powerless in their lairs. Their language was the magic that could liberate me from myself, transform me into another person, transport me to other places far away.

And when they closed the books, these Chicanos, and went into their own Chicano language, they made barrio life come alive for me in the fullness of its vitality. I began to learn my own language, the bilingual words and phrases explaining to me my place in the universe. Every day I felt like the paper boy taking delivery of the latest news of the day.

Months later I was released, as I had suspected I would be. I had been guilty of nothing but shattering the windshield of my girlfriend's car in a fit of rage.

Two years passed. I was twenty now, and behind bars again. The federal marshals had failed to provide convincing evidence to extradite me to Arizona on a drug charge, but still I was being held. They had ninety days to prove I was guilty. The only evidence against me was that my girlfriend had been at the scene of the crime with my driver's license in her purse. They had to come up with something else. But there was nothing else. Eventually they negotiated a deal with the actual drug dealer, who took the stand against me. When the judge hit me with a million-dollar bail, I emptied my pockets on his booking desk: twenty-six cents.

One night in my third month in the county jail, I was mopping the floor in front of the booking desk. Some detectives had kneed an old drunk and handcuffed him to the booking bars. His shrill screams raked my nerves like a hacksaw on bone, the desperate protest of his dignity against their inhumanity. But the detectives just laughed as he tried to rise and kicked him to his knees. When they went to the bathroom to pee and the desk attendant walked to the file cabinet to pull the arrest record, I shot my arm through the bars, grabbed one of the attendant's university textbooks, and tucked it in my overalls. It was the only way I had of protesting.

It was late when I returned to my cell. Under my blanket I switched on a pen flashlight and opened the thick book at random, scanning the pages. I could hear the jailer making his rounds on the other tiers. The jangle of his keys and the sharp click of his boot heels intensified my solitude. Slowly I enunciated the words . . . p-o-n-d, ri-pple. It scared me that I had been reduced to this to find comfort. I always had thought reading a waste of time, that nothing could be gained by it. Only by action, by moving out into the world and confronting and challenging the obstacles, could one learn anything worth knowing.

Even as I tried to convince myself that I was merely curious, I became so absorbed in how the sounds created music in me and happiness, I forgot where I was. Memories began to quiver in me, glowing with a strange but familiar intimacy in which I found refuge. For a while, a deep sadness overcame me, as if I had chanced on a long-lost friend and mourned the years of separation. But soon the heartache of having missed so much of life, that which had numbed me since I was a child, gave way, as if a grave illness lifted itself from me and I was cured, innocently believing in the beauty of life again. I stumblingly repeated the author's name as I fell asleep, saying it over and over in the dark: Words-worth, Words-worth.

Before long my sister came to visit me, and I joked about taking her to a place called Kubla Khan and getting her a blind date with this *vato*

named Coleridge who lived on the seacoast and was *malías* on mor-
phine. When I asked her to make a trip into enemy territory to buy me
a grammar book, she said she couldn't. Bookstores intimidated her,
because she, too, could neither read nor write.

Days later, with a stub pencil I whittled sharp with my teeth, I
propped a Red Chief notebook on my knees and wrote my first words.
From that moment, a hunger for poetry possessed me.

Until then, I had felt as if I had been born into a raging ocean where
I swam relentlessly, flailing my arms in hope of rescue, of reaching a
shoreline I never sighted. Never solid ground beneath me, never a resting place. I had lived with only the desperate hope to stay afloat—that
and nothing more. But when at last I wrote my first words on the page,
I felt an island rising beneath my feet like the back of a whale. As more
and more words emerged, I could finally rest: I had a place to stand for
the first time in my life. The island grew, with each page, into a conti-
nent inhabited by people I knew and mapped with the life I lived.

I wrote about it all—about people I had loved or hated, about the bru-
talities and ecstasies of my life. And, for the first time, the child in me
who had witnessed and endured unspeakable terrors cried out not just
in impotent despair but with the power of language. Suddenly, through
language, through writing, my grief and my joy could be shared with
anyone who would listen. And I could do this all alone; I could do it
anywhere. I was no longer a captive of demons eating away at me, no
longer a victim of other people's mockery and loathing that had made
me clench my fist white with rage and grit my teeth to silence. Words
now pleaded back with the bleak lucidity of hurt. They were wrong,
those others, and now I could say it.

Through language I was free. I could respond, escape, indulge;
embrace or reject earth or the cosmos. I was launched on an endless
journey without boundaries or rules, in which I could salvage the floating fragments of my past or be born anew in the spontaneous ignition
of understanding some heretofore concealed aspect of myself. Each
word steamed with the hot lava juices of my primordial making, and
I crawled out of stanzas dripping with birth-blood, reborn and freed
from the chaos of my life. The child in the dark room of my heart, who
had never been able to find or reach the light switch, flicked it on now;
and I found in the room a stranger, myself, who had waited so many

years to speak again. My words struck in me lightning crackles of elation and thunderhead storms of grief.

When I had been in the county jail longer than anyone else, I was made a trustee. One morning, after a fist fight, I went to the unlocked and unoccupied office used for lawyer-client meetings, to think. The bare white room with its fluorescent tube lighting seemed to expose and illuminate my dark and worthless life. And yet, for the first time, I had something to lose—my chance to read, to write; a way to live with dignity and meaning that had opened for me when I stole that scuffed, second-hand book about the Romantic poets. In prison, the abscess had been lanced.

"I will never do any work in this prison system as long as I am not allowed to get my G.E.D." That's what I told the reclassification panel. The captain flicked off the tape recorder. He looked at me hard and said, "You'll never walk outta here alive. Oh, you'll work, put a copper penny on that, you'll work."

After that interview I was confined to deadlock maximum security in a subterranean dungeon, with ground-level chicken-wired windows painted gray. Twenty-three hours a day I was in that cell. I kept sane by borrowing books from the other cons on the tier. Then, just before Christmas, I received a letter from Harry, a charity house samaritan who doled out hot soup to the homeless in Phoenix. He had picked my name from a list of cons who had no one to write to them. I wrote back asking for a grammar book, and a week later received one of Mary Baker Eddy's treatises on salvation and redemption, with Spanish and English on opposing pages. Pacing my cell all day and most of each night, I grappled with grammar until I was able to write a long true-romance confession for a con to send to his pen pal. He paid me with a pack of smokes. Soon I had a thriving barter business, exchanging my poems and letters for novels, commissary pencils, and writing tablets.

One day I tore two flaps from the cardboard box that held all my belongings and punctured holes along the edge of each flap and along the border of a ream of state-issue paper. After I had aligned them to form a spine, I threaded the holes with a shoestring, and sketched on the cover a hummingbird fluttering above a rose. This was my first journal.

Whole afternoons I wrote, unconscious of passing time or whether it was day or night. Sunbursts exploded from the lead tip of my pencil, words that grafted me into awareness of who I was; peeled back to a burning core of bleak terror, an embryo floating in the image of water, I cracked out of the shell wide-eyed and insane. Trees grew out of the palms of my hands, the threatening otherness of life dissolved, and I became one with the air and sky, the dirt and the iron and concrete. There was no longer any distinction between the other and I. Language made bridges of fire between me and everything I saw. I entered into the blade of grass, the basketball, the con's eye and child's soul.

At night I flew. I conversed with floating heads in my cell and visited strange houses where lonely women brewed tea and rocked in wicker rocking chairs listening to sad Joni Mitchell songs.

Before long I was frayed like a rope carrying too much weight that suddenly snaps. I quit talking. Bars, walls, steel bunk, and floor bristled with millions of poem-making sparks. My face was no longer familiar to me. The only reality was the swirling cornucopia of images in my mind, the voices in the air. Midair a cactus blossom would appear, a snake-flame in blinding dance around it, stunning me like a guard's fist striking my neck from behind.

The prison administrators tried several tactics to get me to work. For six months, after the next monthly prison board review, they sent cons to my cell to hassle me. When the guard would open my cell door to let one of them in, I'd leap out and fight him—and get sent to thirty-day isolation. I did a lot of isolation time. But I honed my image-making talents in that sensory-deprived solitude. Finally they moved me to death row, and after that to "nut-run," the tier that housed the mentally disturbed.

As the months passed, I became more and more sluggish. My eyelids were heavy, I could no longer write or read. I slept all the time.

One day a guard took me out to the exercise field. For the first time in years I felt grass and earth under my feet. It was spring. The sun warmed my face as I sat on the bleachers watching the cons box and run, hit the handball, lift weights. Some of them stopped to ask how I was, but I found it impossible to utter a syllable. My tongue would not move, saliva drooled from the corners of my mouth. I had been so heavily medicated I could not summon the slightest gesture. Yet inside me a small voice cried out, I am fine! I am hurt now but I will come back! I am fine!

Back in my cell, for weeks I refused to eat. Styrofoam cups of urine and hot water were hurled at me. Other things happened. There were beatings, shock therapy, intimidation.

Later, I regained some clarity of mind. But there was a place in my heart where I had died. My life had compressed itself into an unbearable dread of being. The strain had been too much. I had stepped over that line where a human being has lost more than he can bear, where the pain is too intense, and he knows he is changed forever. I was now capable of killing, coldly and without feeling. I was empty, as I have never, before or since, known emptiness. I had no connection to this life.

But then, the encroaching darkness that began to envelop me forced me to re-form and give birth to myself again in the chaos. I withdrew even deeper into the world of language, cleaving the diamonds of verbs and nouns, plunging into the brilliant light of poetry's regenerative mystery. Words gave off rings of white energy, radar signals from powers beyond me that infused me with truth. I believed what I wrote because I wrote what was true. My words did not come from books or textual formulas but from a deep faith in the voice of my heart.

I had been steeped in self-loathing and rejected by everyone and everything—society, family, cons, God, and demons. But now I had become as the burning ember floating in darkness that descends on a dry leaf and sets flame to forests. The word was the ember and the forest was my life.

I was born a poet one noon, gazing at weeds and creosoted grass at the base of a telephone pole outside my grilled cell window. The words I wrote then sailed me out of myself, and I was transported and metamorphosed into the images they made. From the dirty brown blades of grass came bolts of electrical light that jolted loose my old self; through the top of my head that self was released and reshaped in the clump of scrawny grass. Through language I became the grass, speaking its language and feeling its green feelings and black root sensations. Earth was my mother and I bathed in sunshine. Minuscule speckles of sunlight passed through my green skin and metabolized in my blood.

Writing bridged my divided life of prisoner and free man. I wrote of the emotional butchery of prisons and of my acute gratitude for poetry. Where my blind doubt and spontaneous trust in life met, I discovered empathy and compassion. The power to express myself was a welcome storm rasping at tendril roots, flooding my soul's cracked dirt. Writing was water that cleansed the wound and fed the parched root of my heart.

I wrote to sublimate my rage, from a place where all hope is gone, from a madness of having been damaged too much, from a silence of killing rage. I wrote to avenge the betrayals of a lifetime, to purge the bitterness of injustice. I wrote with a deep groan of doom in my blood, bewildered and dumbstruck, from an indestructible love of life, to affirm breath and laughter and the abiding innocence of things. I wrote the way I wept, and danced, and made love.

Thirty Minutes

R. DWAYNE BETTS

Sixteen years hadn't even done a good job on my voice. It cracked in my head as I tried to explain away the police car driving my one hundred and twenty-six pounds to the Fairfax County Jail. Everything near enough for me to touch gleamed with the color of violence: the black of the deputy's holstered guns, the broken leather of the seat I sat on and the silver of the cuffs that held my hands before me in prayer. When I closed my eyes I thought about the way the gun felt in my palm. I tried to remember what caliber pistol it was but couldn't. It was automatic and weighed nothing in my palm, and I couldn't figure how something that weighed nothing could have me slumped in the back of a car driving me away from my life. My wrists almost slipped through cuffs that held me captive as jailhouse dangers swirled red in my head.

I want to tell you that I could talk tough, that I was going over every way I knew how to say fuck you. But I wasn't. There were titles of movies and books on my mind: *Shawshank Redemption; American Me; Blood In, Blood Out; Makes Me Wanna Holler; Racehoss; The Autobiography of Malcolm X*. Every movie or book I'd ever read about prison bled with violence, and I knew the list I was making in my head could go on forever. Stories of robbery, rape, murder, discrimination, and what it means to not be able to go home. Sixteen years old and I was headed to a jail cell, adding my name to the toll of black men behind bars. Not even old enough to buy liquor or cigarettes, but I knew I'd be stepping into the county jail in minutes and that my moms was at home somewhere crying.

When I tried to part my hands I thought about the violence, about how real it is when a cell door closes behind you at night. I thought about needing a knife, 'cause from what I knew everyone needed a knife. I stared at my shackled feet. I hadn't seen my Timberlands since the day I was arrested, three months earlier.

I was getting ready to learn what it meant to lock your thoughts inside of yourself and survive in a place governed by violence, a place where violence was a cloud of smoke you learned to breathe in or choked on. Sometimes there's a story that's been written again and again, sometimes a person finds himself with a story he thinks will be in vogue forever. The story is about redemption, about overcoming. A person finds that story and starts to write it, thinking it will do him some good to tell the world how it really was. That's not this story. This is about silence, and how in an eight-year period I met over a dozen people named Juvenile or Youngin or Shorty, all nicknames to tell the world that they were in prison as young boys, as children. We wore the names like badges of honor, because in a way, for some of us, it was all we had to guard us against the fear. And we were guilty and I was just like everyone else: I thought about the edge of a knife.

My world before incarceration was black and white. Suitland, Maryland, the closest thing to the black belt that I'd ever seen. And it wasn't just that there were no white people in my community, it was that as kids we always saw the white people around us as intruders or people looking to have power. Teachers, firefighters, cops, or the white folks we saw on buses and trains who we imagined driving into D.C. from their nice neighborhoods to work. One night at a mall in Springfield, Virginia, changed my world. It only took thirty minutes. Brandon and I walked into a mall that literally had more white people in it than I'd even seen at one time. And we had walked in looking for someone to make a victim. Both of us were in high school. We should have been thinking homework, basketball, and pretty girls. Driving to the jail brought the night in Springfield fresh to my memory. Somewhere between pulling out a pistol that fit nicely in the palm of my hand, tapping lightly on the window of a forest green Grand Prix and waking the sleeping middle-aged white man with the muzzle of the burner, I committed six felonies. It was February of 1996 and I was a high school junior. I'd never held a gun before and was an honor student who could almost remember every time the police had spoken to me, but I knew none of that mattered as my face pressed against the window of the cruiser.

I wore a sweater of swirling greens and oranges woven and layered as collage; a cheap imitation Gucci that I had buried long ago in my closet. I remember when my moms bought it. I begged for the sweater, thinking if it fooled me I would fool my friends. I was dead wrong. The first time I wore it to school six people joned on me, cut me up so bad that I dumped it under a rack of old clothes and books. It happened a year before I got locked up, when I was in tenth grade and impressing the finest girl in my chemistry class ruled every other ambition. The sweater resurfaced when I needed court clothes. My mother told me that I needed something nice to wear to court. The judges were always white. There may have been black judges, but I never saw or stood before one the entire time I trekked back and forth to court. The juvenile judge who watched me stand uncomfortable in the sweater I ended up wearing to the jail didn't care how I looked. He stared at the charges before me and agreed with the prosecutor to pass me over to adult court before I could speak. It was all policy, a formality that my lawyer knew about. He told me, "Don't worry. This was a formality I knew was coming. The law says that certain charges are automatically certifiable, and carjacking is one of them, but in Circuit Court the judge will have more discretion."

What he was really saying was that nothing I wore mattered. Clothes could hide me no more than days of smoking weed made people think I was built for running the streets. The law said the gun, the carjacking, the robbery all made it an argument we couldn't win. Three things that meant my past didn't matter and certification as an adult was automatic. It's like the car, the cuffs, the shackles, and even the drive were as good as guaranteed when I pulled a pistol on that sleeping white man.

All I had with me was my body and a black trash bag that an officer took from me as they led me to a bench in the corner. On my lips and in my head was the start of a new language defined by the way words changed meanings, all because I'd decided to make a man a victim. New words like *inmate*, *state number*, and *juvenile certification* had crept into my vocabulary. An *inmate* is what I'd become as soon as the deputies picked me up from the juvenile detention center. It meant that I was in the custody of the Fairfax County Jail, and the most important thing anyone needed to know about me was my *state number*. It was a five-digit number I soon learned meant more than my name. It said I was who I said I was whenever I walked around the jail with the band they attached to my arm.

At Landmark we weren't inmates, we were juvenile offenders, which was a nice way of saying black boy in jail from what I saw, because that's all we were at Landmark. Landmark Detention Center was a juvenile facility that housed boys and girls. Mostly the kids were in there for fighting or truancy or selling drugs. There was one white boy in there with us; everyone else was black. Four small units that were as secure as any prison. Everything was electronic and you could only move when told to. But you got to go to school, had to go to school, and the uniform was sweatpants and a T-shirt. That meant if you tried hard enough you could have imagined yourself at the extended camp. Unless of course you were me, given a single cell in the corner and note on your door that said no roommate because you were waiting to be transferred to the jail.

It didn't take long for me to move from inside the squad car to inside the jail. Voices jumped around me in a chaos that belongs to jails and prisons. The same officers who'd driven me to the jail were with me. "You know this jail isn't like the place we're taking you from. All you kids in there running around trying to be tough. Well, you're going where they say the tough guys are." The officer wanted to scare me. He was standing as I sat, looking down and probably imagining a scene from the nightly news of a gun-toting young black man gone crazy. He probably thought about the victim and what they say on TV about black boys who pull guns on people. Fear was a commodity everyone traded in. In three months I'd learned that everyone from lawyers to the judges to the other kids around me thought their power rested in getting someone to fear you. After the arrest warrant had been signed there was only fear and violence. But there had been fear and violence in my life before. Fights in the streets when my arms stopped working after taking too many jabs, or afternoons I spent running from fights. It all caught up with me when I started believing that fear and violence were the things power was made of, and I wanted to touch it if only for a moment.

Thirty minutes changed my life. It took less than thirty minutes for me to find the sleeping man in his car, and it took less than thirty minutes for me to get to the jail. When I walked in, the rank smell of the place hit my nostrils like the fat end of a bat. It made me feel like a man who'd spent a week sleeping in his own piss and shit, breathing it until shit was the only important thing left in the world. Outside the sun lit up the sky but in there it was past dark. A toothless man in the holding cell across from where I stood drooled and yelled at the bars before him. I was embarrassed. It had taken thirty minutes for me to commit the crime that made me a statistic. *Statistic*—another word that took on new meaning after I found my hands in cuffs. I was on a bench in the basement of the Fairfax County Jail waiting for an officer to tell me what cell I'd be spending the night in. I was a *statistic*, another word for failure, and it hurt because no matter what the prosecutors thought, I not only didn't want to be in jail, I really didn't want to be the person pulling guns on people. The jail's smell was funky, but since people were used to the smell eyes kept drifting to me, the young boy sitting on the bench in the corner. The smell was somebody's breath after they've thrown up a plastic cup of Hennessy; piss saturated into someone's clothes, into their skin; but not as noticeable to them as my shaking hands and fresh face.

"Good luck, kid." The female officer shook her head as my escorts left. Maybe she heard my mother crying. I watched their backs and only knew they were leaving the drabness of the county jail, walking outside, not even twenty feet, to where the freedom I couldn't touch shone bright under the sun. I was falling deeper and deeper into a hole I'd dug myself into but couldn't dig myself out of. If I'd seen that hold three months before, I would have run away from the man sleeping in his car. As I looked around the jail, I realized that my days as a juvenile were done. And they were. Once you were in the system there wasn't anything saying you came as a kid. You were just in, shut out with the light of day. All I had behind me were the snatches of small talk exchanged with guards before the court dates, where they heard twelve million black voices crying out to a juvenile court judge for mercy. They were tired of the parade.

Fight

GREG BOTTOMS

Mark came out of the back bedroom of his hot, dark house, shirtless, with eight or ten of the Polaroids of the naked blonde woman from the box under Bill's bed duct-taped to his bare, bony chest and stomach. He had on his blue corduroy shorts, socks, and the construction boots he sometimes wore when he earned extra money helping Bill out by cleaning up at a job site. He was holding a half-drunk forty-ounce bottle of Milwaukee's Best.

It was the day of the fight. I was nervous, feeling absent from myself again, had spent the better part of the morning in the bathroom, stomach churning, talking tough in the mirror. I said, "What's with the pictures?"

He took a long pull from the bottle. "Protection," he said. "Maybe he won't want to punch this woman in the sweet spot. *Please, Darryl*"—his voice high—"*don't hurt my nice cooch.*" He smiled. Then he looked at his boots. "Steel toe. Teeth removers."

He had muscles like—like what?—like a gerbil, like a hamster. He barely showed any evidence of having entered puberty. Darryl, with his mustache and weight, was going to kill him.

"Don't go," I said. "It'll take him a while to get to you."

"I'm going, dude." He took a drink. "I'm feeling good." He belched. "Bill said, 'Never back down.' Bill said, 'Take a beating but don't ever run.'" He slow-moed a punch combo with the bottle in his hand, careful not to spill. "I'm going to fuck him up. Rusty said, 'First punch, first punch. Relaxed, just checking the situation, *wham*. And the face. And the face. And the face. And the throat.' Rusty said, 'Bite nuts, thumb eyes, bend fingers.'"

"You're going to die," I said.

"We're friends."

"Friends. I'll put him off you."

"You can't help. If I put up a good fight, he'll leave me alone. 'Respect,' Rusty said, 'that's all a man needs.' Square up. Face. Throat. Eyes. Nuts. Nobody's going to take from me. Nobody's going to intimidate me. Nobody's going to crowd me out. I'm a man, *bitch*. I'm a man, *faggot*." More punches—*pah pah pah*.

It was the late morning; we were off, walking along that grid of city streets I can still see vividly even now—all these years, all these *lifetimes*, later—past the school and the basketball courts, the fields and neighborhoods, the strip mall and the car dealership and the diner. Mark did look pretty cool, pretty Mad Max, shirtless and half-drunk, with pictures of a naked woman taped all over his chest like so much armor. Some people beeped as they drove by. We raised our fists—shirtless warriors. Who was going to take down a couple of badass twelve-year-olds like us?

We went past Hazel and Sissy's house. Mark said, "Dumped you?"

I said, "Dumped her. She's crazy, man. Totally psycho. Wouldn't leave me alone. Crazy bitch."

"Over there enough."

I wanted to say, *I love her.* I wanted to tell him that I couldn't sleep, couldn't eat, that my thoughts only contained her and parts of her, that I sat in my closet and *cried* about it, that in my mind I took her apart and looked at her pieces and even now, after only a few days, I was having a hard time putting her back together as a single vision without distortions. I said, "I never liked her, man. Just trying to get some."

"That's it, dude," Mark said. "Fucking and fighting and getting fucked up." He punched the air, ducked and moved. "Fucking and fighting and getting fucked up. That's all we're about. We should start a gang. A fucking gang, dude. The fort will be our headquarters."

At the playground, twenty, maybe thirty kids stood around, all boys, ages twelve to fifteen or sixteen. Darryl stood in the middle of the open circle, punching his fist into his open hand, wearing the same ripped-up shirt he wore on the day he ate the bird. Dust blew across the playground. The swings creaked in the wind.

"Fight fight fight fight fight," all the boys shouted, some laughing and pushing each other, as Mark and I approached, Mark somehow still thinking—with the help of alcohol—that he might be able to hold his own in a fight with Darryl, who had fifty or sixty pounds on him. Even with a knife or a stick, he would have lost, would have had the knife or stick thrust right through him, as if he were no more substantial than the carcass of a bird.

This was all ridiculous, of course, the whole mess, a kind of necessary retroactive punishment. Darryl and Sissy were now boyfriend-girlfriend (for only a few weeks, it turned out). All over school property were vile slogans and epithets about Sissy. Everyone, including Sissy, knew that Mark had written them, carved them, drawn them: "Turbo-Diesel Dyke." It wasn't that Darryl cared about Sissy—he was just hoping to have sex with her; it was that Mark had mocked and harassed something—a person, a girl, but it could have been something else, any piece of his property—that Darryl now felt was his and his alone. If anyone was going to ridicule, degrade, humiliate, or violate Sissy, it was going to be Darryl—and Darryl would do all those things soon. And Darryl was also pissed at Mark and me for leaving him under the porch at the house that day, where he woke up in darkness among insects and dust, half-covered in the sticks and pine cones we threw at him. (I was safe from him only because I had a brother tougher and bigger than he was.)

As we neared the open circle, neared Darryl with his mustached snarl, his big fists, his hair, I backed away from Mark and settled into the yelling like all the rest of the boys. Mark had to enter the fight arena, formed of young male bodies, alone. This was part of the ritual of THE FIGHT, and there were FIGHTS all the time.

Mark started screaming, screaming as loud as he could, nonsensical gibberish. His armor of amateur pornographic Polaroids taken by his father flapped in the wind, caught bits and dots of sun and threw them around in our faces.

I'm not going to describe most of what happened next, though it is, I suppose, the *dénouement*, our climax. We live in a violent culture, it goes without saying. But you don't need someone interrupting the narrative flow and getting all *soapboxy* about it. And if you have ever had a fist hit you just below the eye, on the hard bone there, or had a boot on your neck, or had a belt across your back, your legs, or had a foot striking you as you scurried away on all fours, or if you have ever had the wind knocked out of you by a knee or an elbow or a fist, or had your head dunked in a toilet until you squirmed and screamed bubbles, or had your teeth cracked in your mouth so that you feel and taste their sandy residue on your tongue, or if you have ever had the explosion of pain—literally the stars—that comes when a fist or a stick or a bottle crashes into your nose, bending cartilage, breaking bone, or if you have ever been undressed in a way you do not wish in front of a mocking audience of boys, all rabidly homophobic yet interested in shoving their cocks and balls up toward your face for a laugh, their genitals turned to weapons, or if you have ever been tied up or taped up in a basement by kids bigger than you, laughing kids, or if you have ever had the back of your skull smashed against the ground while tufts of your hair are ripped from your scalp, if you have experienced even *one* of these things, then you already know about the distance and distortion of most of the violence we see, which we can watch in our recliners. And if you have experienced even *one* of these things, then maybe you already know about the blunt banality and quick stupidity of real violence, about that room I mentioned earlier, the one where the door is locked and the devil's stereo is on and it is so tiring to either fear or hate all the time and how that kind of thing burns a little ulcer in your soul and how that kind of ulcer can be contagious, *is* contagious, gets passed on to others so that they might one day know about the room and the devil's stereo and later, some years later, not be able to help themselves from locking someone else up in that room because they've been immersed in the banality of stupidity of violence, have been *shaped* by the banality and stupidity of violence, and they have an ulcerated soul, a soul—maybe this is all I'm really trying to say—full of holes. And if you have experienced any of these things, then you also already know that what Mark wanted, all Mark really wanted at this moment, because he was a kid shaped by the blunt banality and quick stupidity of real violence, just as I was a kid partially shaped by the blunt banality and quick stupidity of real violence, was for everyone to know that he was a tough

tough tough tough tough tough tough tough tough tough tough tough
tough tough tough tough tough tough tough tough tough tough tough
tough tough tough tough tough tough tough tough tough tough tough
tough tough tough tough tough tough tough tough tough tough tough
tough tough tough tough tough tough tough tough tough tough tough
tough tough tough tough tough tough tough tough tough tough tough
tough tough tough tough tough tough tough tough tough tough tough
tough tough tough tough tough tough tough tough tough tough tough
tough tough tough tough tough tough tough tough tough tough tough
tough tough tough tough tough tough tough tough tough tough tough
tough tough tough tough tough tough tough tough tough tough tough
tough tough tough tough tough tough tough tough tough tough tough
tough tough tough tough tough tough *motherfucker.*

There were no surprises in the fight between Darryl and Mark, if you could call it a fight, no interesting angles or slow-motion shots; none of the good moves were replayed five or six times for clarification or viewing pleasure while someone explained them. Darryl picked Mark up over his head, slammed him mercilessly onto the hard, gravelly dirt, and beat his face to a bloody, swollen pulp until he was tired of doing so, until the crowd of boys—one day, men—me included, stopped yelling "fight fight fight" and collecting all the loose pornographic photos flying in the wind and started to worry, silently, in fidgeting fashion, about whether Darryl was going to kill, actually *kill*, Mark, who was passive on the ground, arms flung out, with a face—can't you just see it?—made for punching.

I remember us walking home after the fight, Mark's arm over my shoulder, his face barely recognizable under all the swelling, large blobs of blood exploding onto the asphalt and concrete and grass as we went.

When we got to his house, no one was home and the doors were locked. It started raining. I helped him over toward the garage and we rolled open the door with a *ratatatatatatat* and he sat down on the stained concrete. He bled a small puddle from the cuts on his face, which he kept covered by his hands, the blood flowing like tears through his fingers, over his wrists, and onto the floor and out toward the lawn mower and the gas can and hedge clippers and hoes and shovels and rakes and some orange construction cones Bill used to mark off danger. I thought he needed to go to the hospital—in my memory he lost enough blood to die twice—but he said he'd be fine until Bill got home, that he'd roll up his shirt and put it on his face to stop the bleeding, that Bill had been in lots of fights in his time, that Bill would know what to do, Bill would help out, Bill would be home soon, any time now, soon.

I had to get going, because my dad would be getting back from work at the shipyard and my mom would be getting back from the Air Force base—I was reminded by the jet plane roaring overhead—and I needed to beat them home and change out of my bloody clothes and stuff my bloody T-shirt down to the bottom of the trash. As I walked away, I could hear Mark starting to cry, and it got louder and louder, echoing inside the belly of his garage, or through the rainy street, and I knew it was about the pain he was feeling in his face and body, about the humiliation, about the degradation, about the anger, about losing every time, over and over and over, but I also knew, even back then, even as that dimwitted kid drifting around those neighborhoods, that it was about everything else, too, *everything*, every disastrous little thing.

Instructions on the Use of Alcohol

JAMES BROWN

I

You're young, maybe nine or ten, and your parents are throwing a party. All the adults are laughing and talking too loudly, just in general having a good time, and you put two and two together. What makes them happy comes out of those bottles on the kitchen counter. The brown ones, you learn soon enough, contain whiskey and scotch. The clear ones hold vodka and gin, and that odd-shaped bottle with the long neck, something called *Midori*, contains a thick syrupy green liquid. That's the one that intrigues you most, and when the adults aren't looking you pour yourself a glass. You sneak it into your room. You lock the door. At first you sniff at it, the green liquid, and because it doesn't smell so good you pinch your nostrils shut before you take a swallow.

It burns the back of your throat. It makes your eyes water. You shake your head violently, and for a few minutes, until the alcohol takes effect, you can't understand how anyone in their right mind could drink this stuff. But then a tingling sensation begins to spread through your chest, your face is warm and flushed, and you're suddenly light-headed. You feel good. In fact, you feel great, and now you understand why it's worth braving the foul taste, the burn in your throat and the watery eyes. It's as if you've made a major discovery, a real inroad to the secret of a good life, and it only makes sense that if one drink has this effect on you that a second will make you feel even better. You finish the glass and sneak another. You repeat this action several more times.

The party ends around midnight but you wouldn't know it because you're deathly ill. Because you've lost all that sugary green liqueur along with dinner and hors d'oeuvres before you promptly passed out in bed. In the morning you wake with a miserable headache. Your mouth is so dry you can hardly swallow, you're still nauseous, too, and right then and there you vow never again to so much as look at a bottle of Midori. But what the seasoned drunk knows that the apprentice does not is that those of us predisposed to alcoholism are hardwired to quickly forget our unfortunate drinking experiences. In a day or two all you remember is how good the liquor made you feel, and when you go over to a relative's house for dinner that following weekend you find yourself sneaking into the kitchen again. You open the cupboard with the colorful bottles, and instead of the green stuff this time, because there is no green stuff in this household, you choose the liquid in the clear bottle with that weird Russian name of *Stolichnaya* or simply Stoli, as you learn to call it many years later, sidling up to the bar. This brand burns more than the Midori, but it also packs a faster, more powerful punch, and that's exactly what you're after. Drunk, you find yourself smarter and funnier and stronger and braver and even better looking. For the budding alcoholic, booze seems to do more for you than it does others, and your only regret, at least to date, is that you didn't come across this miracle potion sooner.

II

You're older now, maybe fifteen or sixteen, and by no stretch of the word would anyone outside of an uptight substance abuse counselor consider you a problem drinker, let alone alcoholic. Liquor has actually lost some of its initial luster, and you rarely sneak drinks anymore, say, only once or twice a week. What currently interests you is marijuana and the intrigue that surrounds it. Booze just isn't as cool, and besides you like the subterfuge, the cloak-and-dagger melodrama of doing something forbidden. Breaking the law is a high in itself, and just as importantly it befits the rebel image of your teenage years. You enjoy scoring the weed behind the bleachers at your high school almost as much as you do smoking it. You enjoy showing off to your friends how well you can roll a joint, and because the dope world has its own language, all the slang and clever code words, you feel special when you speak it. Tough. Streetwise. And don't for a minute believe all those lies you hear about marijuana being addicting. About how it damages the brain. If you want proof, just ask someone who's been smoking it daily for twenty years, but ask him slowly and be prepared to repeat yourself.

Then one day you try to connect with that kid behind the bleachers, the guy with all the Bob Marley stickers on his notebook, and it isn't happening.

"It's bone-dry out there," he says. "Fucking drought season, man."

Apparently some big bust went down in Humboldt County where they grow some of the world's best sensimilla, and now everyone's hoarding what they have and scrambling to find more. But he does have something else, if you're interested, this stuff he calls blow, a white powder you put up your nose. "It's good shit," he tells you. "Eighty percent pure." Since you've been such a loyal customer he's willing to cut you a deal, a gram for fifty bucks, or an eightball, three and a half grams, for a hundred and twenty. It's too good to pass up, especially since there's no weed around, and there's also a party this weekend where you'd look pretty cool laying out some lines of coke in the bathroom for a few select friends. Or that girl you like. With some good dope and a little luck, you might even get laid. Blow, you've been told, is something of an aphrodisiac.

You enjoy making the buy, even more so now, because the stakes are higher with narcotics, the penalties worse if you're caught. You enjoy the preparations, carefully chopping the crystals with a shiny razor blade, drawing out neat even lines and scraping the bag, or bindle, for every last particle. And as it happens with your first drink, so it is with the coke. It makes you feel great. It makes you stronger and smarter and braver and even better looking. All your fears and insecurities fall to the wayside when you're wired, and you dismiss those lies you've heard about coke being addicting. Getting hooked is for weaklings, the idiots who can't control themselves, those losers who end up broke and penniless, wandering the streets at night like zombies, like the walking dead. You'll never be one of them, though you can see how the stuff might drain your bank account, since the rush is so short, and the more you use, the more it takes to get the same high. Where a couple of grams used to last you a week, now you're lucky if you can stretch that amount a full day. For the budding addict, the supply is never enough, but your only regret, at least to date, is that you didn't come across this miracle powder sooner.

III

You survive your teenage years. You even make it through college drinking and drugging whenever you get a chance, which is about every other night, with all stops pulled on the weekends. At this point you're in your late twenties and still have no idea that you might have a slight problem. Who, after all, doesn't like to party? Who, after all, doesn't deserve a couple of drinks at the end of a hard day? A joint now and then never killed anybody, either. The same goes for a few lines of coke, a hit of Ecstasy now and then, or LSD, and a little heroin is actually a good thing if you're strung out on speed and need to settle your nerves.

Imagine how boring life would be if you had to live it straight twenty-four seven. Imagine how boring you'd be as a person if you couldn't get a little loose, a little crazy from time to time. The whole idea is to escape our dull existence, to find some amusement, some relief from the monotony of the day-to-day grind. This is how you rationalize it, anyway, and through the years you become very good at it.

If you have a rough day, it's reason to drink. If you had a good one, it's reason to celebrate. And if you get into it with your wife, because somewhere in this chemical fog you fall in love and marry, that is definitely grounds for storming out of the house and holding up in the neighborhood bar. Lately this is the only place you seem to find any real peace, among men and women like yourself, the ones who don't judge you. So what if you like to drink yourself into a stupor. So what if you have a DUI or two. Half the people in this bar do, and like you, they all chalk it up to the same thing, bad luck, being in the wrong place at the wrong time. You actually drive better now after a couple of drinks, because you're safer, you take less chances, because you don't want to get busted again. And furthermore, if anyone's complaining, your drinking hasn't caused you to miss a day of work in months. That you're so hung over or strung out and frequently have to go home after lunch doesn't count.

You just can't understand why your wife continues to nag or break down in tears. All the bills are paid. The kids are clothed and fed and you and she both drive newer cars. For a real drunk, you think, for a real junkie, none of this would be possible. You'd have already lost it all or never made it to begin with. But whether you know it or not, and you don't, things are changing deep inside you and have been for some time: hormones, genes, brain chemistry, all of it adapts to the alcohol and drugs you continually dump into your body. The cells habituate. The cells literally mutate to accommodate your cravings, and now they crave, too. Now your addiction has more to do with physiology than psychology. Now it's the body that robs the mind of its power to choose, and it's not long before you'll wish you never came across that miracle potion, those powders and pills.

IV

Add a few years to this story and you're in your thirties, still going strong. God knows what happened to your old college buddies who used to match you shot for shot, line for line. They can't keep up with you anymore and not a single one even wants to try. How they just turned their back on you and the partying life simply because they landed good jobs and married and had kids, you can't understand. What you think has been your dirty little secret for years has in fact been no secret at all to anyone who's ever made the mistake of loving or caring about you.

"It's time to grow up," one says, when you call him late at night, drunk out of your mind.

Grow up, you think. Sure. Your friends have sold out to the doldrums of suburban middle age. The truth is, you are and always have been tougher than them, blessed from the beginning with an iron constitution. A special ability to tolerate alcohol and whatever other poisons you consume. What you don't realize, however, is that this high tolerance is no gift but a liability, another sign and symptom of your addiction. And oddly enough, as you continue along this ever narrowing path, your tolerance will work exactly in the reverse, at least for the alcohol: where before it took ten drinks to get you reasonably drunk, now five will have you stumbling.

If you're not quite to this point yet, you're close. Your liver is enlarged. Your doctor has warned you, as has your boss for all the days of work you've been missing lately, assuming she hasn't already fired you. As for your marriage, it's in ruins, and you're up to your neck in debt. It makes you cringe to think of the thousands of dollars you've put up your nose or slapped down on the bar. The shame and guilt just compels you to drink more and to start earlier, sometimes first thing in the morning if only to quell the horrible hangover from imbibing too heavily the night before.

Hair of the dog.

That's the cure, and since you're always worn out, since you're not getting any younger, you need a little bump—compliments of meth-amphetamine—to get you through the long hard day. Crank is cheaper than blow and better fits your budget. Crank is also stronger than blow, seven times stronger on the central nervous system, and at night you absolutely have to drink if you hope to sleep at all. At this stage of your addiction, your drinking and using has little to do with pleasure, or even escape. From here on out it's about maintenance. From here on out it's about feeding those mutated cells, fighting off the intense depression that follows a binge, and trying, to the best of your weak-ened abilities, to carry on the bare semblance of a life. You are teetering on the edge of becoming the very thing you most feared, another loser, another zombie, one of the walking dead who wander the streets late at night, nameless, lost and forgotten.

V

Believe it or not, you hobble along like this for a couple more years. Obviously you've lost your job by now, or more likely several jobs, and your wife has left you and taken the kids. You're at a cold, ugly place in your life, and there doesn't appear to be any way out, any hope or chance of going anywhere but down. Then something happens. It could be a number of things. A close brush with death. A tragedy in the fam-ily, say, another DUI, a bad car wreck, or just a realization one morn-ing when you look in the mirror and barely recognize the man before you. Somewhere in this haze, between sobering up and getting wasted again, it finally dawns on you that maybe, just maybe you might have a problem.

These moments, however, are fleeting, especially when you try to quit, and you'll try many times in the next several months, only to find that by noon your hands are shaking so badly you can't hold a pen to sign your own name. Nausea quickly sets it, you sweat profusely, your head throbs, and you think to yourself: What the fuck am I doing? Give me a drink. A line. A pill. Anything to stop the pain. The cure is worse than the illness, and you're far less sick when you're drinking and using than when you attempt to stop. Inside of a day you're back at square one, and you hate yourself, as you lift the bottle to your lips, as you split open the bindle of coke or crank or whatever you could get your hands on. You hate yourself because you made a promise not to drink or drug for one measly day, and here you are, loaded again.

You're weak.

You're pathetic. You consider killing yourself, since that's what you're doing anyway, albeit slowly, and you probably would if you didn't have kids. If you'd lost entirely your ability to love. Sometimes that is the only difference between life and death, and it surprises you, it takes you completely off guard that anyone in your family, that any of your old friends still actually care about you. How is it that they see something in you that you can't see in yourself, something worth salvaging, when for the most part you've caused them nothing but disappointment, hurt and shame. But they do, and one day when you come home to your crummy little apartment, or motel room if you've sunk that far, and find a half dozen friends and family waiting for you, the same ones who wouldn't return your late night calls because they knew you'd only phoned to ask for money.

"You're sick," they tell you. "You need help. This is something you can't do alone."

In a matter of minutes you're in the backseat of a friend or relative's car, being kidnapped really, whisked away to a hospital for junkies and drunks and where you remain for the next twenty-eight days.

That first week is a blur. To combat the onset of delirium tremens, the nurses give you round-the-clock doses of Valium, and because your blood pressure has rocketed off the charts you're also administered Clonidine, a powerful antihypertensive, to further reduce the possibility of stroke. For some of us, the harder cases, detoxing from drugs and alcohol without medical supervision can and occasionally does kill. Fortunately this is not your case, and just days after you've weathered the worst of it, you wake up one morning actually feeling rested, actually sober for the first time in you don't know how many years, and it occurs to you right then and there that you might have a chance. That there is at least hope, even for a sorry bastard like yourself.

VI

You're pushing forty now, a little beaten up for all the years of abuse, but for the most part you're still mentally and physically intact. You have no right to whine. No right to bitch. It's a minor miracle you're alive at all, and after a year or so of sobriety you start to get back some of the things you lost. Maybe it's your job, if you have an understanding boss. Maybe it's visitation rights with your kids, if only for every other weekend. But don't count on patching it up with your wife. She's already moved on to another man, the guy who consoled her while you were out partying. The house, too, she's keeping that and everything in it. You feel so much guilt for destroying your marriage that you don't dare fight for what's yours.

Where every night you used to get whacked out of your head, now you attend A.A. meetings. You arrive early and make the coffee. You set out the donuts and fold-out chairs, and when things are underway and you're called on to speak, when you're asked to "share," you follow the A.A. protocol and first announce yourself as an alcoholic and addict. This is an important tenet of your sobriety: to remember always and forever that you are marked, that there is no cure for your affliction. Once drink triggers the craving, and once the craving is on you're off and running—next stop the dope man's house. Beating the physical part of addiction is a cake-walk compared to silencing that voice in your head, the one that never goes away, telling you it's okay to have a drink, a line, or a pill, because you've been clean and sober for a while. Because you can control it now. Compulsion is your soul mate, till death do you part, and your hold on sobriety is never more than tenuous.

But cheer up.

You've lost a lot but you've gained too. If not wisdom, at least the return of your self-esteem. Your self-respect. And even though you've been condemned to a life sentence of A.A. meetings, even though you'll always be struggling with your addiction and may wind up back in rehab, at least for now, if only for this day, you are free of the miracle potions, powders, and pills. If only for this day, you are not among the walking dead.

When My Father Was Beating Me

TOI DERRICOTTE

I'd hear my mother in the kitchen preparing dinner. I'd hear the spoons hitting the mixing bowl, the clatter of silver falling into the drawer. I'd hear the pot lids clink and rattle. The normality of the sound was startling; it seemed louder than usual, as if she weren't ashamed, as if she were making a point. Perhaps the house was cut in two by a membrane, and, though her sounds could come to my ears, my screams and cries and whimpers, his demands and humiliations, the sounds of his hands hitting my body, couldn't pierce back the other way. I learned to stretch time and space so I could think what she was thinking. I learned to hear things far away, to live in a thought that could expand itself even until now: what Einstein said is true—everything slows down the farther you get from your mother.

It seemed as if she wanted it, that either I was taking her place, or maybe she thought I deserved it. Maybe there was an overload of violence in the universe, a short in a wire that had to spill its electricity, and she was glad, this time, she hadn't felt it.

Maybe there was some arcane connection between her and my father's hand, his arm let loose and flying, maybe she was in command, making him hit, telling her side of the story—that I was evil, that I had to be beaten, not just for the crime I had committed, but for the crime of who I was: hungry, trying, in every way, to get through barriers set up for my own good. "You're tearing me apart, you're driving me crazy," my mother would scream.

Sometimes I saw the world from her perspective: she *was* beautiful and pitiful and overwhelmed, she was also some blood-sucking witch—not a whole being—able to stretch and contort herself like a cry, something that hated and was flexible. She wanted to beat me in the same way my father did, but she knew she couldn't, because I'd fight back, I'd cry that cry that made her go crazy. "You can't manipulate your father the way you can manipulate me." She meant it as a compliment for herself, as if she loved me more.

They wanted a stillness, a lack of person, place, agony swallowed. They wanted me to die, or, not to die, to exist with a terrible pain, but have it sewn up—as if they could reach into my ribs, crack them open, put a handful of suffering in there and stitch it back, as if my body had a pocket, a black pocket they could stick a thought in that they couldn't stand.

I would fold, collapse like a marionette. (I beat my dolls for years, pounded and pounded and nobody seemed to notice.) "Just keep trying," my father'd say just before he'd strike me. And I did. I kept trying to be beaten.

ᕙ ᕤ ᕦ ᕥ

Serving the dinner plates with her face bland, as if it were virtuous not to take sides, serving the beautiful food that she had cooked all day—her great gift—to say, *I've given everything I could, I've got nothing left.* Often when my father would hit me she'd say, as if he and I were man and wife, "I'm not going to come between the two of you. You two have to work this out for yourselves." He'd give me a warning. "Wipe that look off your face or I'll knock it off. Dry up," he'd scream, "and eat."

same again

NICK FLYNN

The usual I say. Blood of Christ I say. Essence. Spirit. Medicine. A hint.
A taste. A bump. A snort. I say top shelf. Straight up. Two fingers. A
shot. A sip. A nip. I say another round. I say brace yourself. Lift a few.
Hoist a few. Work the elbow. Bottoms up. Belly up. Leg up. Set 'em up.
Freshen up. What'll it be. Name your poison. Mud in your eye. A jar.
A jug. A pony. I say a glass. I say same again. I say all around. I say
my good man. I say my drinking buddy. I say git that in ya. Then an
ice-breaker. Then a quick one. Then a couple pops. Then a nightcap.
Then throw one back. Then knock one down. Working on a scotch and
soda I say. Fast & furious I say. Could savage a drink I say. Guzzle I say.
Chug. Chug-a-lug. Gulp. Sauce. Mother's milk. Home brew. Everclear.
Moonshine. White lightning. Firewater. Antifreeze. Wallbanger. Zombie.
Rotgut. Hootch. Relief. Now you're talking I say. Live a little I say. Drain
it I say. Kill it I say. Feeling it I say. Slightly crocked. Wobbly. Another
dead sailor I say. Breakfast of champions I say. I say candy is dandy
but liquor is quicker. I say beer that made Milwaukee famous. I say
Houston, we have a drinking problem. I say the cause of, and solution
to, all of life's problems. I say ain't no devil only god when he's drunk. I
say god only knows what I'd be without you. I say thirsty. I say parched.
I say wet my whistle. I say awful thirst. Dying of thirst. Lap it up. Hook
me up. Beam me up. Watering hole. Hole. Knock a few back. Pound
a few down. Corner stool. My office. Out with the boys I say. Unwind
I say. Nurse one I say. Apply myself I say. Tie one on I say. Make a
night of it I say. Dive. Toasted. Glow. A cold one a tall one a frosty I say.
One for the road I say. A drinker I say. Two-fisted I say. Never trust a
man who doesn't drink I say. Drink any man under the table I say. A
good man's failing I say. Then a binge then a spree then a jag then a
bout. Coming home on all fours. Rousted. Roustabout. Could use a

drink I say. A shot of confidence I say. Steady my nerves I say. Drown my sorrows. I say kill for a drink. I say keep 'em comin'. I say a stiff one. I say fast as possible. I say the long haul. Drink deep drink hard hit the bottle. Two sheets to the wind then. Half-cocked then. Knackered then. Showing it then. Holding up the wall then. Under the influence then. Half in the bag then. A toot. A tear. A blowout. Out of my skull I say. Liquored up. Rip-roaring. Slammed. Fucking jacked. The booze talking. The room spinning. Primed. Feeling no pain. Buzzed. Giddy. Silly. Glazed. Impaired. Intoxicated. Lubricated. Stewed. Tight. Tiddly. Juiced. Plotzed. Potted. Pixilated. Pie-eyed. Cock-eyed. Inebriated. Laminated. Stoned. High. Swimming. Elated. Exalted. Debauched. Rock on. Drunk on. Shine on. Bring it on. Pissed. Then bleary. Then bloodshot. Glassy-eyed. Mud-eyed. Red-nosed. Thick-tongued. Addled. Dizzy then. Groggy. On a bender I say. On a spree. On a drunk. I say off the wagon. I say gone out. I say on a slip. I say in my cups. I say riding the night train. I say the drink. I say the bottle. I say the blood bank. I say drinkie-poo. I say a drink drink. A drink a drunk a drunkard. Swill. Swig. Faced. Shitfaced. Fucked up. Stupefied. Incapacitated. Raging. Seeing double. Shitty. Take the edge off I say. That's better I say. Loaded I say. Wasted. Looped. Lit. Off my ass. Befuddled. Reeling. Tanked. Punch-drunk. Mean drunk. Maintenance drunk. Sloppy drunk happy drunk weepy drunk blind drunk dead drunk. Serious drinker. Hard drinker. Lush. Drink like a fish. Boozer. Booze hound. Absorb. Rummy. Alkie. Sponge. Sip. Sot. Sop. Then muddled. Then maudlin. Then woozy. Then clouded. What day is it? Do you *know* me? Have you *seen* me? When did I *start*? Did I ever *stop*? Slurring. Reeling. Staggering. Overserved they say. Drunk as a skunk they say. Falling down drunk. Crawling down drunk. Drunk & disorderly. I say high tolerance. I say high capacity. I say social lubricant. They say protective custody. Sozzled soused sloshed. Polluted. Blitzed. Shattered. Zonked. Ossified. Annihilated. Fossilized. Stinko. Blotto. Legless. Smashed. Soaked. Screwed. Pickled. Bombed. Stiff. Fried. Oiled. Boiled. Frazzled. Blasted. Plastered. Hammered. Tore up. Ripped up. Ripped. Destroyed. Whittled. Plowed. Overcome. Overtaken. Comatose. Dead to the world. Beyond the beyond. The old K.O. The horrors I say. The heebie-jeebies I say. The beast I say. The dt's. B'jesus & pink elephants. A hummer. A run. A mindbender. Hittin' it kinda hard they say. Go easy they say. Last call they say. Quitting time they say. They say shut off. They say ruckus. They say dry out. Pass out. Lights out. Blackout. Headlong. The bottom. The walking wounded. Saturday night paralysis. Cross-eyed & painless. Petroleum dark. Gone to the world. Gone. Gonzo. Wrecked. Out. Sleep it off. Wake up on the floor. End up in the gutter. Off the stuff. Dry. Dry heaves. Gag. White knuckle. Lightweight I say. Hair of the dog I say. Eye-opener I say. A drop I say. A slug. A taste. A swallow. A pull. Sadder Budweiser I say. Down the hatch I say. I wouldn't say no I say. I say whatever he's having. I say next one's on me. I say match you. I say bottoms up. Put it on my tab. I say one more. I say same again.

from *Beyond Desert Walls: Essays from Prison*

KEN LAMBERTON

Introduction

In 1986, during the summer of my twenty-eighth year, I abandoned my pregnant wife and two small children for someone half my age. Seven months later, I would be on my way to prison.

Until that summer I had been a predictable, if oblivious, husband and father. I was a successful teacher, having just been named Teacher of the Year by my school district. When I wasn't teaching, I spent my summers working as a program director for a YMCA youth camp near Oracle, Arizona—the same camp where I had met and married my wife Karen. Together, we developed environmental and outdoor programs, trained staff, and supervised an operation involving sixty adults and more than fifteen hundred children over the course of the ten-week season. I considered camp my primary focus. Teaching was what I did in the off-season. I was young, but I had a career, a home in a subdivision, a new family, and some direction in my life. I was unstoppable, invincible, as only youth can make one believe. I could do no wrong.

I felt this way even as I left it all behind—such was the nature of my obsession. The girl was one of my students, whom I had hired to work at camp, and what began with mutual infatuation grew like a tumor into a romance, complete with all the emotional energy of secret letters and clandestine glances and dangerous meetings. We were intoxicated with each other, with the electricity of something forbidden. If I allow it to, that summer still seems as magical to me as the one years earlier when I fell in love with Karen. Sleep was impossible and I was losing weight, but the stars were chiseled from glacial ice and scattered over a desert redolent with the scents of mesquite and mistletoe and newly washed hair. Moonlight spread on the landscape like a rumor—it was not a landscape of charmed hills and quiet arroyos, however, but of fear and desperation. Not of tranquility but of trembling. For the romance had spread beyond my control. I thought that running away with her would solve everything. We could start a new life together. I was a fool. More than our romance ended with my arrest two weeks after we left Arizona for Aspen, Colorado. I was twenty-seven years old. She was fourteen.

The affair—the crime—would send me to prison for twelve years . . . and change the way I think about myself.

Karen's response to my crime amazes me still. Anyone else would have divorced me. I had humiliated her in public, betrayed her in the worst way a man can betray a woman. I was her husband and I had deserted her and my children for someone younger, too young. But Karen set her feelings aside. Against advice from my family and friends, she flew to Aspen to collect me, and found me in the Pitkin County Jail in a state she would later describe as near-catatonic. While I faced bond restrictions and lawyers and indictments, she sold all that we owned, moved to Tucson, and began trying to salvage our relationship by drawing me to our children and the approaching birth of Melissa.

Some have said that Karen is weak for choosing to stay with me, that she's a coward, afraid—like many women in abusive marriages—to stand on her own. People have compared her to women who'd rather suffer quietly than admit failure, women who'd rather question their own self-worth and normalize the indignity than face life alone. They've said this to her, many times, usually after she's spoken of her religious convictions. She no longer talks about where she originally found guidance concerning her role with my unfaithfulness. I think she regrets ever reading about Hosea, an Old Testament prophet commanded by God to return to his adulterous wife, Gomer, and to love her. Religious convictions or no, Karen's motivations stem more from stubbornness than fear. Stubbornness and the need to be in control. These are her words. Divorce was never an option for her—separation, possibly, but not divorce. And certainly not another relationship. She could never do to me what I had done to her. Karen has told me—or warned me—that one reason she's stayed with me is because of her power over me, the power of being right. She's given me other reasons even more base: guilt-free sex. She would have to wait a long time for that.

After I went to prison, Karen enrolled in college to study criminal law. She specialized in legislative histories, concentrating on the law behind my crime. She researched the similar statutes of other states and met with legislators. She spoke at conferences and appeared on local radio and national talk shows. Without arguing against the fact that I was guilty, she began using the law and the media, suggesting that my twelve-year sentence was what the constitution called "Cruel and Unusual Punishment." She eventually—after more than seven years—won my release.

Today Karen regrets the time, money, and effort, the emotional energy she devoted to my post-conviction relief, because my release would be only temporary. Karen no longer believes in the equality of our justice system; she knows it was politics not law that returned me to prison. But I see the nineteen months of freedom as a gift. Prison never allowed me, outside the occasional visits, to be a part of my family, to be a husband again, a father. I had made the decision to return to my wife and daughters shortly after Melissa's birth, just prior to my sentencing, despite my own emotional ruin and the disparate feelings I had for them and for the girl. Karen's gift allowed me not so much a second chance but a way to continue with our lives. It was forgiveness; it was something beyond—and better than—forgiveness. I could be involved with my wife and children again, facing the consequences of what I had done to them. I could support Karen in her new career with a Tucson law firm, keeping house, washing laundry. I could help my daughters with their schoolwork, ride bikes with them, take them fishing.

My temporary release came in 1994 after one of my arresting officers, who no longer worked for the prosecutor's office, approached Karen, expressing his concern about the harshness of my sentence and offering to testify on my behalf if Karen could get us back into the courtroom. Detective Terrance Wesbrock described my case as a thorn in his side from the day it was assigned to him, saying, "I did not want the case, I did not enjoy working the case, nor was I satisfied with the outcome of the case." Somewhat encouraged, Karen sought out lawyers to file a Rule 32, post-conviction relief, that she had started preparing. The Sherick Law Firm agreed to hire her as a paralegal and take me as a client. Superior Court Judge Alan Minker accepted my case, a rare event in itself, listened to two days of court testimony, and then took three months to make his decision. My lawyers used evidence the state had collected to convict me originally, together with new testimony from both arresting officers, to argue for my release. At my resentencing, Judge Minker overturned my conviction, saying it was time for all of us to move on with our lives. He placed me on probation for the remainder of my sentence and allowed me to go home. Unfortunately, the Arizona Court of Appeals did not agree. A year and a half after my prosecutor appealed the decision to free me, three justices ordered my return to prison, reinstating my original twelve-year term, which I wouldn't complete until September 25, 2000. Twice in my life have three men I never saw beaten me senseless. This was the first time. The second time came shortly after I returned to prison. No one, including the appellate court, goes easy on sex offenders.

I wrote the first drafts of all but the last four of these essays from inside a concrete, eight-by-twelve, two-man cell, propped against the wall at the head of my bunk. It's one thing much of these words have in common, the first thing, although the essays in this collection don't necessarily always deal with prison in a direct context. I've already written that book. Prison (and by the term I mean not only the place but its larger significance—prison as it defines me: criminal, failure, outcast of society) plainly leaks onto many of the pages here. There are other places, however, where prison is not so clear, so conscious, but ringing in the background like tinnitus. Even now I occasionally uncover in my writing some new metaphor or irony that exposes me, and every time I'm amazed.

Rick Bass says that he writes to "make stories of order out of elements of disorder." In the same way, I wrote these essays to try to make sense of my place, struggling through words to understand the insanity of my own choosing, to look inside myself and know my passions and my flaws. This kind of insight—if I may claim any insight at all—didn't come in the beginning but slowly evolved as I persisted with writing draft after draft, "to fill up my empty days and nights," as my wife says. In the beginning I wrote to hold on to an intimacy with places that were at the time only memories—places and events, and the people I loved associated with these, that I could sense whenever a familiar scent or sound or sight trespassed those fences. In this, I wrote to discover and to embrace the loss, attempting to preserve all that I knew would change in my absence, and at the same time, to unwittingly punish myself.

My early drafts focused largely on natural history. With my science background and personal experiences, I grew to know the desert well, and I had begun to find success in writing informative articles for nature magazines, profiling individual species and particular locations. I was teaching again. Still, something was missing; my words lacked emotion.

In 1993, more than six years into my sentence, I published an article on the barn swallows that had recently adopted the prison. I had been watching the birds on their seasonal migration for several years, since three tentative pairs arrived to construct their adobe nests under the visitation ramada. Each April, with a rise in temperature and its accompanying insect bloom, the swallows darted in on narrow wings. And every September they disappeared with the first Pacific cold front. The article profiled the natural history of barn swallows in general, focused on the breeding (from scientific research sent to me by a kind woman at the Tucson Audubon Library), and hypothesized a reason for the birds' continuing presence at the prison (insect availability due to our wastewater treatment practices). I believed the article was one of my best, mostly because it included direct observations over several years, but it was still only information.

Then, in 1997, after my nineteen-month "temporary release," when I came back to the same facility, the barn swallows were the first to greet my return. It was a poignant meeting. I immediately wrote, "Of Swallows and Doing Time," revising the earlier barn swallow article. I wanted to know why I felt so connected with these diminutive, razor-winged birds. Why migrating swallows? The answer came almost as an afterthought at the end of the essay:

> I gauge my life by the swallows. Their nature, like many things in the world, is cyclic; they live inside the regular heartbeat of the land. Ebb and flow, flex and flux, rise and fall. It's a pattern I can live with, one that gives me hope. As long as the swallows come in the spring and go in the fall, come and go and come, I'll feel their rhythm, measuring it out as a change of seasons. This is the source of my hope: the swallows don't only make me feel the weight of time, they cue me to

the passage of time. Where ancient peoples raised stones to track equinoxes and solstices, the swallows are my Stonehenge. In a place where clocks and calendars are meaningless, where hours and days and months percolate into one homogenous, stagnant pond, I mark the swallows.

In subsequent essays, those that would eventually become my first book, *Wilderness and Razor Wire: A Naturalist's Observations from Prison*, I found other profound meanings—toads that tied me to my children, trees that cut holes in the fences, connections to beetles and weeds and whimbrels that I valued more than freedom itself.

I wrote the seeds of the following essays during my early prison years up through the months of my temporary release—before I wrote *Wilderness*—so these essays are a kind of prequel to that book. As I looked them over for a possible collection, I saw some of the same meaningful connections, connections to my crime as well as my place, to the people who remained in my life and those who didn't. What's revealed in *Beyond Desert Walls: Essays from Prison* seemingly arose (I believe) through the language itself, as if I had no choice in the matter: a wonderful, deeper, frightening understanding of myself, of a human nature.

Desert's Child

KEN LAMBERTON

From the upper bunk where I write, a narrow window allows me a southern exposure of the desert beyond this prison. Saguaro cacti, residents here long before this rude pueblo, fill the upper part of my frame. If I could open the window and reach out across the razed ground, sand traps, and shining perimeter fence, I might touch their fluted sides, their glaucous and waxen skins. But it's enough for now just to see them, standing erect in the distance among the creosote, prickly pear, and paloverde. The saguaro is the literal soul of the Sonoran Desert; its slender columns spell this out, uplifted and arranged like the Greek letter psi. There was a time when I couldn't see this, a time when I looked at saguaros and saw only dark hands with fingers poised in obscene gestures. And I connected with the significance. It was what I admired: an arrogant defiance of this extreme place.

☙ ☙ ☙ ☙

When I first came to this desert in 1968 as a child, I killed things. Whether spined, scaled, feathered, or furred, they all fell to my slingshot and BB gun. In the desert lot behind my house, I hunted whiptail lizards to near-extirpation, hanging their broken bodies on the spines of a prickly pear cactus as if they were trophies of my budding manhood. Around my neighborhood I stalked songbirds to skin and mount following the directions of a mail-order taxidermy kit. I imagined I was James Ohio Pattie, Daniel Boone of the Southwest, using my skills as a trapper and explorer to survive off the land. But in truth the animals I killed were sacrifices offered up to my own selfish curiosity and ignorance. It had nothing to do with survival. Killing was my way of dealing with an environment I didn't understand, a brutal, arrogant reaction to its incomprehensible and awful strangeness. And because everything was strange, I killed over and over again. It was my first religion.

I paid particular attention to saguaros. At first I did this by using them for targets when throwing rocks, launching spears, or practicing with an archery set. Once, while I was trundling boulders in Pima Canyon, the collision between the opposing energies (kinetic versus potential) of a falling rock and stationary saguaro snapped four feet off the cactus's crown. The break was clean and sharp and exposed a circlet of skeleton wrapped in white, spongy flesh. It reminded me of a zucchini chopped in two. When I took to probing another saguaro with a sharpened stick, someone taught me another way to pay attention to saguaros.

"*What* are you doing there?" the man behind me asked. I tried to hide my sap-bloodied weapon and turned to face my punishment. He had trapped me in his yard. To my surprise, however, he wasn't interested in scolding me and sending me home with burning ears. Instead, he diagramed a cactus in the dirt (with my stick) and explained the damage I was causing, damage like introducing bacteria into the wounds I had made. It was a good lecture, but it would be awhile before I stopped persecuting saguaros.

As I got older, I began visiting the front range of the Santa Catalina Mountains: Pusch Ridge, Pima Canyon, Finger Rock, Sabino Canyon. Hiking here was intimate and absorbing. I learned the well-traveled trails and then avoided them, choosing instead to bushwhack over *bajadas* and along drainages and scale cliff faces. Each time I returned, I became more attuned to the inconspicuous—the furtive call of a mourning dove in 110 degree heat, the pulse of water constricted by rock. I learned that cicadas, "cold-blooded" insects, love the heat. Their electric whine heralds the approach of the summer monsoon: precisely six weeks following their first song, according to local folklore. I often came across the discarded skins of their larvae shortly after their emergence, the keratinous casings clinging to branches and twigs of mesquite trees like split seedpods. For a few short weeks, the male's monotonous serenade calls females to breed, completing the annual cycle. I loved them for their constancy. They cued me to the rhythms of the desert, and even now I hear their seasonal chorus; my ears fairly ring with it. For me, it is an epiphany, not unlike the advent of our summer thunderstorms.

Returning to the Catalinas again and again always brought new experiences. The familiar defiles and outcrops, the canyons and ridges and peaks offered deeper layers of detail with each trip. I wasn't satisfied only to make an acquaintance with the landscape. I desired romance. Even more, I wanted the kind of relationship where romantic chance encounters would be the interlocking strands of some new and profound ecological vision, where I wasn't a mere observer but a participant, where I was connected and my place made sense.

Not surprisingly, the killing didn't stop. But the killing—actually, I preferred the term "collecting"—did become less meaningless. There was a kind of intimacy within the act. Body parts became my personal tutors. A four-foot pelican wing modeled flight mechanics. A tray of skulls illustrated eating habits. I notice how the imbricated scales of reptiles matched the same pattern in the feathers of birds. I started keeping more dead things in the freezer. My dresser drawers doubled as museum drawers, socks making room for the skin tubes of snakes and birds, underwear for mammal hides. When friends discovered my taxidermy hobby, they brought me gifts of roadkills, deceased pets, victims of pool drownings. My driver's license was my salvage permit. No still shape in the road got past my scrutiny; I was always looking for new species. I grew fond of certain stretches of road, particularly on night drives, expecting additional specimens for my collections.

I collected pets, too. I set up aquariums for fish, and I built terrariums for snakes and toads. I hatched Gambel's quail in a homemade incubator and trained a red-tailed hawk for hunting. Throughout my high school years, my bedroom was a menagerie. I wanted two of every kind, but unlike Noah, the only freedom I ever gave my animals came by way of their death. I had no ethics, a serious flaw in my desired ecological vision. The desert had opened up to me and taught me about its intricacies, its relationships and dependencies among living things and their nonliving environment. I understood that death was necessary for life, that birth was the beginning of death. I even grasped the importance of sex (years before puberty). I had watched house finches tumble and roll over each other in the dust, screaming with their bird voices, the red faced males mad with lust, scrabbling for females. I saw how the victor, after driving away its rivals, mounted its prize, flushing its wings and shuddering with heat for that two-second, cloacal "quickie." And then there were the cottontails, furry reproductive perfectionists. The males were nearly as fast, coupling and inseminating in a moment's thumping, finishing with a drunken plop, pleasure dazed. And anyone who has seen lesser long-nosed bats feeding deep within the recesses of a saguaro flower, their elongated snouts perfectly (and erotically) fitting the canal of the bloom, can't miss the coital parallel.

I knew about sex from an early age. I knew it was the essence of existence, of life. Even the insects at my doorstep did it, box elder bugs with their sterns locked together, scuttling around like two beads on a string. But what I didn't know about was how human babies were born. I had asked my mother when I was five after my little sister was born. What she told me I believed. She showed me her scar, a white vertical blaze on her belly. "This is where babies come from," she explained. "When the baby's ready to come out, the doctor cuts you open and the baby is born." For years this made perfect sense to me. It was the way I and my brothers and sister had arrived. The fact that, shortly after this revelation, I had seen the live birth of ten kittens, their perfect cat-forms slipping wet and bloody from the uterus of my pet, didn't bother me. Nor was I confused when I witnessed a deer drop her fawn, wrapped in its amniotic sack, umbilical cord trailing from its mother. People were different. I had seen the evidence. And what better evidence is there than a scar?

I remember when I was eleven or twelve, visiting my friends Mark and Todd Svane at their farm in northern Texas. They told me how babies are born, and I, in turn, explained how they are made. "They come out of their mothers the same way calves come out of cows," they said. I didn't believe them but they didn't believe me either when I insisted that our parents mate like animals. Before the end of that summer, the truth settled into place. My mother hadn't really lied to me. My siblings and I had been born under a surgeon's knife, cesarean section—but she *had* misled me. How convenient for her, those C-sections, at least when it came to answering a child's awkward questions.

My own sex education aside, what I continued to ignore was that I was wrong about many things. I was out of balance. There wasn't any purpose to my desert education. I was taking, and giving nothing back.

Immediately following high school, I went to college to study biology, unavoidably, it seems. This formal education attempted to redefine my background experiences with nature, labeling them and tying them up into neat packages like cuts of beef. But it seemed necessary at the time, this idea of a concrete foundation in science. I benefited from upper-level courses like invertebrate zoology and marine biology. But my favorite classes lacked textbooks altogether. In one class called "Selective Studies in Malacology," the professors outnumbered the students. We spent a week together in the mountains of northern Mexico searching for snails. I returned with a tiny boojum tree that I had shoveled from the ground at Punta Cirio, the only place the rare succulent grows on mainland Mexico. Border officials quarantined the boojum, but a fat chuckwalla, hidden under my shirt, escaped detection. This course offered more than knowledge and experience. It offered specimens for my collections, new species to catalogue and file away.

When I married in my senior year, Karen, born and raised in the desert, became the perfect partner for me. She was the assistant curator of my collections, accompanying me to the beaches of Mexico and the mountains of the Southwest. She also had taken lessons in the Catalinas. As we moved from homes to dorm rooms to apartments, she learned to care for fish tanks, birds of prey, and chuckwallas. It wasn't until I finally graduated and settled into teaching that my collections found a purpose outside my own pleasure. Now, everything, my entire life's experiences and all its natural extensions—hobbies, interests, and talents—came to focus on teaching biology. It seemed my life was making sense.

Within a few years of teaching, I had branched out into extracurricular programs that included a science club, which traveled around the state on monthly wilderness expeditions; an after-school taxidermy class; and an annual cooking and eating event we called "the Beast Feast." My collections, caged and displayed in the classroom, attracted much attention. Now my students brought me gifts, both alive and dead—so many, in fact, that I didn't have cages for them all. Some I just let roam free in my room. Jerald, the science department chair, complained about the smells, the loose (lost) creatures, and the potential dangers of rattlesnakes and biting varmints. But he supported me. When another teacher objected to the condition of my refrigerator, he even defended me. "That refrigerator belongs to the science department," he told her. "If you don't want animal hair in your lunch, there's another one in the teachers' lounge." *My* refrigerator got a lot of use. I had packed its freezer compartment with the skins of javelina and deer, owls and snakes, and a menu of donated meats for our wild food feast. When a fellow teacher and hunting friend gave me the whole carcass of a mule deer he had killed, I had to remove the shelves and vegetable crisper to fit it inside while the meat cured. One night an alarmed janitor found a pool of watery body fluids blossoming on the floor. (He probably thought it belonged to one of my belligerent students.) He wasn't happy about cleaning it up, and he let me know about it the next morning. But soon he too was bringing me desert treasures.

Because teaching took Karen and me to another city away from Tucson, our hometown, we traveled a lot the first years. One strip of road along Highway 89 called the Pioneer Parkway was our favorite. The parkway, a botanical reserve with rest stops, monuments, and picnic areas, was less congested and more interesting than the freeways. It was also a grocery store for roadkills.

Training hawks for falconry demanded quantities of fresh meat, preferably with the roughage intact (skin, bone, fur, feathers). Not only did the parkway provide this roadkill cuisine, but it also produced the salvage for my taxidermy students. On the parkway, great horned owls were accustomed to preying on rodents as they skittered across the warm pavement, their cheek pouches stuffed with the seeds of grasses that thrived on the road's margins. Unfortunately, the owls' habits for easy pickings periodically cost them their lives. One night, I found two of them, lying like feather pillows in the road, their bodies warm and eyes bright as though only resting. Whereas other animals usually melded with the asphalt, their broken forms like divots of turf, heavy with death, the owls seemed as though they might take flight at any moment. Driving home with them on the floor of my cab, I wondered what I'd do if one suddenly rose up in life, huge talons slashing at me for freedom.

It was this apparent vitality, even limp in death, that made great horned owls such appealing subjects for taxidermy. One of my students, Jody, became an expert at mounting them. She never complained about the delicate (and messy) flesh removal, but blow drying the owls' thick plumage did try her eighth grade patience. We discovered that a horned owl's feathers outweigh its bones.

At about the time Jody had finished a pair of owls, a local newspaper ran a feature story about my taxidermy class. My students gave the reporter and his photographer quite a performance, scraping hides, shampooing birds, and touching up head mounts, while providing interviews. The article appeared as a full-page spread in the lifestyle section. The publicity pleased me, but I had one concern. The reporter failed to mention any permit to salvage and preserve wildlife for educational purposes. I didn't have a permit, only a letter from the Game and Fish Department.

That week, the *Associated Press* picked up the article and it went national. I didn't know this. I also didn't know that certain government wildlife agencies had become very interested in my after-school activities. I was in the middle of teaching third period Life Science when two uniformed wildlife officers walked into my room. They were serious. I left my class and followed them to the teachers' area. "We need to see your animals and your permit," the man in the U.S. Fish and Wildlife uniform said. "Okay," I answered. I directed them to my lab area, dug out some paperwork, and opened the freezer. The Fish and Wildlife officer was not happy with my paperwork. "You should have a federal salvage permit," he told me. "You're in possession of federally protected animals." I knew this, and knew about the need for the permit. I had just neglected to get one. Fortunately, my letter was enough to disappoint them. They gave me a lecture but no citations. After they were gone, the principal of the school told me how they had charged into her office, threatening to arrest me. The whole incident unnerved me; it was the "saguaro lecture" all over again. My behavior hadn't changed.

As a hunter and angler, I had had a few encounters with wildlife officials and other law enforcement people. My falconry activities invariably drew attention, whether I was driving down the road with a hawk on my fist or following a hunting bird onto private property. Once, a police officer stopped me for faulty taillights when I was returning from an evening of dove hunting. He noticed that my hands were soaked with blood and asked if I had injured myself. I should have been embarrassed about this foolish macho tradition of unwashed hands following a hunt. (My hunting partner and best friend, Terry Hutchins, and I always bought cherry Cokes at the same Circle K, blood and feathers sticking to our hands, after cleaning our kill.) The officer checked my limit of birds and my hunting license, and told me to get my lights fixed. He must have thought I was sadistic.

Maybe I was. This business of blood held a measure of fascination for me. My wife thought it was juvenile, but she didn't understand. She had had enough of blood. To her, blood meant weakness and loss and pain: the blood of menstruation, of irrevocable innocence, of childbirth. Blood was personal and private; when confronted with it she always washed her hands. But to me, the pride of life was blood. It was a sign of strength. Blood on my hands, extraneous blood, meant that I was a survivor, that I could dominate my world. I could protect my family and provide flesh for them. Karen preferred to work in her garden among chlorotic vegetables.

It would be a long time before my bloodlust would begin to surrender to a more mature ecological awareness, a conservation ethic. A long time confined to one place. But the desert is patient, and it would eventually lead me, little by little, away from killing (and its antiquated relationship to manhood) to a simple and more profound appreciation of living things. And in this, I could find intimacy. The child of the desert, nursed, weaned, and raised with heat and thirst, thorn and wound, would grow into a naturalist.

This began in prison, where I worked as an education aide, with changes to my teaching style. Instead of focusing on the structure of lectures, notes, and books (of which we didn't have much), my teaching took on a more open approach. I discarded the dry, ineffective methodology I had learned in college and used in public school, looking to my fellow inmate students for another structure. Rather than my curious collections and displays, my students became the center of learning. I took a seat next to them, scribbling notes instead of regurgitating facts in the traditional, spoon-feeding teaching style. I looked for ways to teach tangentially. I relied on what I called "teachable moments," gifts from the desert that come by chance, by serendipity. Lesson plans were obsolete here, even sacrilege. In our "prison classroom," we might find a tarantula out prowling for a mate after a storm, or we might get a soaking looking for toads. Both could be lessons. I had to become a teacher's aide to the desert, allowing it to try on my students the same methods it had used on me. I could only master teaching by giving it up.

Outside my window, Gila woodpeckers argue among the saguaros for the best nesting cavities. Their voices, a shrill *huit huit huit*, carry all the way into my cell. The giant cacti, obscene gestures aside, really aren't as defiant as I have said. They, like me, have adapted themselves to this place over time. They've accepted the desert for what it is, on its terms. Their roots, shallow mats of tough rope, radiate out more than fifty feet to take advantage of only a few inches of rain each year. Their storage-jar columns have pleats to maximize water containment when water is available and a thick, waxy cuticle to minimize water loss from evaporation when it's not. The spines, splayed from areoles along each rib, also help conserve moisture by providing shade and creating pockets of insulating air while discouraging thirsty browsers.

But saguaros aren't selfish either. During the driest, hottest, most wicked time of year, the foresummer of May and June just before the monsoon season, the cactus offers sweet refreshment. At a time when many other plants are either dead or dormant, the saguaro bears fruit, its figlike *pitahayas* splitting like chapped lips to ooze a bloody pulp studded with tiny black seeds. It is a boon to wildlife. Curve-billed thrashers and mourning doves relish the feast. What they knock to the ground, coyotes and javelina and tortoises gladly consume. Even the harvester ants will celebrate, single-filing away the nutritious seeds.

By this, the saguaro gives back some of the wealth it has acquired in its kinship with the desert. As part of a larger community, it is only natural. And so, I, too, could do the same. What I have taken I might now give back; what I have learned I could teach. To do otherwise would be arrogant and childish, contrary to the desert's way, my way.

Turtle Suit: A How-To Guide

TERRA LYNN

How to Get There

If you are a danger to yourself or others, you will be separated from population, like Nikki, who had the habit of swallowing things like lighters and razors, tampons, sporks, erasers, parts to pens.

You will be taken to the mental health pod, where you will be monitored by specially trained mental health nurses and psychiatrists. Do not mention suicide. Do not mention depression. Do not mention the ever-present desire to find any object to bash against your head.

Accommodations

You will be put in a room called the "Bubble Room," with a steel bed cemented in the middle of the cell. The front wall of your cell, approximately 6' x 7', will be made of Plexiglas. You will have absolutely no privacy. The cell will also have a video camera, which will record all but the bathroom area; what the camera can't see, everyone else outside of the room can. The bright lights will not turn off in the cell.

What to Wear

You will be stripped of your clothes. You will bend-squat-and-cough. Depending on the CO or nurse on duty, and what mood they might be in, you may be asked to perform this twice. This will be purely for embarrassment. Simply because they have the authority to ask you to do this. Twice.

Once you're finished, they will hand you a large, green, turtle-looking, heavy, quilted nylon gown, Velcro at the shoulders and in the back—it is called the "suicide gown." But remember: do not mention suicide.

It will cover you from your shoulders down to your knees—if you are of normal height, that is. If you are of shorter stature, the gown might fall as far down as your shins. If this happens, consider yourself lucky. At least you are covered.

Due to the risk of injury, you will be forbidden undergarments, blankets, socks, shoes, pillows, or anything else sharp or dangerous. Even if you remember not to say it, no one has forgotten suicide.

You will freeze during your stay in the bubble room. This cell is very cold all year round. Heat is unheard of. The tips of your fingers and toes, your face will get so cold they will practically go numb. Huddle in a corner.

The Ladies Room

In order to establish trust that you won't attempt to swallow and choke on toilet paper, you must ask for an allotment each time nature calls.

Meals

Meals will be given to you on a tray, through a slot in the door, three times a day. You will be given a Styrofoam cup filled with "jail juice." The general consensus is that "jail juice" is some rendition of Kool-Aid. You may also drink water from your sink. From your hands.

You will be given a paper medicine cup to use as a "spoon."

At the end of each meal, everything will be collected.

Rules

Anytime you have the "turtle suit" on, you will not be permitted to have recreation or visitations from friends or family. You will also be prohibited from ordering commissary. You will be let out daily to get a shower in the morning once the other inmates have taken their showers and are locked in their cells. You are to have no contact with the other inmates. You are not to remind the other inmates of suicide, of depression, of bashing their heads in.

Health

You will be seen by a psychiatrist daily to check on your progress. Once you are cleared by the doctor, you will earn back your clothes and blankets and the rest of the things the other inmates have—just as long as you can behave yourself, stop the suicidal threats or threatening other people.

Stopping the suicidal threats will certainly keep you a lot warmer and you'll get commissary.

Staff

You will realize that some of the staff you encounter will be understanding, or at least make an attempt at understanding what you will go through. They may even help you. Even when you are uncooperative. But there will be other staff, too. Those whose only concern is collecting a paycheck. They will arrive, do the bare minimum, and go home.

Be prepared. These staff will treat you like a diseased, puss-filled abscess containing MRSA, a thing that could have been prevented. A thing that should not have been allowed to fester. You will be a festering, preventable sore to these staff.

Behavior

Because of good behavior, you will earn staff's trust.

You will receive your first set of burgundy ACJ scrubs with a handy, dandy pocket on the front. You will receive blankets and a regular cell where the lights actually shut off. This will seem lavish. You will participate in rec and visits, buy commissary. You will use an actual spork for your meals.

Things won't get much better than this.

Eventually, you will be taken to another pod. If you're lucky, the Hope Pod.

Eventually, you will stop saying the word *suicide*. You will stop mentioning it, speaking its name aloud. To say it, you will realize, is redundant.

from *How to Stop Time: Heroin from A to Z*

ANN MARLOWE

addiction

The nearest I can come to explaining to someone who doesn't take illegal drugs the unrecapturable specialness of your first heroin high is to invoke the deep satisfaction of your first cup of coffee in the morning. Your subsequent coffees may be pleasant enough, but they're all marred by not being the first. And heroin use is one of the indisputable cases where the good old days really were. The initial highs did feel better than the drug will ever make you feel again.

The chemistry of the drug is ruthless: it is designed to disappoint you. Yes, once in a while there's a night when you get exactly where you're trying to go. Magic. Then you chase that memory for a month. But precisely because you so want to get there it becomes harder and harder. Your mind starts playing tricks on you. Scrutinizing the high, it weakens. You wonder if you're quite as high as you should be, if the cut's different, if there's something funny about your jaw or lower back, if it used to feel this speedy. . . . Ah for the time when heroin felt instantly, overwhelmingly wonderful. If I had to offer up a one sentence definition of addiction, I'd call it a form of mourning for the irrecoverable glories of the first time. This means that addiction is essentially nostalgic, which ought to tarnish the luster of nostalgia as much as that of addiction.

Addiction can show us what is deeply suspect about nostalgia. That drive to return to the past isn't an innocent one. It's about stopping your passage to the future, it's a symptom of fear of death, and the love of predictable experience. And the love of predictable experience, not the drug itself, is the major damage done to heroin users. Not getting on with your life is much more likely than going to the emergency room, and much harder to discern from the inside.

aging

Dope can make you bad looking, especially if you're using a lot: you retain water, so your face grows puffy and aged, you develop blemishes, your skin looks green. And after quitting, you look worse for months before your former looks return. But heroin also seems to retard the aging process. People who've been involved with dope are pickled by it, preserved from decay.

What happens might be purely chemical—heroin does slow the metabolism. Or it might be psychological, an arrest of life experience. Think about those commercials for skin care products that point out that laughing or frowning ages your skin. Life on heroin doesn't lend itself to lots of animated facial expressions. Your lows are higher and—because of the physical annoyances of addiction—your highs are lower. There are not a lot of surprises, which is often the point; your rhythms are defined by the familiar and predictable arc of the drug's breakdown in your body, rather than the hazards of time. It is absence of pain that you are looking for, but absence of living that you get. Your last few years of use are like suspended time, and this absence of living tells on your face, and, alas, on your heart.

alphabet

Sanctified only by usage, but nevertheless immutable, alphabetical order is an obvious enemy of chance. While there is an underlying arbitrariness—which words to alphabetize, which letters they happen to begin with—once a commitment is made to the principle, all is fixed. Alphabetical order is the schoolchild's first lesson in the implacability of fate: he may be assigned to a seat solely on the basis of his last name, and he will learn to listen for that name each morning in the roll call, in its proper place.

When you stop to think about it, alphabetical order is emphasized in early schooling more than its intellectual importance warrants. Learning the alphabet is conventionally the first step in learning to read, but it's not necessary for the process. Given a basic vocabulary, you can read in a language without knowing its alphabetical order. True, you can't use a dictionary, a phone book or many other reference works without great trouble. But digital culture makes it likely that the importance of alphabetical order will erode rapidly in the near future. We won't use paper dictionaries or reference works; we will just query a database.

Our early training in the alphabet is mainly about submitting for the first time to an arbitrary discipline. The implacable order of letters will not be rearranged to please the child; no cute pleas or frightening howls will change it. Memorizing the order of the letters is an induction into the child's inherited culture, a set of rules that initially appear equally arbitrary, but which make human society possible. Rules are the enemy of entropy. The sonata and the sonnet, the haiku and the lipogram, the blues lyric and Scrabble, the civil statute and the religious injunction all set up artificial forms that comfort distress at the uncertainty of human fate (see **vertigo**).

arrest

The olive skin and curly black hair that made me an anomaly in my childhood town allowed me to blend into the heavily Hispanic Lower East Side street scene, but it is probably just dumb luck that saved me from the embarrassments of arrest. I tried to minimize risk: street lore had it that copping during the day was more dangerous than at night, because the police were more motivated to make arrests in daylight. Buying below Houston Street was said to be more dangerous than above, since that area had been targeted for a police crackdown. You were supposed to drop the dope bags if you thought a cop was behind you; looking back over your shoulder was a tip-off that you'd been copping.

Before leaving the house, I made sure I had my license because if you're arrested you get released faster with ID. And of course I had to have the right money, which sometimes meant getting reverse change, a ten or twenty for ones or fives. Stores in the neighborhood often refused this request. But almost no dealers would take ones. If they knew you, fives were OK, but tens were the only sure thing. You could usually get change for larger bills, but it wasn't the best idea. If the guy took your twenty and only gave you a bag, or would only give you two bags, not a ten and a bag, what were you going to do?

Whenever I went out to cop, I was watchful. I liked going for a reconnaissance by bicycle, to check to see if a particular spot was open. (You don't take a car, because the new laws let the cops confiscate it if you're busted.) The odds that you would arrive when the spot was open were maybe fifty-fifty. If it was closed, you had probably passed by a bunch of undercover cops, who had watched you walk to a known dope spot and turn around and walk away. The more times the cops saw you the more likely it was they'd pick you out and arrest you some other day when you were walking away from buying. It was too much exposure—hence the bicycle. There were also supposed to be video cameras aimed at notorious cop spots and if you showed up a lot they knew you were using.

If the lookouts or another user told you to come back in five minutes, you had to kill time. Sometimes I spent those stressful moments lingering in a bodega, searching for an imaginary need on the dusty shelves of Goya canned goods waiting forlornly in their off-colored sunfaded labels, or searching among the stale bags of dried black and red beans. Many of the stores were drug fronts, but they wouldn't sell to Anglos, or dealt in crack rather than dope. Or I pretended to be waiting for a friend outside, reading a band poster pasted on a lamppost, or one of those signs, handwritten when I first moved to the East Village but later printed out on home computers, announcing the finding or losing of a pet.

The worst was being told to come back in twenty minutes, so you had to go home or somewhere else and repeat the whole procedure. What with all this, I sometimes just sought out a friend of Dave's named Stan, a prematurely decrepit and unexpectedly sweet white handyman who would get you a bag or two for cost plus five bucks or a taste. You could spend your waiting time in Max Fish (see **Max Fish**), get high there without having to go home, and start your evening more smoothly.

Under the Influence

SCOTT RUSSELL SANDERS

My father drank. He drank as a gut-punched boxer gasps for breath, as a starving dog gobbles food—compulsively, secretly, in pain and trembling. I use the past tense not because he ever quit drinking but because he quit living. That is how the story ends for my father, age sixty-four, heart bursting, body cooling and forsaken on the linoleum of my brother's trailer. The story continues for my brother, my sister, my mother, and me, and it will continue so long as memory holds.

In the perennial present of memory, I slip into the garage or barn to see my father tipping back the flat green bottles of wine, the brown cylinders of whiskey, the cans of beer disguised in paper bags. His Adam's apple bobs, the liquid gurgles, he wipes the sandy-haired back of a hand over his lips, and then, his bloodshot gaze bumping into me, he stashes the bottle or can inside his jacket, under the workbench, between two bales of hay, and we both pretend the moment had not occurred.

"What's up, buddy?" he says, thick-tongued and edgy.

"Sky's up," I answer, playing along.

"And don't forget prices," he grumbles. "Prices are always up. And taxes."

In memory, his white 1951 Pontiac with the stripes down the hood and the Indian head on the snout jounces to a stop in the driveway; or it is the 1956 Ford station wagon, or the 1963 Rambler shaped like a toad, or the sleek 1969 Bonneville that will do 120 miles per hour on straightaways; or it is the robin's-egg blue pickup, new in 1980, battered in 1981, the year of his death. He climbs out, grinning dangerously, unsteady on his legs, and we children interrupt our game of catch, our building of snow forts, our picking of plums, to watch in silence as he weaves past into the house, where he slumps into his overstuffed chair and falls asleep. Shaking her head, our mother stubs out the cigarette he has left smoldering in the ashtray. All evening, until our bedtimes, we tiptoe past him, as past a snoring dragon. Then we curl in our fearful sheets, listening. Eventually he wakes with a grunt, Mother slings accusations at him, he snarls back, she yells, he growls, their voices clashing. Before long, she retreats to their bedroom, sobbing—not from the blows of fists, for he never strikes her, but from the force of words.

Left alone, our father prowls the house, thumping into furniture, rummaging in the kitchen, slamming doors, turning the pages of the newspaper with a savage crackle, muttering back at the late-night drivel from television. The roof might fly off, the walls might buckle from the pressure of his rage. Whatever my brother and sister and mother may be thinking on their own rumpled pillows, I lie there hating him, loving him, fearing him, knowing I have failed him. I tell myself he drinks to ease an ache that gnaws at his belly, an ache I must have caused by disappointing him somehow, a murderous ache I should be able to relieve by doing all my chores, earning A's in school, winning baseball games, fixing the broken washer and the burst pipes, bringing in money to fill his empty wallet. He would not hide the green bottles in his tool box, would not sneak off to the barn with a lump under his coat, would not fall asleep in the daylight, would not roar and fume, would not drink himself to death, if only I were perfect.

I am forty-two as I write these words, and I know full well that my father was an alcoholic, a man consumed by disease rather than by disappointment. What had seemed to me a private grief is in fact a public scourge. In the United States alone, some ten or fifteen million people share his ailment, and behind the doors they slam in fury or disgrace, countless other children tremble. I comfort myself with such knowledge, holding it against the throb of memory like an ice pack against a bruise. There are keener sources of grief: poverty, racism, rape, war. I do not wish to compete for a trophy in suffering. I am only trying to understand the corrosive mixture of helplessness, responsibility, and shame that I learned to feel as the son of an alcoholic. I realize now that I did not cause my father's illness, nor could I have cured it. Yet for all this grown-up knowledge, I am still ten years old, my own son's age, and as that boy I struggle in guilt and confusion to save my father from pain.

◌   ◌   ◌   ◌

Consider a few of our synonyms for *drunk:* tipsy, tight, pickled, soused, and plowed; stoned and stewed, lubricated and inebriated, juiced and sluiced; three sheets to the wind, in your cups, out of your mind, under the table; lit up, tanked up, wiped out; besotted, blotto, bombed, and buzzed; plastered, polluted, putrefied; loaded or looped, boozy, woozy, fuddled, or smashed; crocked and shit-faced, corked and pissed, snockered and sloshed.

It is a mostly humorous lexicon, as the lore that deals with drunks—in jokes and cartoons, in plays, films, and television skits—is largely comic. Aunt Matilda nips elderberry wine from the sideboard and burps politely during supper. Uncle Fred slouches to the table glassy-eyed, wearing a lampshade for a hat and murmuring, "Candy is dandy but liquor is quicker." Inspired by cocktails, Mrs. Somebody recounts the events of her day in a fuzzy dialect, while Mr. Somebody nibbles her ear and croons a bawdy song. On the sofa with Boyfriend, Daughter giggles, licking gin from her lips, and loosens the bows in her hair. Junior knocks back some brews with his chums at the Leopard Lounge and stumbles home to the wrong house, wonders foggily why he cannot locate his pajamas, and crawls naked into bed with the ugliest girl in school. The family dog slurps from a neglected martini and wobbles to the nursery, where he vomits in Baby's shoe.

It is all great fun. But if in the audience you notice a few laughing faces turn grim when the drunk lurches on stage, don't be surprised, for these are the children of alcoholics. Over the grinning mask of Dionysus, the leering mask of Bacchus, these children cannot help seeing the bloated features of their own parents. Instead of laughing, they wince, they mourn. Instead of celebrating the drunk as one freed from constraints, they pity him as one enslaved. They refuse to believe *in vino veritas*, having seen their befuddled parents skid away from truth toward folly and oblivion. And so these children bite their lips until the lush staggers into the wings.

My father, when drunk, was neither funny nor honest; he was pathetic, frightening, deceitful. There seemed to be a leak in him somewhere, and he poured in booze to keep from draining dry. Like a torture victim who refuses to squeal, he would never admit that he had touched a drop, not even in his last year, when he seemed to be dissolving in alcohol before our very eyes. I never knew him to lie about anything, ever, except about this one ruinous fact. Drowsy, clumsy, unable to fix a bicycle tire, throw a baseball, balance a grocery sack, or walk across the room, he was stripped of his true self by drink. In a matter of minutes, the contents of a bottle could transform a brave man into a coward, a buddy into a bully, a gifted athlete and skilled carpenter and shrewd businessman into a bumbler. No dictionary of synonyms for *drunk* would soften the anguish of watching our prince turn into a frog.

◎　◎　◎　◎

Father's drinking became the family secret. While growing up, we children never breathed a word of it beyond the four walls of our house. To this day, my brother and sister rarely mention it, and then only when I press them. I did not confess the ugly, bewildering fact to my wife until his wavering walk and slurred speech forced me to. Recently, on the seventh anniversary of my father's death, I asked my mother if she ever spoke of his drinking to friends. "No, no, never," she replied hastily. "I couldn't bear for anyone to know."

The secret bores under the skin, gets in the blood, into the bone, and stays there. Long after you have supposedly been cured of malaria, the fever can flare up, the tremors can shake you. So it is with the fevers of shame. You swallow the bitter quinine of knowledge, and you learn to feel pity and compassion toward the drinker. Yet the shame lingers in your marrow, and, because of the shame, anger.

◎　◎　◎　◎

For a long stretch of my childhood we lived on a military reservation in Ohio, an arsenal where bombs were stored underground in bunkers and vintage airplanes burst into flames and unstable artillery shells boomed nightly at the dump. We had the feeling, as children, that we played in a minefield, where a heedless footfall could trigger an explosion. When Father was drinking, the house, too, became a minefield. The least bump could set off either parent.

The more he drank, the more obsessed Mother became with stopping him. She hunted for bottles, counted the cash in his wallet, sniffed at his breath. Without meaning to snoop, we children blundered left and right into damning evidence. On afternoons when he came home from work sober, we flung ourselves at him for hugs, and felt against our ribs the telltale lump in his coat. In the barn we tumbled on the hay and heard beneath our sneakers the crunch of buried glass. We tugged open a drawer in his workbench, looking for screwdrivers or crescent wrenches, and spied a gleaming six-pack among the tools. Playing tag, we darted around the house just in time to see him sway on the rear stoop and heave a finished bottle into the woods. In his good night kiss we smelled the cloying sweetness of Clorets, the mints he chewed to camouflage his dragon's breath.

I can summon up that kiss right now by recalling Theodore Roethke's lines about his own father:

> The whiskey on your breath
> Could make a small boy dizzy;
> But I hung on like death:
> Such waltzing was not easy.

Such waltzing was hard, terribly hard, for with a boy's scrawny arms I was trying to hold my tipsy father upright.

For years, the chief source of those incriminating bottles and cans was a grimy store a mile from us, a cinder block place called Sly's, with two gas pumps outside and a moth-eaten dog asleep in the window. A strip of flypaper, speckled the year round with black bodies, coiled in the doorway. Inside, on rusty metal shelves or in wheezing coolers, you could find pop and Popsicles, cigarettes, potato chips, canned soup, raunchy postcards, fishing gear, Twinkies, wine, and beer. When Father drove anywhere on errands, Mother would send us kids along as guards, warning us not to let him out of our sight. And so with one or more of us on board, Father would cruise up to Sly's, pump a dollar's worth of gas or plump the tires with air, and then, telling us to wait in the car, he would head for that fly-spangled doorway.

Dutiful and panicky, we cried, "Let us go in with you!"

"No," he answered. "I'll be back in two shakes."

"Please!"

"No!" he roared. "Don't you budge, or I'll jerk a knot in your tails!"

So we stayed put, kicking the seats, while he ducked inside. Often, when he had parked the car at a careless angle, we gazed in through the window and saw Mr. Sly fetching down from a shelf behind the cash register two green pints of Gallo wine. Father swigged one of them right there at the counter, stuffed the other in his pocket, and then out he came, a bulge in his coat, a flustered look on his red face.

Because the Mom and Pop who ran the dump were neighbors of ours, living just down the tar-blistered road, I hated them all the more for poisoning my father. I wanted to sneak in their store and smash the bottles and set fire to the place. I also hated the Gallo brothers, Ernest and Julio, whose jovial faces shone from the labels of their wine, labels I would find, torn and curled, when I burned the trash. I noted the Gallo brothers' address, in California, and I studied the road atlas to see how far that was from Ohio, because I meant to go out there and tell Ernest and Julio what they were doing to my father, and then, if they showed no mercy, I would kill them.

☙   ☙   ☙   ☙

While growing up on the back roads and in the country schools and cramped Methodist churches of Ohio and Tennessee, I never heard the word *alcoholism,* never happened across it in books or magazines. In the nearby towns, there were no addiction treatment programs, no community mental health centers, no Alcoholics Anonymous chapters, no therapists. Left alone with our grievous secret, we had no way of understanding Father's drinking except as an act of will, a deliberate folly or cruelty, a moral weakness, a sin. He drank because he chose to, pure and simple. Why our father, so playful and competent and kind when sober, would choose to ruin himself and punish his family, we could not fathom.

Our neighborhood was high on the Bible, and the Bible was hard on drunkards. "Woe to those who are heroes at drinking wine, and valiant men in mixing strong drink," wrote Isaiah. "The priest and the prophet reel with strong drink, they are confused with wine, they err in vision, they stumble in giving judgment. For all tables are full of vomit, no place is without filthiness." We children had seen those fouled tables at the local truck stop where the notorious boozers hung out, our father occasionally among them. "Wine and new wine take away the understanding," declared the prophet Hosea. We had also seen evidence of that in our father, who could multiply seven-digit numbers in his head when sober, but when drunk could not help us with fourth-grade math. Proverbs warned: "Do not look at wine when it is red, when it sparkles in the cup and goes down smoothly. At the last it bites like a serpent, and stings like an adder. Your eyes will see strange things, and your mind utter perverse things." Woe, woe.

Dismayingly often, these biblical drunkards stirred up trouble for their own kids. Noah made fresh wine after the flood, drank too much of it, fell asleep without any clothes on, and was glimpsed in the buff by his son Ham, whom Noah promptly cursed. In one passage—it was so shocking we had to read it under our blankets with flashlights—the patriarch Lot fell down drunk and slept with his daughters. The sins of the fathers set their children's teeth on edge.

Our ministers were fond of quoting St. Paul's pronouncement that drunkards would not inherit the kingdom of God. These grave preachers assured us that the wine referred to during the Last Supper was in fact grape juice. Bible and sermons and hymns combined to give us the impression that Moses should have brought down from the mountain another stone tablet, bearing the Eleventh Commandment: Thou shalt not drink.

The scariest and most illuminating Bible story apropos of drunkards was the one about the lunatic and the swine. We knew it by heart: When Jesus climbed out of his boat one day, this lunatic came charging up from the graveyard, stark naked and filthy, frothing at the mouth, so violent that he broke the strongest chains. Nobody would go near him. Night and day for years this madman had been wailing among the tombs and bruising himself with stones. Jesus took one look at him and said, "Come out of the man, you unclean spirits!" for he could see that the lunatic was possessed by demons. Meanwhile, some hogs were conveniently rooting nearby. "If we have to come out," begged the demons, "at least let us go into those swine." Jesus agreed, the unclean spirits entered the hogs, and the hogs rushed straight off a cliff and plunged into a lake. Hearing the story in Sunday school, my friends thought mainly of the pigs. (How big a splash did they make? Who paid for the lost pork?) But I thought of the redeemed lunatic, who bathed himself and put on clothes and calmly sat at the feet of Jesus, restored—so the Bible said—to "his right mind."

When drunk, our father was clearly in his wrong mind. He became a stranger, as fearful to us as any graveyard lunatic, not quite frothing at the mouth but fierce enough, quick-tempered, explosive; or else he grew maudlin and weepy, which frightened us nearly as much. In my boyhood despair, I reasoned that maybe he wasn't to blame for turning into an ogre: Maybe, like the lunatic, he was possessed by demons. I found support for my theory when I heard liquor referred to as "spirits," when the newspapers reported that somebody had been arrested for "driving under the influence," and when church ladies railed against that "demon drink."

If my father was indeed possessed, who would exorcise him? If he was a sinner, who would save him? If he was ill, who would cure him? If he suffered, who would ease his pain? Not ministers or doctors, for we could not bring ourselves to confide in them; not the neighbors, for we pretended they had never seen him drunk; not Mother, who fussed and pleaded but could not budge him; not my brother and sister, who were only kids. That left me. It did not matter that I, too, was only a child, and a bewildered one at that. I could not excuse myself.

On first reading a description of delirium tremens—in a book on alcoholism I smuggled from the university library—I thought immediately of the frothing lunatic and the frenzied swine. When I read stories or watched films about grisly metamorphoses—Dr. Jekyll becoming Mr. Hyde, the mild husband changing into a werewolf, the kindly neighbor taken over by a brutal alien—I could not help seeing my own father's mutation from sober to drunk. Even today, knowing better, I am attracted by the demonic theory of drink, for when I recall my father's transformation, the emergence of his ugly second self, I find it easy to believe in possession by unclean spirits. We never knew which version of Father would come home from work, the true or the tainted, nor could we guess how far down the slope toward cruelty he would slide.

How far a man *could* slide we gauged by observing our back-road neighbors—the out-of-work miners who had dragged their families to our corner of Ohio from the desolate hollows of Appalachia, the tight-fisted farmers, the surly mechanics, the balked and broken men. There was, for example, whiskey-soaked Mr. Jenkins, who beat his wife and kids so hard we could hear their screams from the road. There was Mr. Lavo the wino, who fell asleep smoking time and time again, until one night his disgusted wife bundled up the children and went outside and left him in his easy chair to burn; he awoke on his own, staggered out coughing into the yard, and pounded her flat while the children looked on and the shack turned to ash. There was the truck driver, Mr. Sampson, who tripped over his son's tricycle one night while drunk and got so mad that he jumped into his semi and drove away, shifting through the dozen gears, and never came back. We saw the bruised children of these fathers clump onto our school bus, we saw the abandoned children huddle in the pews at church, we saw the stunned and battered mothers begging for help at our doors.

Our own father never beat us, and I don't think he ever beat Mother, but he threatened often. The Old Testament Yahweh was not more terrible in his wrath. Eyes blazing, voice booming, Father would pull out his belt and swear to give us a whipping, but he never followed through, never needed to, because we could imagine it so vividly. He shoved us, pawed us with the back of his hand, as an irked bear might smack a cub, not to injure, just to clear a space. I can see him grabbing Mother by the hair as she cowers on a chair during a nightly quarrel. He twists her neck back until she gapes up at him, and then he lifts over her skull a glass quart bottle of milk, the milk running down his forearm, and he yells at her, "Say just one more word, one goddamn word, and I'll shut you up!" I fear she will prick him with her sharp tongue, but she is terrified into silence, and so am I, and the leaking bottle quivers in the air, and milk slithers through the red hair of my father's uplifted arm, and the entire scene is there to this moment, the head jerked back, the club raised.

When the drink made him weepy, Father would pack a bag and kiss each of us children on the head, and announce from the front door that he was moving out. "Where to?" we demanded, fearful each time that he would leave for good, as Mr. Sampson had roared away for good in his diesel truck. "Someplace where I won't get hounded every minute," Father would answer, his jaw quivering. He stabbed a look at Mother, who might say, "Don't run into the ditch before you get there," or, "Good riddance," and then he would slink away. Mother watched him go with arms crossed over her chest, her face closed like the lid on a box of snakes. We children bawled. Where could he go? To the truck stop, that den of iniquity? To one of those dark, ratty flophouses in town? Would he wind up sleeping under a railroad bridge or on a park bench or in a cardboard box, mummied in rags, like the bums we had seen on our trips to Cleveland and Chicago? We bawled and bawled, wondering if he would ever come back.

He always did come back, a day or a week later, but each time there was a sliver less of him.

In Kafka's *Metamorphosis*, which opens famously with Gregor Samsa waking up from uneasy dreams to find himself transformed into an insect, Gregor's family keep reassuring themselves that things will be just fine again, "When he comes back to us." Each time alcohol transformed our father, we held out the same hope, that he would really and truly come back to us, our authentic father, the tender and playful and competent man, and then all things would be fine. We had grounds for such hope. After his weepy departures and chap-fallen returns, he would sometimes go weeks, even months, without drinking. Those were glad times. Joy banged inside my ribs. Every day without the furtive glint of bottles, every meal without a fight, every bedtime without sobs encouraged us to believe that such bliss might go on forever.

Mother was fooled by just such a hope all during the forty-odd years she knew this Greeley Ray Sanders. Soon after she met him in a Chicago delicatessen on the eve of World War II, and fell for his butter-melting Mississippi drawl and his wavy red hair, she learned that he drank heavily. But then so did a lot of men. She would soon coax or scold him into breaking the nasty habit. She would point out to him how ugly and foolish it was, this bleary drinking, and then he would quit. He refused to quit drinking during their engagement, however, still refused during the first years of marriage, refused until my sister came along. The shock of fatherhood sobered him, and he remained sober through my birth at the end of the war and right on through until we moved in 1951 to the Ohio arsenal, that paradise of bombs. Like all places that make a business of death, the arsenal had more than its share of alcoholics and drug addicts and other varieties of escape artists. There I turned six and started school and woke into a child's flickering awareness, just in time to see my father begin sneaking swigs in the garage.

He sobered up again for most of a year at the height of the Korean

War, to celebrate the birth of my brother. But aside from that dry spell, his only breaks from drinking before I graduated high school were just long enough to raise and then dash our hopes. Then during the fall of my senior year—the time of the Cuban missile crisis, when it seemed that the nightly explosions at the munitions dump and the nightly rages in our household might spread to engulf the globe—Father collapsed. His liver, kidneys, and heart all conked out. The doctors saved him, but only by a hair. He stayed in the hospital for weeks, going through a withdrawal so terrible that Mother would not let us visit him. If he wanted to kill himself, the doctors solemnly warned him, all he had to do was hit the bottle again. One binge would finish him.

Father must have believed them, for he stayed dry the next fifteen years. It was an answer to a prayer, Mother said, it was a miracle. I believe it was a reflex of fear, which he sustained over the years through courage and pride. He knew a man could die from drink, for his brother Roscoe had. We children never laid eyes on doomed Uncle Roscoe, but in the stories Mother told us he became a fairy tale figure, like a boy who took the wrong turning in the woods and was gobbled up by the wolf.

The fifteen-year dry spell came to an end with Father's retirement in the spring of 1978. Like many men, he gave up his identity along with his job. One day he was a boss at the factory, with a brass plate on his door and a reputation to uphold; the next day he was a nobody at home. He and Mother were leaving Ontario, the last of the many places to which his job had carried them, and they were moving to a new house in Mississippi, his childhood stomping grounds. As a boy in Mississippi, Father sold Coca-Cola during dances while the moonshiners peddled their brew in the parking lot; as a young blade, he fought in bars and in the ring, winning a state Golden Gloves championship; he gambled at poker, hunted pheasants, raced motorcycles and cars, played semi-professional baseball, and, along with all his buddies—in the Black Cat Saloon, behind the cotton gin, in the woods—he drank. It was a perilous youth to dream of recovering.

After his final day of work, Mother drove on ahead with a car full of begonias and violets, while Father stayed behind to oversee the packing. When the van was loaded, the sweaty movers broke open a six-pack and offered him a beer.

"Let's drink to retirement!" they crowed. "Let's drink to freedom! to fishing! hunting! loafing! Let's drink to a guy who's going home!"

At least I imagine some such words, for that is all I can do, imagine, and I see Father's hand trembling in midair as he thinks about the fifteen sober years and about the doctors' warning, and he tells himself *Goddamnit, I am a free man,* and *Why can't a free man drink one beer after a lifetime of hard work?* and I see his arm reaching, his fingers closing, the can tilting to his lips. I even supply a label for the beer, a swaggering brand that promises on television to deliver the essence of life. I watch the amber liquid pour down his throat, the alcohol steal into his blood, the key turn in his brain.

Soon after my parents moved back to Father's treacherous stomping ground, my wife and I visited them in Mississippi with our five-year-old daughter. Mother had been too distraught to warn me about the return of the demons. So when I climbed out of the car that bright July morning and saw my father napping in the hammock, I felt uneasy, and when he lurched upright and blinked his bloodshot eyes and greeted us in a syrupy voice, I was hurled back helpless into childhood.

"What's the matter with Papaw?" our daughter asked.

"Nothing," I said. "Nothing!"

Like a child again, I pretended not to see him in his stupor, and behind my phony smile I grieved. On that visit and on the few that remained before his death, once again I found bottles in the workbench, bottles in the woods. Again his hands shook too much for him to run a saw, to make his precious miniature furniture, to drive straight down back roads. Again he wound up in the ditch, in the hospital, in jail, in treatment centers. Again he shouted and wept. Again he lied. "I never touched a drop," he swore. "Your mother's making it up."

I no longer fancied I could reason with the men whose names I found on the bottles—Jim Beam, Jack Daniels—nor did I hope to save my father by burning down a store. I was able now to press the cold statistics about alcoholism against the ache of memory: ten million victims, fifteen million, twenty. And yet, in spite of my age, I reacted in the same blind way as I had in childhood, ignoring biology, forgetting numbers, vainly seeking to erase through my efforts whatever drove him to drink. I worked on their place twelve and sixteen hours a day, in the swelter of Mississippi summers, digging ditches, running electrical wires, planting trees, mowing grass, building sheds, as though what nagged at him was some list of chores, as though by taking his worries on my shoulders I could redeem him. I was flung back into boyhood, acting as though my father would not drink himself to death if only I were perfect.

I failed at perfection; he succeeded in dying. To the end, he considered himself not sick but sinful. "Do you want to kill yourself?" I asked him. "Why not?" he answered. "Why the hell not? What's there to save?" To the end, he would not speak about his feelings, would not or could not give a name to the beast that was devouring him.

In silence, he went rushing off the cliff. Unlike the biblical swine, however, he left behind a few of the demons to haunt his children. Life with him and the loss of him twisted us into shapes that will be familiar to other sons and daughters of alcoholics. My brother became a rebel, my sister retreated into shyness, I played the stalwart and dutiful son who would hold the family together. If my father was unstable, I would be a rock. If he squandered money on drink, I would pinch every penny. If he wept when drunk—and only when drunk—I would not let myself weep at all. If he roared at the Little League umpire for calling my pitches balls, I would throw nothing but strikes. Watching him flounder and rage, I came to dread the loss of control. I would go through life without making anyone mad. I vowed never to put in my mouth or veins any chemical that would banish my everyday self. I would never make a scene, never lash out at the ones I loved, never hurt a soul. Through hard work, relentless work, I would achieve something dazzling—in the classroom, on the basketball floor, in the science lab, in the pages of books—and my achievement would distract the world's eyes from his humiliation. I would become a worthy sacrifice, and the smoke of my burning would please God.

It is far easier to recognize these twists in my character than to undo them. Work has become an addiction for me, as drink was an addiction for my father. Knowing this, my daughter gave me a placard for the wall: WORKAHOLIC. The labor is endless and futile, for I can no more redeem myself through work than I could redeem my father. I still panic in the face of other people's anger, because his drunken temper was so terrible. I shrink from causing sadness or disappointment even to strangers, as though I were still concealing the family shame. I still notice every twitch of emotion in the faces around me, having learned as a child to read the weather in faces, and I blame myself for their least pang of unhappiness or anger. In certain moods I blame myself for everything. Guilt burns like acid in my veins.

◌ ◌ ◌ ◌

I am moved to write these pages now because my own son, at the age of ten, is taking on himself the griefs of the world, and in particular the griefs of his father. He tells me that when I am gripped by sadness he feels responsible; he feels there must be something he can do to spring me from depression, to fix my life. And that crushing sense of responsibility is exactly what I felt at the age of ten in the face of my father's drinking. My son wonders if I, too, am possessed. I write, therefore, to drag into the light what eats at me—the fear, the guilt, the shame—so that my own children may be spared.

I still shy away from nightclubs, from bars, from parties where the solvent is alcohol. My friends puzzle over this, but it is no more peculiar than for a man to shy away from the lions' den after seeing his father torn apart. I took my own first drink at the age of twenty-one, half a glass of burgundy. I knew the odds of my becoming an alcoholic were four times higher than the sons of nonalcoholic fathers. So I sipped warily.

I still do—once a week, perhaps, a glass of wine, a can of beer, nothing stronger, nothing more. I listen for the turning of a key in my brain.

Everything Is White

MERSIHA TUZLIC

Everything is white. It feels like I am here, but when I try to look down, I feel the motion of my neck, but there's nothing! My body is missing.

I hear a voice saying my name, but not my nickname, Mia.

I hear it.

"MerSiha," I hear it a bit louder now.

I stop to listen, but my body is not present. I feel the motions of legs and arms moving, but it's so bright and orange now that I don't even realize how weird this is. I'm completely out of my element—but it feels so fucking right.

"MerSiha," I hear it again.

And again. A short, few seconds pass.

"MerSiha," and now the voice is drifting farther away. I start to panic, because it just doesn't feel right anymore. I start to walk toward the sound of the unfamiliar voice, but my body is M.I.A.

"MerSiha!"

It's so much farther away now, so I do the only thing that feels right— I run. I run toward the sound of my name being called out, almost like a chant now. I'm completely and utterly driven by feelings and emotions, which I've hardly ever acknowledged before. My life is filled with suppression of them, with masks I wear as camo to protect myself. I'm a chameleon. I want to get by, unnoticed, because I got shit to do.

I open my eyes. I'm nowhere . . . great. Nothing exciting or amazing here. I'm in my fucking bathroom. I see the paramedics. To my right is a chubby guy and behind him is a heart monitor. There are two cops standing by the doorway, looking at me. Oh shit. What did I do now?

I'm looking around my bathroom. There are beige and brownish tiles in the shower and a line of embroidered tiles with a symbol that almost looks like an "S." My father picked them out right before the cancer ate him straight to six feet under. I like to think that he chose them because his name was Sabo. Everything in my bathroom was remodeled just to fit those tiles in. Now, every time I look at them, I think of my father.

One of the cops snaps me back into the moment.

"You're having a pretty eventful evening here."

I realize what is going on, because I see the glass vial of Narcan by the paramedic working by my feet. I overdosed again. I try to get up, but they start yelling at me to lie back down.

"I'm fine—I'm fine. I can stand up," I say, as I attempt to stand up again, but they make me lie down. I feel something wet and moist under my right thigh, but I just figure it is something the paramedics spilled.

The chubby guy with the chinstrap reaches for my chest and I twitch back.

"I'm just getting these off of you."

I look down and I see two big pads stuck to my chest. One on my upper right, slightly to the right of the center of my B-cup boobs. The other one is below my left boob. The chubby, yet cute, paramedic peels them off. I look behind the two cops standing by the doorway and see my boyfriend.

"You're supposed to be dead," Ryan says.

Supposed? What the fuck does that mean? I think.

"Don't be so thrilled I made it, please," I snap back. I notice he's been crying, and his eyes are swollen red.

"You scared the shit out of me, Mia."

I'm still lying on the floor, my head by the toilet now. My bathroom, I notice, no longer smells of Glade's Hawaiian Breeze automatic plug-in. It smells like rubbing alcohol and plastic.

The tall, lean cop with a buzz cut says, "You gotta go to the hospital."

"I'm fine," I say and start to get up now with a paramedic's help. The whole right side of my jeans is wet. "What's this shit?"

"Your bladder released while we were using the defibrillator."

"You died, Mia. You had no heartbeat," Ryan yells at me from the hallway.

"I'm fine. I don't need to go to the hospital," I tell them, but the cops have something else in mind.

"Well, you have two options: you either go to the hospital and get yourself checked out or we take you to jail."

Fuck. I really don't want to go to a hospital. It's bullshit. A complete waste of time. They don't do shit to you. But I wasn't going to jail, that was for sure. My P.O. would leave me in there for violating probation again.

"Fine. I'll go, but I gotta change my pants." Ryan finally has access to me and hugs me so tight, my eyes feel like they will pop out. He smells of the cologne I got him for his birthday—Burberry Weekend. We go to my bedroom and I grab the first pair of gray sweatpants I find in my closet.

"Did you put my shit away?" I ask him.

"Of course, Mia."

Ryan has school in the morning and I really don't want him to miss out on his college education just because I choose a different lifestyle. In the end, I win and he goes home, while I go to Mercy.

I can't recall the experience there. I was probably sleeping. It is 6 a.m. by the time I am released. I have about 1,800 dollars with me and no ride home. I decide to call a cab, because Ryan is probably on his way to school and I really don't need a lecture. I feel like shit and just want to go home to get well.

I have my scripts to sell, but I am so sick, the first thing I want to do the minute I walk out of the hospital is any kind of opiate. Withdrawal from heroin is so fucked up. My head is pounding and my palms are clammy. I feel a surge of heat come over my body, and I continue to sweat the whole car ride home. My stomach is in pain, and I know diarrhea is soon to follow. I feel like puking and shitting my pants all at the same time. The cab finally arrives at my house, and I know that sweet relief is near. I get out of the cab. The air hits my face and I feel so cold walking up to my front door. Almost make it. Except for one thing—the keys are inside my locked house.

I can't believe the luck I'm having. My withdrawals are getting worse and worse. I just need to get one more. Just one! I decide to go to the rear of my house and climb to the balcony on the second floor. It's not like I lack the ability to scale it. I've done it hundreds of times when I've forgotten my keys. There's just one problem: I've never done this dopesick. My body is so heavy and my stomach churning with pain. I feel weak from the burden of gravity, but I have no choice, and no time to waste, for I'm certainly not far from a visit from the grim reaper.

I start to climb the first couple of steps, and even though my hands were so weak a few minutes ago, I climb higher and higher. I feel like I am saving a baby from a burning car, and a surge of energy takes over. I am on the balcony safely when I try to open the back door to my house, but it's locked too! What the fuck?

I don't know what else to do, so I think, fuck it, and hit the glass with my elbow. It shatters all over the tiles, and I slip my hand through the door and unlock it. I am so glad to finally be inside my home. I go straight for my needle, a new one, because I have no idea where Ryan has stashed anything. But I know I have a couple extra bags in my dresser. I get some water and a spoon.

Next, I go through the ritual I hold so dear to my heart. I reach into the gray sweatpants I changed into due to my accident the previous night. I can't believe what I'm holding in my hand. I can feel the four edges of waxy squares. I pull out six black bags. Same brand I overdosed with the night before. "Now we're talking," I think. "My luck's finally turning around. Yes!"

I decide it's a great idea to combine them with the five other bags, because the Narcan wiped out any trace of opiate in my body. I'm so sick, this is about to fix everything.

I mix the powder up and suck it up through a cotton ball. I'm pinching my ass cheeks, as I search for a good angle on my vein, now bulging from the shoestring I used to get it that way. I find a perfect spot and trace my index finger over it. The needle pierces my skin first and then the vein. I draw back the blood and excitement starts to build in my body. I push the plunger in and as I'm finishing the push, I start to feel the dope, like poison in my veins. My head tingles and it feels like pins and needles are attempting to escape from inside me. My body gets a surge of heat all over it and I know this is it—the old familiar game. Should I stay or should I go? The sweet relief turns to fatal attraction and suddenly intensifies. Everything goes black and, fuck—not again.

I can't believe I'm in jail.

And I'm stuck, too. Why the fuck did I walk Brownsville Road and refuse to stay on the backstreets? I knew I had a warrant for three probation violations—all charges I'd gotten in the craziness of the last six months. I was selling narcotics and getting high when I got set up by some bitch from my neighborhood. A warrant was issued when I told a cop I wasn't setting anyone up. I dodged that warrant for five months in a part of the city where every cop knew me by name.

I was walking to the store to get a pack of Newports, some K2, and a blunt wrap. My brother's girlfriend was walking with me. I saw a Brentwood cop drive past me and look straight at me.

"Dude, he's definitely turning around, Court, we gotta get off Brownsville."

So we walked all backstreets to the convenience store, purchased the goods, and went back through the backstreets. We smoked on the way back. The problem was, my house was right on Brownsville.

I didn't even want to go two hundred yards on the road, but Court said, "It's all good. We'll be fine."

"Yeah," I shot back. "How bad would you feel if I get arrested?"

"You'll be fine, girl," she said.

I had this knot in my stomach, and I know now—that was my gut telling me *don't do it, bitch.*

Needless to say, I wasn't even on this road for three minutes when I got arrested. I was so mad. Mad I was arrested. Mad I was cuffed. Mad I was tired. Mad I hadn't had a chance to finish my brick of heroin— thirteen bags. I was pissed, but most of all, I was scared. Not of the jail experience that was coming, but because four months earlier, the Dollar Tree pregnancy test had shown up positive.

Yes, I used while pregnant. I couldn't stop. I wouldn't stop. Addiction had me tying my own noose and I knew I wasn't far from kicking away the chair.

The disease of addiction is cunning and baffling. It told me there wasn't room for a child. I was too inadequate to care for a baby. It told me I couldn't be a real mother, that this simply wasn't the time for a baby. Pregnancy meant I had to stop using everything. And once I realized that, any possible excitement at being a mother faded. Quitting wasn't an option. The very thought of not using was unacceptable, and I also believed it was unattainable, due to several failed attempts in rehabs.

And so I continued life like I wasn't even pregnant. I was in a tremendous amount of denial that had me convinced I wasn't even pregnant anymore.

Until a fat, bearded woman in her fifties told me I was pregnant at the Allegheny County Jail (ACJ). Reality sunk in then, and I began to understand I was most likely having this baby in jail. And that was what I feared the most.

I'm not a religious person, but I find myself saying a prayer to a God I have no understanding of. Tears stream down my cheeks as I lie four months pregnant on my metal slab of a bed. I feel hopeless and desperate. Desperate enough to jerk myself off the bed and get a legal pad and pen.

Before I even know it, I find myself writing a special prayer for the health of this baby, and for God to please, please, please not let me have this baby in the Allegheny County Jail. As I'm writing my special God-willing magical prayer, tears are dropping down on the paper. When I'm done, I carefully fold the paper into a football and place it under my ghetto-style pillow made of an itchy, fireproof blanket and a jail-issued white T-shirt.

I end up falling asleep—dopesick as fuck. When I wake up two hours later, my body feels like bugs are crawling all over it. I'm sweating, and beads are falling down my forehead as I attempt to stay still so I don't induce diarrhea or vomiting. It's very difficult to hold still, because my legs are so restless. I can't help but wish I could just jump out of my skin.

The next two weeks are fucked up. I get put on Methadone because I'm pregnant and withdrawing. I'm selfishly glad to have some relief and something to look forward to each morning.

One morning the intercom goes off, and the pod officer tells me I have an attorney visit. I wake fast from my sleep and try to get decent.

My attorney informs me of the severity of my charges and probation violation. Over the next seven and a half months, he will work on getting me into Drug Court. Drug Court is a court-stipulated program for repeat offenders with drug charges. It mandates you go to treatment, and I am more than eager to go. My attorney tells me I have a minimum of five years, realistically speaking, in prison, if I don't get accepted into the program. I pray every night for God's help.

Life in jail is repetitive. I'm locked up in my cell with a woman who showers only two or three times a week. Like herds of cattle, we're guided through our days. Fights break out nearly every day. Women who are usually feminine in the outside world now flex their muscles as a coping mechanism. Their red or maroon uniforms, each with the branding of "Allegheny County Jail" on the backs, are now sagged to expose their boxer shorts. My world is reduced to the size of a quarter of a football field. The only way to survive the time, I find, is to forget there *is* a world beyond these walls.

My attorney visits and informs me I've been accepted into Drug Court. Relief sweeps over me, and a small glimmer of hope starts to shine. Now I just have to try and not go into labor before December 5, 2012.

But my unborn son has other plans. On October 7, 2012, my water breaks and I'm completely freaked. I'm not due until November 12. I don't blame him for wanting out of this hellhole himself.

On October 9, Chaseton Kurtz is born, via C-section. Six pounds, one ounce of a perfectly beautiful baby boy. I get to spend four days with him, until I'm escorted by a sheriff, shackled and cuffed, back to the Allegheny County Jail.

I haven't even named him yet, but they want me to leave my baby, alone in the hospital, unnamed, to be picked up by my mother and Ryan. Thankfully the sheriff is someone I know, and he tells the nurse we don't have to go anywhere until I name my child. I'm so thankful to at least have that privilege.

I spend the next two months detoxed completely from methadone and anxious for my court hearing in December. I yearn for the day I will look into the perfect baby-blue gems of my firstborn child, but I have nothing but time, and thankfully, time waits on no one.

At least that's the one thing they can't control.

I'm staring at the reflection of myself in a little metal mirror that's hanging on a wall, scrubbed to perfection with pads—the sight of a woman who's getting ready to find out her fate. I don't look much different, apart from my well-done makeup, made of pencil shavings and one cheap wet n wild mascara. I'm not using my Kool-Aid blush today because I feel hot; the baby-powdered coffee mix will do. I look at my sad little 2 x 4 cell.

I spruced it up as best I could with magazine clippings and pictures hanging above my single metal bed. I earned this cell. I've been here seven months, and I finally got a single cell. No more junkies coming in and out, detoxing and smelling like pussy sweat. No more fights with bitches because they won't shower every day. I'm so fucking glad to be past that nightmare.

I get my "ironed" reds from under my mattress. The creases are just right. I hope my whites are dried, the ones I washed in my sink the previous night, wrung out by my calloused hands. I think back to my first time in jail—a scared little girl with big-girl consequences.

"When can I post bail?" I had asked the manly looking woman who held the keys to my freedom.

"You have a detainer. You ain't going nowhere, Snowbunny." Tears started to well up into my eyes, and before the stinging started, I retreated to my cell. Couldn't let them see me cry—advice I got from my brother a long time ago.

"Tears are a sign of fresh meat, don't ever let anyone see you sweat," he had said.

I threw the covers over my head and prayed my celly was too busy playing spades on the pod to come take a piss. God forbid anyone needed me at this very moment. Indisposed, I prayed to a God I never talked to unless I was in a jam.

"Please, dear God, just let me get out and I promise I'll never do it again"

I cried like a baby, not knowing I'd be released in seven days.

Now, I sit on my bed, getting dressed to the best of my ability for the courtroom—a hearing I've been waiting four months for. I know my fate lies in another man's hands, yet I am eerily calm. I made this little cell my home. I hear the C.O. over the intercom, "Tuzlic, you ready?"

I look around and park my eyes on a picture of my son . . . the son I don't even know. Today, I'll find out if I'll meet him at two months or five years. I stand and walk toward the cell door, saying a prayer to the same God I talked to on that first bust in jail. I take one more look in my metal mirror before popping my cell door. Here goes nothing.

I open my eyes to a window bleached with the vague sunlight of dawn. The radio is playing the current hit, "Can't Hold Us." It's 6:44 a.m. and time to start my day.

Chaseton's still sleeping and off into whatever dreamland babies go to each night. I'm exhausted but have to force my body with all my might to sway my legs off the bed.

Today, there's no kryptonite to get my day started. No lines of anxiety meds to shove up my nostril. No needle will be meeting the pit of my arm to give me that illusion of a boost for my day ahead. I'm not thinking about having to mix up some dope to find relief of withdrawal. The only relief I'm in desperate need of today is for my bladder.

Life is so much more intense sober. The tastes of food, sounds of cars, and the real world are deepened. My eyes see the same colors but more vividly.

This is what the majority of the world deals with on a daily basis, and today, I finally feel a part of it. I don't feel alone. For once in my life, I'm doing something productive. I drink my coffee and read the paper. I change my son's diaper and get him dressed for the day. I take a shower and have no need to rush, other than to see my son. I finally know what it's like to be a productive member of society, dealing with life on life's terms.

I was nervous to come to a place where I knew I would have to start opening the can that holds my secrets and fears. I was escorted to my social worker, who had hundreds of questions for me regarding my drug use and medical coverage. All I could think about was my son, though. I anticipated his arrival, which was to be at any moment. Every time the doorbell rang, my heart skipped a few beats. The last time I had seen my now two-and-a-half-month-old son had been right after giving birth to him at Magee Women's Hospital. A tiny boy with ten little fingers and ten tiny toes stared up at me. His eyes so blue, you could see crystals in them like little gems. Having to have him in that hospital, shackled and cuffed like a woman on death row, escorted by a sheriff in a paddy wagon, back to the ACJ, was one of the most disturbing times of my life. I felt unloved and abandoned, including by him, for using my womb and deserting me for the worthless mother I was. I hated him for abandoning me and had had dreams of watching him fall out of a window, his blanket swaddle slowly unraveling as he fell toward his death.

Now I was filled with anticipation and excitement to see those eyes again. The doorbell rang, and my heart skipped a beat again. My social worker took me to the front door, and there was my boyfriend with a car seat, seat cover over it. Ryan pulled it off.

"Look at our boy."

Chaseton was sleeping, and when I touched his hand, my eyes filled with tears as he opened his baby-blue gems and we locked eyes again. I no longer hated him and wanted to die. I finally had a reason to live.

Men We Reaped

JESMYN WARD

It was 1982 and my mother was pregnant with my sister Nerissa. New Edition crooned; Joshua and I loved New Edition. My father would grab my hand, and then he'd grab Joshua's, and I'd grab Joshua's small moist palm in my own, and we'd dance a ring in the middle of the kitchen. My mother shook her head at us, smiled, waved my father away when he tried to get her to dance with him. She would have been feeling pressure then as her family grew, as my father continued to cheat and plead his innocence and devotion and cheat more. She was afraid of what she saw on the horizon. She could not dance in the kitchen. She fried eggs sunny side up, and as a family, we sat at the table and ate.

But my father could be dark, too. He was attracted to violence, to the basic beauty of fighting, the way it turned his body and those he fought into meticulously constructed machines. He taught his purebred pit bull to fight with deflated bike tires. Alternately he coddled his dog, treated it as tenderly as one of his children, but the dog's ability to fight was paramount, and my father had little mercy for him in his quest to make him harder to kill. Like my brother, my father's dog required a hard hand if he would be his toughest.

My father stood in the doorway of the house with a machete in his hand, the blade so dark gray it looked black. He held it lightly, loosely. My mother was in her room watching television, and Joshua and I crowded around my father's legs, looking out at the yard, at Homeboy, squat and as finely muscled as my father. Homeboy gleamed back and panted with his tongue out. He smiled at us.

"Stay inside," my father said, and he trotted down the steps. Joshua and I dug into the door jamb, waited until Daddy walked around the house, leading Homeboy by his studded collar, to lean far out. We were determined to watch. One of my father's first cousins, also shirtless in white shorts, grabbed Homeboy's tail, held it down still and tight over a pillar of cinder blocks. Homeboy waited patiently, quietly, glanced back over his shoulder, and then snapped at a gnat. He trusted my father. Daddy whipped the machete up and brought it down hard on Homeboy's tail, inches below where the tail merged into his backside. Blood spurted across the gray cinder in a steady gush. Homeboy yelped and jerked. My father dropped the machete and tied a bandage around Homeboy's stump, and then smoothed his sides. Homeboy whimpered and quieted.

"Good boy," my father said. Homeboy licked my father's hand, butted him with his head.

Later, Joshua and I lay in our room, a room that was still decorated only for me; there were Cinderella curtains at the windows, and a rough Cinderella bedspread on my twin bed. When we moved in, Joshua had had his own room, but when my father decided he wanted a room for his weight bench and his kung-fu weapons, they moved Joshua into my room. This made me angry for a week or so because I felt territorial; this was my space. But that night Joshua and I lay quietly in our small beds, Joshua breathing softly, almost snoring, while I lay awake and listened to my father and his cousin in the other room, listened to them take smoking pipes down off the wall where my father had mounted them for decoration, listened to the clink of the weights, all this drifting down the hot hallway in the dark. The wind blew my curtains; they wafted out and stilled. The humid air coming into all the open windows of the house drew the smell of weed into my room. I knew this was some sort of smoke, like cigarettes. My father smoked it and my mother didn't. Maybe my father and his cousin talked about their dogs. Maybe they talked about their cars. Maybe they whispered about women.

My mother had given birth to Nerissa by then. She'd also come to realize the hopelessness of her dreams that our growing family would bind my father to her and encourage his loyalty to her. She'd carried Nerissa to term, and my sister had been a hard birth. She'd been the heaviest of all of us, and had refused to descend down the birth canal, so the doctors and nurses had to drive her out of my mother by taking their forearms and sweeping down my mother's stomach from rib cage to hip, and then grabbing Nerissa's head with forceps. *She didn't want to leave me,* my mother says. When Nerissa was born, she looked the most like my father: she had black hair and large, black eyes shaped like quotation marks in her face when she smiled.

The violence of my sister's birth and the slow unraveling of our family marked my mother when she came home. She was more withdrawn. She turned inward. When her patience waned, she argued with my father over his infidelities, and while my father was dramatic and flamboyant with his anger, flipping mattresses from beds, my mother was curt. I imagine she wanted to spare us the spectacle of their arguments, the way violence hovered at the edges of their confrontations. They never touched each other in anger, but the small things in that house suffered.

That year, the world outside our house taught me and my brother different lessons about violence. Our play taught us that violence could be sudden, unpredictable, and severe, soon.

My mother's brother took Joshua for a ride on his moped. Uncle Thomas was around nineteen, and his moped was white with a maroon seat. My brother sat on my uncle's lap, and my uncle whooped and hollered as they rode in circles around the yard. My uncle had the kind of face that was so hard when he was serious that I could hardly believe it was the same face when he smiled. I wanted a turn on the moped. Joshua leaned forward and grabbed the handlebars, and pretended to steer. The moped accelerated. My uncle clicked the clutch so he could slow down while my brother pressed the gas, and they surged forward. My uncle cut the wheel to stop and they crashed in the sandy ditch. Joshua screamed. Blood ran steadily from his mouth. My uncle apologized again and again: *I'm sorry I'm sorry I'm sorry,* he said. My mother held Josh's mouth wide to look inside and saw that the thin film of flesh that held his tongue to the floor of his mouth had been ripped. They made him suck on ice to dull the pain, to bring the swelling down. His sobs subsided and he went to sleep. They did not take him to the hospital. Perhaps they thought it would heal on its own, or they were afraid of the bill, or they were distracted by their failing relationship. Regardless, the slice healed.

My own lesson in sudden violence involved pit bulls, of course. My father had just purchased a full-grown white pit bull from another man in DeLisle; the dog's name was Chief. One of my father's dogs, Mr. Cool, the gentle white half-breed pit bull who'd comforted me when I was younger, had recently gotten sick. My cousin Larry had taken him out into the backyard into the deep woods behind the house with a rifle in hand, a job my father didn't have the heart to do himself. My father planned to fight the new dog, Chief, along with Homeboy, whom he'd had since he was a puppy. This new dog was twice Mr. Cool's size and less interested in my father's human brood. Homeboy could be tender like Mr. Cool. He would shield me with his body, while Chief looked at me, unmoved.

On an unexceptional hot and bright day, I met Farrah and her brother Marty in the middle of the gravel driveway. Homeboy was asleep under the house. A stray girl dog trotted around us. Chief wandered over to investigate her. He stood to her side very stiffly, smelled her rear, her tail, her belly. He found something to interest him. Both of them stood still before me, entranced with each other. The sun was high. I was hot and cross, and Chief stood in my way.

"Move," I said.

Chief's ear twitched.

"Move, Chief!"

Farrah laughed.

"Move!" I said, and I hit Chief on his broad white back.

He growled and leapt at me. I fell, screaming. He bit me, again and again, on my back, in the back of my head, on my ear; his stomach, white and furry, sinuous and strong, rolled from side to side over me. His growl drowned all sound. I kicked. I punched him with my fists, left and right, over and over again.

Suddenly he was off me, yelping, running away with his back curved. My great-aunt Pernella, who lived in the smallest house in the field, was beating Chief away with a yellow broom. She picked me up off the ground. I wailed.

"Go home," she told Marty and Farrah.

She placed a palm tenderly where my neck met my back, and she walked me down the long drive to our house. My head and back and arms were burning, red, hotter than the day. Walking was a scream. My mother stood in the doorway of our house. I was barefoot: blood plain on my face and streaming down my body to my feet. The back of my shirt was torn and turning black. Years later, my mother told me, "I saw him attacking you in front of Pernella's house, saw her beating him off. I couldn't move." She was paralyzed by fear.

"The dog. It bit Jesmyn," my aunt said.

Her voice freed my mother from her shock. She called my father, who turned on the water in the bathtub. He picked me up, put me in the water. I hollered. The water turned red. My mother pulled off my shirt, took the cup she kept near the tub to rinse us with when she gave us a bath and poured water over my head. The cuts and gashes sizzled. I screamed.

"We have to wash you off, Mimi," they said. "It's okay."

My mother bloodied her towels as they dried me off, and when she dressed me, I bled through my T-shirt. My father drove us to the hospital. Joshua sat quietly and solemnly in the passenger seat. My mother and I sat in the back of the car, and I lay my head on her lap; my mother laid her hands lightly on the cotton towel they'd wrapped around my head, the cotton staining red. At the hospital, a nurse, tall and White, said to me: "Oh, you got bit by a dog, did you?" My wounds throbbed, and I thought she was stupid. What did she think happened? When the doctors gave me a rabies shot, they called in four men, and each held one of my five-year-old limbs. I bucked against them. Afterward, they sewed me up. I had three deep puncture wounds on my back. I had a three-inch gash running from the top of my left ear, parallel to my collarbone, back to the nape of my skull. They did not sew any of these. These they disinfected and bandaged. What they did sew was the bottom of my left ear, which had been nearly ripped off, and which hung on by a centimeter of flesh and skin.

"A pit bull did this?" the doctor asked.

"Yes," my father said.

"She fought," my mother said.

"These dogs go for the neck," the doctor said. "If she hadn't fought . . ."

"I know," my father said.

My parents brought me home and I crept around the house. Cousins and neighbors visited. Marty brought my mother the small gold hoop earring I'd worn in my left ear, which he'd found in the bloody gravel. When my father stood in the middle of a gathering of boys and men in the front yard, some who leaned on the hoods of their cars, some who squatted on the ground, some who stood like my father, some of whom were young as fourteen, some of whom were old as sixty, my father said that if I had not fought, I would have died. He said the dog had been trying to rip out my throat. He said the girl dog must have been in heat, and Chief must have thought I was a threat. All of the men held rifles, some like babies in the crooks of their elbows, some thrown over their shoulders. My father dispersed the men, and they went off to hunt the dog: he'd been slinking around the neighborhood, trying to find his way back home. My father found him and shot Chief in the head and buried him in a ditch. I did not tell them I had started the fight. That I had smacked Chief on his back. I felt guilty. Now, the long scar in my head feels like a thin plastic cocktail straw, and like all war wounds, it itches.

My dog bites had healed to pink scars when my mother and father had their last fight in that house, and it must have been spring because the windows were open. We were preparing to move again, this time to the small trailer that we would live in for a year, my parents by degrees driving each other to even more misery, my brother and sister and I the happiest we'd ever been in our young lives, ignorant of their fights because my parents became so adept at hiding their arguments from Nerissa and Joshua and me. But that night in 1984, they broke and could not contain their ire, my father because he felt shackled by the fact that he had a wife and kids who needed loyalty and fortitude, and my mother because my father had told her he could give us those things, and she was realizing he couldn't. By that time, he'd had his first child out of wedlock. With that, my mother was realizing that soon her mother's story would be hers.

My parents were screaming at each other, their voices loud and carrying out of the windows, but I could not understand what they were saying. I heard one word repeated over and over again: *you. You* and *you* and *you* and *you!* This was punctuated by throwing things. The sun had set, and the evening sky was fading blue to black. Above Joshua's and my head, bats swooped, diving for insects. The windows shone yellow. Nerissa, one year old then, was in the house with our parents, and she was crying. Joshua and I sat on the dark porch, and I held him around his thin shoulders. He was shaking, and I was shaking, but we could not cry. I hugged my brother in the dark. I was his big sister. My mother and father yelled at each other in the house, and as the bats fluttered overhead, dry as paper, I heard the sound of glass shattering, of wood splintering, of things breaking.

POETRY

23

JOHN AMEN

That birthday, I swallowed valiums with vodka,
drove dark back-roads, both headlights broken.
I made it to the driveway, crashing into an oak,
passing out behind the airbag. Jul called an ambulance,
and I came to in intensive care, sunlight flooding
through barred windows, tubes flowing like power lines.
I'd been here before, each survival bolstering some
myth of invincibility, but this time I knew I was treading
a bloody shark pool, the inglorious end converging like teeth.
I told the doctor I intended to get clean. He shrugged
when I declined his offer to check me into a treatment center,
railed that the odds were mounded against me. Death
sat on the edge of the gurney, smiling like a mentor.

Bed Sheets

JEN ASHBURN

When I remember that night, I can't recall
if we had pork chops and broccoli for dinner,
or ham and beans, or fried bluegill
with stewed tomatoes. I don't know
if we watched TV or sat on the back patio
listening to crickets. I can say it was summer;
the evening light soaked everything
in the color of plums—not the skin of plums, or the flesh,
but that deep orange-red that bleeds in between.

She was gentle at first, my mother. Then she said,
"This is how they restrain you in hospitals."
She tucked the sheets hard under the mattress,
trapping my arms, legs, shoulders, my surprised ribs.

How old was I? Strong enough to untuck the sheets
and crawl out of bed, but I didn't. Into the night
I listened for her return footsteps and startled
at every old-house creak. What I remember
from that night is this: my mother's unsteady eyes
behind her thick-rimmed glasses, and squares of light
gliding across the bedroom wall. Light through the window.
Light from the station wagons and pickup trucks
that said, so patiently, there is a road. My mother
was breaking. Even the light on the wall knew.

Schubert's Unfinished Symphony

JEN ASHBURN

My mother played the piano. The whole
of our years together she'd play the piano,
and I'd dance as if I were Dorothy Hamill
and Mary Lou Retton wrapped into one, except
my pre-teen limbs moved like tree trunks.

My mother would play the piano, twisting over 16th notes,
driving   driving   faster faster   and I'd dance
just as fast and just as hard. Stop.

My mother would begin again,
begin with the deep bass notes. She clung
and lived in the dark old tones.
My mother lived in a garden
of darkness, and I'd spin
behind her back until exhausted,
          until I collapsed and followed her
into the shadows of her song. She
did not see me follow. I listened
to her music—an echo from the depths
of an unknown forest that vibrated
from our living room walls.

My mother played the piano. She looked
over her shoulder and hid in her forest.
And I danced or I followed. Some days
I still listen for the tremor of her song.

Ghazal

R. DWAYNE BETTS

Men bleed without insight in prison?
A hand on neck starts a fight in prison.

He held the night's air in his fist and screamed,
then sent word by scribbled kite in prison.

Steve's eyes broke open to the bluest black,
then he wore homemade tights in prison.

Marquette splintered, deranged, pigeon insane.
He learned there is never flight in prison.

You wouldn't use a rusted blade to pull
a wrist vein, but a man just might in prison.

We read *Midsummer Night's Dream* on the yard,
then Snoop said, "I am a sprite in prison."

Tim stared at lipstick on his forehead—
believed passion ignites in prison.

Evan celled with his father at Augusta,
some discovery—birthright in prison.

But, for real, why does any of it matter?
Some men never pray at night in prison.

Blame me. Write another poem, a sad psalm.
Shahid, sing for the gods, right in prison.

Red Onion State Prison

R. DWAYNE BETTS

A warehouse of iron
bunks: straight lines
& right angles

flush against the gutted
side of a mountain.
Inside, white paint

cracks into a thousand
pockmarks and listens
to the sound of a padlock

splitting a man's scalp &
voices of guards in shot-
guns or the hand that tilts

a slender metal rod,
then scrapes it against
concrete & stretches night

longer than a sinner's
prayer in Red Onion's small
ruined cells where ten thousand

years of sentences
beckon over heads & hearts,
silent, a promise, like mistletoe.

Ode to the Man
Who Grabbed My Arm in the Bar

ROGER BONAIR-AGARD

(for Patrick)

When you leaned in and made the decision
to grab my arm, you did not know
the cautionary tale you would become.
You'd left work earlier for a few drinks
with friends, and soon you were bar-hopping
and drunk, and happy, and a little in love.
When you finally looked up, and your boy said
yeah, Bar 13 has 2 for 1 specials
and your girl said *awesome!* you did not know
we misfits would be reading poems,
some of them terrible, but so necessary
to us that we couldn't stop even when
we knew they were bad. You did not know
how necessary you were (are)
to everything I've come to believe
and to much that I'm trying to unlearn.
You were loud, yes sir, and you were rude
and you did not know how willing I was
to forgive all this, because you did not know
you required forgiveness. You did not know
you were not allowed every right
you chose to claim and so you leaned in
drunk, to grab a man 40 pounds heavier
and 3 inches taller; and when my hand
pried itself away and made short journey
to your head, I was as surprised as you

to see you actually fall—
the slow-motion tumble of it.

You did not know when you left work
that you'd be struck down (ever).
You had not considered that
even remotely possible
and neither you nor your friend knew
how willing I became then to fight
your entire crew—even the women.
I wanted the ballet of all of you
come to me—I wanted you
to draw blood to my mouth,
to remind me how close to love-
making is the wrestle, have me
believe in gladiators, gargoyles
and the night again.

Small man, you could not know
that I cried after I hit you
that I've always wished myself
beyond the tribe of blood, dirt
and immediate consequence—
but you, you brought me back—
you thought you could put your hands
on anyone you felt like, and I
had to remind you otherwise,
as I slipped out the back door,
to avoid the cops, who surely
would see it your way,
and take my chance instead
with my body, my fists,
my good two legs running,
knowing I could trust only
my hands' self-made laws,
the shadows the buildings make
of the city—the night
for me to hide in.

Ode to the Man
Who Leaned Out the Truck to Call Me Nigger

ROGER BONAIR-AGARD

Before I met you that night, before you leaned out
the truck window to call me nigger, I knew
nothing of my own flesh's surrender
to blood, dust. But I did know speed; I knew
the weight of lumber and the forearm's debt
to torque. I knew (and loved) the sound of shattering glass, the quick snap of a duressed jaw.
I knew the taste of my own blood. I'd had
a fist test the tension of my kneecaps,
my heart's tight buckle.

What you taught me as I leaned out
the window, New York speeding by
at 50mph, to catch you,
was about the song of the air
at night, how—as I braced my foot
against the dash and limboed out
to swing at your windscreen—I craved
the timpani of glass and metal
the soprano of your screams.

So easily I could have fallen
under your truck's wheels. I was
in search of love and somehow
knew you had it to give in blood,
which I needed to husband
my quiet, quiet rage. I had
not thought then about how I wanted
my body disposed, that I loved

a woman to call me names in bed.
I wanted a song that was mine,
something to belong to, a love
I'd recognize when I heard
my true name sung
in the street.

The Mother

GWENDOLYN BROOKS

Abortions will not let you forget.
You remember the children you got that you did not get,
The damp small pulps with a little or with no hair,
The singers and workers that never handled the air.
You will never neglect or beat
Them, or silence or buy with a sweet.
You will never wind up the sucking-thumb
Or scuttle off ghosts that come.
You will never leave them, controlling your luscious sigh,
Return for a snack of them, with gobbling mother-eye.

I have heard in the voices of the wind the voices of my dim killed
    children.
I have contracted. I have eased
My dim dears at the breasts they could never suck.
I have said, Sweets, if I sinned, if I seized
Your luck
And your lives from your unfinished reach,
If I stole your births and your names,
Your straight baby tears and your games,
Your stilted or lovely loves, your tumults, your marriages, aches, and
    your deaths,
If I poisoned the beginnings of your breaths,
Believe that even in my deliberateness I was not deliberate.
Though why should I whine,
Whine that the crime was other than mine?—
Since anyhow you are dead.
Or rather, or instead,

You were never made.
But that too, I am afraid,
Is faulty: oh, what shall I say, how is the truth to be said?
You were born, you had body, you died.
It is just that you never giggled or planned or cried.

Believe me, I loved you all.
Believe me, I knew you, though faintly, and I loved, I loved you
All.

Jojo's

CHRISTOPHER DAVIS

The night my brother was stabbed,
but not quite stabbed to death,
I was drinking wine in a coffeeshop
called Jojo's with some friends.
He'd been walking home drunk
from a party. Two guys who'd shared a case
of beer had picked him up.
After stabbing him, they threw him
down into a canyon. Parasites
kept his wounds clean: two days later,
he climbed out. He was
found at the side of the road by
two guys. He would not let them
touch him. On May 1st,
he died in the hospital.

I've forgotten if I had a good time that night
with my friends. I probably did.
We were all in a band together.
A month later, I
left that town to go to college.
The rest of them moved too, I think.
No: on a trip home at Christmas
I saw Nancy at Jojo's. (They had
found my phone number in his pocket.)
I don't know what
was said, if we did talk.

The Murderer

CHRISTOPHER DAVIS

As I talked, I kept thinking,
You're only guilty if they
can find it: but they'd fixed pads
to my temples and wrists. Now
I want to tell them something.
Last night, in a dream,
I watched a crusted gray whale
dying underwater, the bad end
of a steel harpoon
broken off in its side.
It was going down slowly,
horizontal, turning over
on its back, on its belly,
the blood weaving out
and wrapping around its whole length
like a frayed blanket. Then it
broke through a school of thousands
of tiny silver fish
and disappeared.
I guess it hit bottom. The blanket
kept unraveling up from the shadows,
staining all the water, all
the fish, and even the filtered
weak columns of sunlight.
I woke, and lay half an hour
on my iron bed.
I hardly know what I've done.

Clitoris

TOI DERRICOTTE

This time with your mouth on my clitoris, I will not think
he does not like the taste of me. I lift the purplish hood back
from the pale white berry. It stands alone on its thousand branches.
I lift the skin like the layers of taffeta of a lady's skirt.
How shy the clitoris is, like a young girl
who must be coaxed by tenderness.

The Elephants

NATALIE DIAZ

Hast thou not seen how thy Lord dealt with the possessors of the elephant?
al-Fil, sura 105, Qur'an

My brother still hears the tanks
    when he is angry—they rumble like a herd of hot green
        elephants over the plowed streets inside him, crash through

the white oleanders lining my parents' yard
    during family barbecues, great scarred ears flapping, commanding
        a dust storm that shakes blooms from the stalks like wrecked stars.

One thousand and one sleepless nights
    bulge their thick skulls, gross elephant boots pummel
        ice chests, the long barrels of their trunks crush cans of cheap beer

and soda pop in quick, sparkling bursts of froth,
    and the meat on the grill goes to debris in the flames
        while the rest of us cower beneath lawn chairs.

When the tusked animals in my brother's miserable eyes
    finally fall asleep standing up, I find the nerve to ask him
        what they sound like, and he tells me, *It's no hat dance,*

and says that unless I've felt the bright beaks of ancient Stymphalian birds,
    unless I've felt the color red raining from Heaven and marching
        in my veins, I'll never know the sound of war.

But I do know that since my brother's been back,
    orange clouds hang above him like fruit made of smoke,
        and he sways in trancelike pachyderm rhythm

to the sweet tings of death music circling
    circling his head like an explosion of bluebottle flies
        haloing him—*I'm no saint,* he sighs, flicking each one away.

He doesn't sit in chairs anymore and is always on his feet,
    hovering by the window, peeking out the door, *Because,*
        he explains, *everyone is the enemy, even you, even me.*

The heat from guns he'll never let go
    rises up from his fists like a desert mirage, blurring
        everything he tries to touch or hold— If we cry

when his hands disappear like that, he laughs,
    Those hands, he tells us, *those little Frankensteins*
        were never my friends.

But before all this, I waited for him
    as he floated down the airport escalator in his camouflage BDUs.
        An army-issued duffel bag dangled from his shoulders—

hot green elephants,
    their arsenal of memory, rocking inside.
        He was home. He was gone.

How to Go to Dinner with a Brother on Drugs

NATALIE DIAZ

If he's wearing knives for eyes,
if he's dressed for a Day of the Dead parade—
three-piece skeleton suit, cummerbund of ribs—
his pelvic girdle will look like a Halloween mask.

The bones, he'll complain, make him itch. *Each ulna*
a tingle. His mandible might tickle.
If he cannot stop scratching, suggest that he change,
but not because he itches—do it for the scratching,
do it for the bones.

Okay, okay, he'll give in, *I'll change.*
He'll go back upstairs, and as he climbs away,
his back will be something else—one shoulder blade
a failed wing, the other a silver shovel.
He hasn't eaten in years. He will never change.

Be some kind of happy he didn't appear dressed
as a greed god—headdress of green quetzal feathers,
jaguar loincloth littered with bite-shaped rosettes—
because tonight you are not in the mood
to have your heart ripped out. It gets old,
having your heart ripped out,
being opened up that way.

Your brother will come back down again,
this time dressed as a Judas effigy.
I know, I know, he'll joke. *It's not Easter. So what?*
Be straight with him. Tell him the truth.
Tell him, *Judas had a rope around his neck.*

When he asks if an old lamp cord will do, just shrug.
He'll go back upstairs, and you will be there,
close enough to the door to leave, but you won't.
You will wait, unsure of what you are waiting for.

Wait for him in the living room
of your parents' home-turned-misery-museum.
Visit the perpetual exhibits: *Someone Is Tapping
My Phone, Como Deshacer a Tus Padres,
Jesus Told Me To,* and *Mon Frère*—
ten, twenty, forty dismantled phones dissected
on the dining table: glinting snarls of copper,
sheets of numbered buttons, small magnets,
jagged, ruptured shafts of lithium batteries,
empty 2-liters of Diet Coke with dirty tubing snaking
from the necks, shells of Ataris, radios, television sets,
and the Electrolux, all cracked open like dark nuts,
innards heaped across the floor.

And your pick for Best of Show:
Why Dad Can't Find the Lightbulbs—
A hundred glowing bells of gutted lightbulbs,
each rocking in a semicircle on the counter
beneath Mom's hanging philodendron.

Your parents' home will look like an al-Qaeda
yard sale. It will look like a bomb factory,
which might give you hope, if there were
such a thing. You are not so lucky—
there is no fuse here for you to find.

Not long ago, your brother lived with you.
You called it, *One last shot*, a three-quarter-court
heave, a buzzer-beater to win something of him back.
But who were you kidding? You took him in
with no grand dreams of salvation, but only to ease
the guilt of never having tried.

He spent his nights in your bathroom
with a turquoise BernzOmatic handheld propane torch,
a Merlin mixing magic, then shape-shifting into lions,
and tigers, and bears, *Oh fuck*, pacing your balcony
like Borges's blue tiger, fighting the cavalry in the moon,
conquering night with his blue flame, and plotting to steal
your truck keys, hidden under your pillow.
Finally, you found the nerve to ask him to leave,
so he took his propane torch and left you
with his meth pipe ringing in the dryer.

Now, he's fresh-released from Rancho Cucamonga—
having traveled the Mojave Trail in chains—
living with your parents, and you have come
to take him to dinner—because he is your brother,
because you heard he was cleaning up,
because dinner is a thing with a clear beginning
and end, a measured amount of time,
a ritual everyone knows, even your brother.
Sit down. Eat. Get up. Go home.

Holler upstairs to your brother to hurry.
He won't come right away.
Remember how long it took the Minotaur
to escape the labyrinth.

Your father will be in the living room, too,
sitting in a rocking chair in the dark,
wearing his *luchador* mask—he is El Santo.
His face is pale. His face is bone-white. His eyes
are hollow teardrops. His mouth a dark O—
He is still surprised by what his life has become.

Don't dare think about unmasking your father.
His mask is the only fight he has left.
He is bankrupt of *planchas and topes.*
He has no more *huracanranas* to give.
Leave him to imagine himself jumping
over the top rope, out of the ring,

running off, his silver-masked head
cutting the night like a butcher knife.

When your brother finally appears,
the lamp cord knotted at his neck
should do the trick, so leave to the restaurant.
It will be hard to look at him in the truck,
dressed as a Judas effigy. Don't forget,
a single match could devour him like a neon
tooth, canopying him in a bright tent of pain—
press the truck's lighter into the socket.

Meth—his singing sirens, his jealous jinn
conjuring up sandstorms within him, his Harpy
harem—has sucked the beauty from his face.
He is a Cheshire cat, a gang of grins.
His new face all jaw, all smile and bite.

Look at your brother—he is Borges's bestiary.
He is a zoo of imaginary beings.

Your brother's jaw is a third passenger in the truck—
it flexes in the wind coming in through the window,
resetting and rehinging, opening and closing
against its will. It will occur to you
your brother is a beat-down, dubbed Bruce Lee—
his words do not match his mouth, which is moving
faster and faster. You have the fastest
brother alive.

Your brother's lips are ruined.
There is a sore in the right corner of his mouth.
My teeth hurt, he says. He will ask to go
to the IHS dentist. At a stoplight, you are forced
to look into his mouth—it is Švankmajer's rabbit hole—
you have been lost in it for the last ten years.

Pull into the restaurant parking lot.
Your brother will refuse to wear his shoes.
Judas was barefoot, he will tell you.

Judas wore sandals, you answer.
No, Jesus wore sandals, he'll argue.
Maybe one day you will laugh at this—
arguing with a meth head dressed
like a Judas effigy about Jesus's sandals.

Your brother will still itch when you are seated
at your table. He will rake his fork against his skin.
Look closer—his skin is a desert.
Half a red racer is writhing along his forearm.
A migration of tarantulas moves like a shadow
over his sunken cheeks.

Every time the waitress walks by, he licks his lips
at her. He tells you, then her, that he can taste her.
Hope she ignores him. Pretend not to hear
what he says. Also ignore the cock crowing
inside him. But if he notices you noticing,
Don't worry, he'll assure you, *The dogs will get it.*
Which dogs? You have to ask.
Then he'll point out the window at two dogs humping
in the empty lot across the way.

Go ahead. Tell him. *Those are not dogs,*
you'll say. *Those are chupacabras.*
Chupacabras are not real, he'll tell you,
brothers are. And he'll be right.

The reflection in your empty plate will speak,
Your brother is on drugs again.
You are at a dinner neither of you can eat.

Consider your brother: he is dressed
as a Judas effigy. When the waitress takes your order,
your brother will ask for a beer.
You will pour your thirty pieces of silver
onto the table and ask, *What can I get for this?*

Tiara

MARK DOTY

Peter died in a paper tiara
cut from a book of princess paper dolls;
he loved royalty, sashes

and jewels. *I don't know,*
he said, when he woke in the hospice,
I was watching the Bette Davis film festival

on Channel 57 and then—
At the wake, the tension broke
when someone guessed

the casket closed because
he was *in there in a big wig
and heels,* and someone said,

*You know he's always late,
he probably isn't in there yet—
he's still fixing his makeup.*

And someone said he asked for it.
Asked for it—
when all he did was go down

into the salt tide
of wanting as much as he wanted,
giving himself over so drunk

or stoned it almost didn't matter who,
though they were beautiful,
stampeding into him in the simple,

ravishing music of their hurry.
I think heaven is perfect stasis
poised over the realms of desire,

where dreaming and waking men lie
on the grass while wet horses
roam among them, huge fragments

of the music we die into
in the body's paradise.
Sometimes we wake not knowing

how we came to lie here,
or who has crowned us with these temporary,
precious stones. And given

the world's perfectly turned shoulders,
the deep hollows blued by longing,
given the irreplaceable silk

of horses rippling in orchards,
fruit thundering and chiming down,
given the ordinary marvels of form

and gravity, what could he do,
what could any of us ever do
but ask for it?

Allegheny Ford Trucks

STEPHON HAYES

Looking out a 2nd floor window
I can only see the bridge that
leads to downtown Pittsburgh—
the rivers
and Southside work district.

The sign I can see reads
ALLEGHENY FORD TRUCKS
and I'm going crazy
with teasing myself.

You see, the vehicles are rolling by
and I imagine that someone I
know might get caught
in the 3 o'clock traffic
by my window
and look up to see me.

I would wave
screaming their name:
write me
visit me
I am lonely.
I am lonely.

ALLEGHENY FORD TRUCKS, ALLEGHENY FORD TRUCKS
greets me every day every night until I tear
myself from the window.
Even then the picture in my mind seems to
always read
ALLEGHENY FORD TRUCKS.

Ars Poetica # 789

TERRANCE HAYES

My daddies have voices
like bachelors, like castigators & crooners.
They have busted kneecaps.
They stand behind my mother
in the kitchen pretending to count the hairs
on her neck. One of my daddies
was a carpenter. One lost his tooth
in a fistfight with Jesus. One went to prison.
No, two went to prison. One daddy sits beside me
telling jokes dull as mouthwash.
One can guess how many catfish swim
in every pond. Here is my scar
from a summer working in the glass factory
across from another daddy's home.
My daddy with the pretty gold-tooth smile taps
my shoulder & says, "Look at the booty
on that gal." My daddy, Mr. Blacker-than-most,
wears shades in the house. He says
"Nobody's blacker than me, Boy."
Each of my daddies asks, "Are you writing
another poem about me?" They covet secrets.
No, my daddies covet work above secrets.
We are watching an action movie now,
my daddies & me. There are guns & damsels
& camouflage. There are car wrecks
& cusswords & blood. But my daddies are tired
Some of them sprawl on the carpet.
Some of them go upstairs to the bedrooms,

or through the front door to the porch.
My daddies fall asleep in all the rooms
inside & outside the house. I want to sleep too,
but their snores make the wind chimes tremble.

Sixth Grade

MARIE HOWE

The afternoon the neighborhood boys tied me and Mary Lou Mahar
to Donny Ralph's father's garage doors, spread-eagled,
it was the summer they chased us almost every day.

Careening across the lawns they'd mowed for money,
on bikes they threw down, they'd catch us, lie on top of us,
then get up and walk away.

That afternoon Donny's mother wasn't home.
His nine sisters and brothers gone—even Gramps, who lived with them,
gone somewhere—the backyard empty, the big house quiet.

A gang of boys. They pulled the heavy garage doors down,
and tied us to them with clothesline,
and Donny got the deer's leg severed from the buck his dad had killed

the year before, dried up and still fur-covered, and sort of
poked it at us, dancing around the blacktop in his sneakers, laughing.
Then somebody took it from Donny and did it.

And then somebody else, and somebody after him.
And then Donny pulled up Mary Lou's dress and held it up,
and she began to cry, and I became a boy again, and shouted Stop,

and they wouldn't.
And then a girl-boy, calling out to Charlie, my best friend's brother,
who wouldn't look

Charlie! to my brother's friend who knew me
Stop them. And he wouldn't.
And then more softly, and looking directly at him, I said, Charlie.

And he said Stop. And they said What? And he said Stop it.
And they did, quickly untying the ropes, weirdly quiet,
Mary Lou still weeping. And Charlie? Already gone.

leadbelly in angola prison: down again

TYEHIMBA JESS

this place sucks men firmly in her mouth, swallows them whole and leaves them shrunken masses of muscle, melts them down in a cast iron gut and shits them out with new names. smilin' johnny lee is now dicklicker, james baker became ironhead, joe simms makes himself rat, and roy from brazos county was beaten into tight eye.

they put me in the belly of a place with a name that lifts your tongue to the roof of your mouth with promise, *an'* . . . presses back down and tells you to *go*, just as your lips beg the kiss of surprise, an *oh* that grabs liver and squeezes bowels shut. *la* pushes the dirt of truth beneath myth's fertile topsoil.

someone said this place has a faraway sound, like the songs we sung before the church and jesus lashed us down to this moaners' bench of religion. i say don't nothing sound more american than angola.

Home Girl Talks Girlhood

ALLISON JOSEPH

Remember that longing for hips
and breasts, the rising curves
of womanhood? Honey, I was

so skilled at wishing
for a body I didn't know
what the hell to do with:

round, proud, everything
high and firm, long legs
curved just so, a dancer's

bearing. Just who I was
going to lure with all this,
I didn't know—all I did know

was that I quaked, afraid
each time I had to pass
those boys on the corner,

their eyes inspecting me,
finding what wasn't there,
calling after me—*you ugly,*

too skinny, for real.
How much time did I waste
longing to be a woman,

fooling around in Mother's
make-up—slashes of red vivid
against my lips, loose powder

freed on her dresser top.
I'd forage among bottles
of perfume, spray myself

with musk's dark odor,
fingers stained by mascara,
rouge. And when she'd find

me, she'd demand *just what
you think you doing, you
no damn woman yet*, and I'd

wait again, hoping my body
would begin, hoping to be
like her—all business,

all woman as she wiped
the paint from my face,
smoothing on cream to clean

my skin, bringing me back
to my ashy girlhood self,
muted child of color.

The Black Eye

NATALIE KENVIN

Your fist beat a knot on my face,
Polyphonous, clothed, densely erudite.
The winter was a lovely white.
All gypsy plaques and dewlaps
Could not undo this knobbed insult,
Relentless, misfractured, not painted.
Mazurkas, fandangos, jigs, abrupt
Blisters of music
Did not dampen or soothe
This ripely dark, evasive, shadowed bruise
Growing as a bone-orchard savors decay.
The ephemeral meringue of fog
Rose in a poverty of oxygen,
A mishap of touch.
My eye, mashed blue, adroop in fading light.
The winter was a lovely white.

Beating

NATALIE KENVIN

My father knows only that
There is a humid readiness
About my mother,
Her hair messy, lying in ringlets
That smell of copper.
Now she is going to get it,
He says.
He strikes her once and she falls
Back from the medicinal, calloused skid
Of his right hand.
Now he is balancing on top of
Her fallen body with his left leg,
His right suspended in the air
As one might balance on a log.
She says, "Don't."
For a moment they are caught here
In the spit of craziness.
He lets her up.
They walk to the kitchen.
They sit at the table
In a convalescent indolence,
A queer lassitude.
He pours a curl of cream into her tea,
Turning it a tarnished color.
She drinks, hooking her fingers
Around the cup.
He eats a small cracker.
I stare at them.
They are shameless
And in a great solitude.

Another Poem for Me
(after Recovering from an O.D.)

ETHERIDGE KNIGHT

what now
what now dumb nigger damn near dead
what now
now that you won't dance
behind the pale white doors of death
what now   is   to be
to be what you wanna be
or what white / america wants you to be
a lame crawling from nickel bag to nickel bag
be black brother / man be black
and blooming in the night
be black like your fat brother
sweating and straining to hold you
as you struggle against the straps
be black   be black like
your woman   her painted face floating
above you   her hands sliding
                        under the sheets
to take yours   be black like
your mamma sitting in a quiet corner
praying to a white / jesus to save her black boy

what now dumb nigger damn near dead
where is the correctness
the proper posture
the serious love of living
now that death has fled these quiet corridors

Genealogy

JOAN LARKIN

I come from alcohol.
I was set down in it like a spark in gas.
I lay down dumb with it, I let it erase what it liked.
I played house with it, let it dress me, undress me.
I exulted, I excused.
I married it. And where it went, I went.
I gave birth to it.
I nursed, I plotted murder with it.
I laid its table, paid its promises.
I lived with it wherever it liked to live:
in the kitchen, under the bed, at the coin laundry,
out by the swings, in the back seat of the car,
at the trashed Thanksgiving table.
I sat with it in the blear of TV.
I sat where it glittered, carmine,
where it burned in a blunt glass,
where it stood in a glittering lineup on the bar.
I saw it in the dull mirror, making up my face,
in the weekend silence,
in the smashed dish, in the slammed car door,
in the dead husband, the love.
Alcohol in the void mirror.
My generations are of alcohol
and all that I could ever hope to bear.

Good-bye

JOAN LARKIN

You are saying good-bye to your last
drink. There is no lover
like her: bourbon, big gem
in your palm and steep
fiery blade in your throat,
deadeye down. None like her
but her sister, first
gin, like your first
seaswim, first woman
whose brine took to your tongue,
who could change the seasons of your cells
like nothing else.
Unless it was wine, finally
your only companion, winking
across the table, hinting
in his rubies, his first-class labels,
of her peasant blood
and the coarse way she would open you.

Good-bye, beauties. You don't want to say it.
You try to remember
the night you fell out of the car
and crawled to the curb, the night
two of you stood
screaming over your daughter's crib.
You remember deaths
by gin, by easy capsules—
the friend who fell in silence

and the friend who quoted *Antony* in his suicide note.
All this helps for a moment, till your heart
blooms and stiffens with desire.

I Could Never

HEATHER MCNAUGHER

have a daughter.
God help me
if she dates men.
Or women like her mother,
flighty and demanding, hot-to-trot-to-
tramp over the amber coals
of her lovers' hearts.

I could never have a daughter.
What if she was raped,
or stupid,
or shallow? What if
she rolls her eyes—my eyes—
and yawns in the 11th hour
of *Brideshead Revisited*?
What if she hates herself,
and refuses food, deflecting
warmth, arms, devotion?
Shunning our face in the mirror.

What if she doesn't read,
as I did not and did not and
did not until one day,
I did. It wasn't up to you, Mom.

I could never have a daughter.
What if she loves me,
and hates me the way
I love and love my mother

until it burns to look
or swallow.

What if it's up to me and she listens
to a word I say?

Untitled

HEATHER MCNAUGHER

If, on the other hand, if on that day at noon, a Friday I think it was, I was 23, when I hopped up on that barstool—if you had told me I'd still be sitting there at four with a decision to make: to leave or not to leave, to quit now or have another, to quit now or have however many more I could fit into the next 45 minutes (make that 50, I'll walk fast because honestly, how much time does a girl need to mosey on down Pike Street to meet her girlfriend at five o'clock, roughly 40 minutes from now?).

If you had told me that this decision would become the line I'd cross, that this decision would become the story I'd tell about the line I crossed, that ten years later my story would go, *Well, at 4:55 I still cared about people; at five I said fuck off.* If you had shown me both sides of the line, given me a demonstration—said, *Heath, on this side we have giving a shit about anybody, see, and on the other we have Sierra Nevada Pale Ale on draught; on the Pike Street side of the line we have a redhead who loves you, who will, incidentally, become a model, and who is presently waiting for you at the corner of Pike and Pine, waiting for you right this second, waiting . . . to take you home, the home you share, to love and touch and look lingeringly through you. On the Denny Way side of things, however, we have this cool, dark, clammy bar with its dark woods and empty dark amber light. Here we have the mirror and the TV with the sound turned off and in front of the mirror the bottles, a dewy metropolis of bottles, and in your pocket a credit card, and beneath your denim ass the coveted corner stool, the look-at-me-I'm-not-here-stool you're not likely ever to get again should you decide to leave, so many bottles bending in that mirror, above which ticks a clock.* If you had told me that this would be my story I'd have said, another round please.

Thanks

W. S. MERWIN

Listen
with the night falling we are saying thank you
we are stopping on the bridges to bow from the railings
we are running out of the glass rooms
with our mouths full of food to look at the sky
and say thank you
we are standing by the water thanking it
smiling by the windows looking out
in our directions

back from a series of hospitals back from a mugging
after funerals we are saying thank you
after the news of the dead
whether or not we knew them we are saying thank you

over telephones we are saying thank you
in doorways and in the backs of cars and in elevators
remembering wars and the police at the door
and the beatings on stairs we are saying thank you
in the banks we are saying thank you
in the faces of the officials and the rich
and of all who will never change
we go on saying thank you thank you

with the animals dying around us
our lost feelings we are saying thank you
with the forests falling faster than the minutes
of our lives we are saying thank you
with the words going out like cells of a brain
with the cities growing over us

we are saying thank you faster and faster
with nobody listening we are saying thank you
we are saying thank you and waving
dark though it is

Kindness

NAOMI SHIHAB NYE

Before you know what kindness really is
you must lose things,
feel the future dissolve in a moment
like salt in a weakened broth.
What you held in your hand,
what you counted and carefully saved,
all this must go so you know
how desolate the landscape can be
between the regions of kindness.
How you ride and ride
thinking the bus will never stop,
the passengers eating maize and chicken
will stare out the window forever.

Before you learn the tender gravity of kindness,
you must travel where the Indian in a white poncho
lies dead by the side of the road.
You must see how this could be you,
how he too was someone
who journeyed through the night with plans
and the simple breath that kept him alive.

Before you know kindness as the deepest thing inside,
you must know sorrow as the other deepest thing.
You must wake up with sorrow.
You must speak to it till your voice
catches the thread of all sorrows
and you see the size of the cloth.

Then it is only kindness that makes sense anymore,
only kindness that ties your shoes
and sends you out into the day to mail letters and
purchase bread,
only kindness that raises its head
from the crowd of the world to say
It is I you have been looking for,
and then goes with you everywhere
like a shadow or a friend.

I Go Back to May 1937

SHARON OLDS

I see them standing at the formal gates of their colleges,
I see my father strolling out
under the ochre sandstone arch, the red tiles glinting like bent
plates of blood behind his head, I
see my mother with a few light books at her hip
standing at the pillar made of tiny bricks with the
wrought-iron gate still open behind her, its
sword-tips black in the May air,
they are about to graduate, they are about to get married,
they are kids, they are dumb, all they know is they are
innocent, they would never hurt anybody.
I want to go up to them and say Stop,
don't do it—she's the wrong woman,
he's the wrong man, you are going to do things
you cannot imagine you would ever do,
you are going to do bad things to children,
you are going to suffer in ways you never heard of,
you are going to want to die. I want to go
up to them there in the late May sunlight and say it,
her hungry pretty blank face turning to me,
her pitiful beautiful untouched body,
his arrogant handsome blind face turning to me,
his pitiful beautiful untouched body,
but I don't do it. I want to live. I
take them up like the male and female
paper dolls and bang them together
at the hips like chips of flint as if to
strike sparks from them, I say
Do what you are going to do, and I will tell about it.

The Language of the Brag

SHARON OLDS

I have wanted excellence in the knife-throw,
I have wanted to use my exceptionally strong and accurate arms
and my straight posture and quick electric muscles
to achieve something at the center of a crowd,
the blade piercing the bark deep,
the haft slowly and heavily vibrating like the cock.

I have wanted some epic use for my excellent body,
some heroism, some American achievement
beyond the ordinary for my extraordinary self,
magnetic and tensile, I have stood by the sandlot
and watched the boys play.

I have wanted courage, I have thought about fire
and the crossing of waterfalls, I have dragged around
my belly big with cowardice and safety,
stool charcoal from the iron pills,
huge breasts leaking colostrum,
legs swelling, hands swelling,
face swelling and reddening, hair
falling out, inner sex
stabbed and stabbed again with pain like a knife.
I have lain down.

I have lain down and sweated and shaken
and passed blood and shit and water and
slowly alone in the center of a circle I have
passed the new person out
and they have lifted the new person free of the act
and wiped the new person free of that
language of blood like praise all over the body.

I have done what you wanted to do, Walt Whitman,
Allen Ginsberg, I have done this thing,
I and the other women this exceptional
act with the exceptional heroic body,
this giving birth, this glistening verb,
and I am putting my proud American boast
right here with the others.

If There's a God . . .

GREGORY ORR

If there's a god of amphetamine, he's also the god of wrecked lives, and it's only he who can explain how my doctor father, with the gift of healing strangers and patients alike, left so many intimate dead in his wake.

If there's a god of amphetamine, he's also the god of recklessness, and I ask him to answer.

He's the god of thrills, the god of boys riding bikes down steep hills with their hands over their heads.

He's the god of holy and unholy chance, the god of soldiers crossing a field and to the right of you a man falls dead and to the left also and you are still standing.

If there's a god of amphetamine, he's the god of diet pills, who is the god of the fifties housewife who vacuums all day and whose bathroom is spotless and now it is evening as she sits alone in the kitchen, polishing her chains.

He's the god of the rampant mind and the god of my father's long monologues by moonlight in the dark car driving over the dusty roads.

He's the god of tiny, manic orderings in the midst of chaos, the god of elaborate charts where Greg will do this chore on Monday and a different one on Tuesday and all the brothers are there on the chart and all the chores and all the days of the week in a miniscule script no one can read.

If there's a god of amphetamine, my father was his hopped-up acolyte who leapt out of bed one afternoon to chase a mouse through the house, shouting, firing his .38 repeatedly at the tiny beast scurrying along the wall while Jon wailed for help from the next room.

If there's a god of amphetamine, he's the god of subtle carnage and dubious gifts who lives in each small pill tasting of electricity and dust.

If there's a god of amphetamine, my father was its high priest, praising it, preaching its gospel, lifting it like a host and intoning: "Here in my hand is the mystery: a god alive inside a tiny tablet. He is a high god, a god of highs—he eats the heart to juice the brain and mocks the havoc he makes, laughing at all who stumble. Put out your tongue and receive it."

Dad's at the Diner

SARA RIES

9:30 a.m. I make coffee, open a book.
It's breakfast rush for Dad.
I picture hard spatula scrapes under eggs,
pancake islands in meat grease.
His sneakers scuff the new cream tiles,
a fast morning dance, as the waitress
brews more coffee. The old tiles were worn to black
from his feet, so many times writing:
This is my poetry. When all the orders are cooked,
Dad tosses an egg in his half-eaten sandwich
because a yolk broke and he grew up poor.

Once, during a break from school,
I pointed to the potatoes
frying in bacon grease and said
What about the vegetarians, like me, Dad
and when you add sausage to lentil soup,
shouldn't you write—lentil with sausage—on the board?
He said *Come on, Sara. You've been gone too long.*
You know our customers aren't those kinds of people.

When the waitress took my order,
I said *Hi, I'm Sara and Dave's my father.*
Can I get chocolate chip pancakes
but please write—No meat grease
anywhere near your daughter's food.

I sat beyond the grill. When the waitress
hung my order, Dad turned and said
You want to cook it? I'm busy;

I have my customers to worry about.
I would, I said, *but this is a new shirt.*

I went to the kitchen to hug Dad goodbye.
He was massaging his wrist. He said
I don't know how much longer—
I promised myself long ago
I wouldn't work this way forever.
His face was a sheet of paper so crumpled
it started to tear. I said *I'll help out this summer.*

Before I applied to school, Dad said
Sara, if you want to take over the diner,
I'll work for you as long as I'm able, but I said
I can't. After that, when customers asked
if I'm the future owner, Dad shook his head,
said *She's smarter than that.*

Five years have passed and still, every day,
4 a.m., except Sundays, Dad flips on the lights
and he wonders, how many eggs, how many aprons,
how many mornings will the sign say
Come In, We're Open.

For Brothers Everywhere

TIM SEIBLES

There is a schoolyard that runs
from here to the dark's fence
where brothers keep goin to the hoop, keep
risin up with baske'balls ripe as pumpkins
toward rims hung like piñatas, pinned
like thunderclouds to the sky's wide chest
an' everybody is spinnin an' bankin
off the glass, finger-rollin off the glass
with the same soft touch you'd give
the head of a child, *a chile witta*
big-ass pumpkin head, who stands
in the schoolyard lit by brothers—postin up,
givin, goin, taking the lane, flashin off
the pivot, dealin behind the back, between
the legs, cockin the rock an' glidin
like mad hawks—swoopin black with arms
for wings, palmin the sun, throwin it down,
and even with the day gone, without even
a crumb of light from the city, *brothers*
keep runnin-gunnin, fallin away takin
fall-away j's from the corner, their bodies
like muscular saxophones *body-boppin*
better than jazz, beyond summer, beyond
weather, beyond everything that moves—
an' with one shake they're pullin-up
from the perimeter, shakin-bakin,
brothers be sweet pullin-up from
the edge a' the world, hangin like

air itself hangs in the air,
an' gravidy gotta giv 'em up: the ball
burning like a fruit with a soul
in their velvet hands, while the wrists
whisper backspin, *an' the fingers comb the rock*
once—givin it up, lettin it go, lettin it go
like good news because the hoop is a well,
a well with no bottom, *an' they're*
fillin that sucker up!

Natasha in a Mellow Mood

TIM SEIBLES

(apologies to Bullwinkle and Rocky)

Boris, dahlink, look
at my legs, long
as a lonely evening in Leningrad,
how they open the air
when I walk, the way moonlight
opens the dark. Boris, my hair
is so black with espionage,
so cool and quiet with all those secrets
so well kept—those secret plans
you've nearly kissed
into my ears. Who gives a proletarian
damn about Bullwinkle and that
flying squirrel and that idiot
who draws us? America
is a virgin, the cartoonist who leaves me
less than a Barbie doll under
this dress, who draws me
with no smell—**he** is a virgin.
The children who watch us
every Saturday mornink
are virgins. Boris, my sweet waterbug, I
don't want to be a virgin anymore.
Look into my eyes, heavy
with the absence of laughter
and the presence of vodka. Listen
to my Russian lips muss up
these blonde syllables of English:
Iwantchu. Last night

I dreamed you spelled your
code name on my shoulder
with the waxed sprigs of your
moustache. I had just come
out of the bath. My skin was still
damp, my hair poured like ink
as I pulled the comb through it. Then
I heard you whisper, felt you take
my hand—Oh, Boris, Boris
Badenov. I want your mischief-
riddled eyes to invent
my whole body, all the silken
slopes of flesh forgotten
by the blind cartoonist. I want
to be scribbled all over you
in shapes no pencil would dare. Dahlink,
why don't we take off
that funny little hat. Though
you are hardly tall
as my thighs, I want your pointy
shoes beside my bed, your
coat flung and fallen
like a double-agent
on my floor.

Addiction

SHERYL ST. GERMAIN

—in memory of my brother, Jay St. Germain, 1958–1981

The truth is I loved it,
the whole ritual of it,
the way he would fist up his arm, then
hold it out so trusting and bare,
the vein pushed up all blue and throbbing
and wanting to be pierced,
his opposite hand gripped tight as death
around the upper arm,

the way I would try to enter the vein,
almost parallel to the arm,
push lightly but firmly, not
too deep,
you don't want to go through
the vein, just in,
then pull back until you see
blood, then

hold the needle very still, slowly
shoot him with it.
Like that I would enter him,
slowly, slowly, very still,
don't move,
then he would let the fist out,
loosen his grip on the upper arm—

and oh, the movement of his lips
when he asked that I open my arms.
How careful,
how good he was, sliding

the needle silver and slender
so easily into me, as though
my skin and veins were made for it,
and when he had finished, pulled
it out, I would be coming
in my fingers, hands, my ear lobes
were coming, heart, thighs,
tongue, eyes and brain were coming,
thick and brilliant as the last thin match
against a homeless bitter cold.

I even loved the pin-sized bruises,
I would finger them alone in my room
like marks of passion;
by the time they turned yellow,
my dreams were full of needles.

We both took lovers who loved
this entering and being entered,
but when he brought over the
pale-faced girl so full of needle holes
he had to lay her on her back

like a corpse and stick the needle
over and over in her ankle veins
to find one that wasn't weary
of all that joy, I became sick
with it, but

you know, it still stalks my dreams,
and deaths make no difference:
there is only the body's huge wanting.

When I think of my brother
all spilled out on the floor
I say nothing to anyone.
I know what it's like to want joy
at any cost.

Eating

SHERYL ST. GERMAIN

I have eaten the blueberry pancakes with their rich wells
of butter and syrup, and I have not once thought
about the weight of syrup and butter on heart and hips
already heavy with living. And the crisp, hard bacon,
all four pieces have I eaten, and not once have I thought
about the pig's sufferings, but have enjoyed the
beautiful slabs of fried fat, have taken pleasure in the eating of it,
as some lover may take pleasure in the plumpness of me.

How could I not eat the pancakes with their blueberries
like eyes that bleed blueness everywhere, the fork,
the plate, my lips and tongue stained
with the greedy juices of ripe blueberries.
I want to forget the sad tuna fish sandwiches
and cottage cheese lunches, to hell with the idea
that I could be slim, happy
without pancakes and syrup, butter and bacon.
I'll take hips full and wide as the earth, legs big enough
to swallow the night, a body that shouts the pure delight
of eating, the meat of the earth, the sweet and salty
fruit of the earth. Let me die with a syrupy grin
and bacon breath, blueberry juice
inked thick in my mouth.

Young Night

SHERYL ST. GERMAIN

1

They are standing in shadows,
he reaches under her shirt
to stroke her breast.
It is the beginning,
the young night, his small
hands that feel cool
on her breasts, her nipples
that ache like pennies
wanting to be spent.

2

Years later she will look at herself
in the mirror, hold her breasts
in her hands like gifts.
Now he says they are too large,
they do not fit my hands.
She lets them fall, and touches
her face, which he says he cannot
look at. She can't remember if
she is ugly or pretty.
There is a weight in her
like a stone moon. Mirrors
can no longer be trusted.
She cooks breakfast,
little sausages, fried in fat.

3

A closet is not such a bad place
to be. It is true there is nothing
to read, but since the light burned
out there has been nothing to read by.
There is a pile of clothes on the floor
that she sits on. The smell of it
is like a perfume of family:
the smell of greasy old slippers,
the pepper of vacuum cleaner dust,
wool and cedar, mildew, old magazine
smell, brittle as fire.

She takes her ring off
and puts it in her mouth.
Metal and soap, it is something.
She can hear the children asking
their father again where she is.
Their voices seep like razors
Under the door.

4

She forgives him and sleeps with him
again. After all, there is the rent,
the groceries, the children,
her face—what kind of job
could she get with this face.
But most of all there is his
regular presence, like a light
bulb, there is his cologne,
which she loves, on his cotton
shirts.

 She likes to sit up
at night after everyone is asleep
and breathe in his scent on the shirt
he has worn that day. First under the arms,

then the back. She buries her
face in it.

> A fist,

a kiss, one always follows
the other if she waits long
enough. They are the same.

5

Her friends don't understand
why she doesn't leave him.
She would point to his kindnesses,
which are many. She knows
the world is not black and white.
It is a bruise of splendid and various
blues, purples and blacks that stretches
as far as she can see.

Relapse Suite

CHRISTINE STROUD

1: New Orleans

Jade, the night you
flayed your calf muscle
with a hunk of PBR bottle,
after you drank a case of beer
and a fifth of Old Crow
I heard Joe held you down—
knees on your chest, hands
clamped over your
wiry arms. He tried to stop
the pulsing blood
with his black t-shirt and dirty
socks. You screamed
your own poetry and Gits' lyrics,
and hissed at him   *let me die*

2: Asheville

After New Orleans you started
building boundaries, tattooed
dont doit across your knuckles
and locked your liquor
cabinet. For a whole year
at the French Broad bar
you served gin and tonics,
sliced lime wedges, poured
heavy whiskey shots. Not once
did you take a beer at the party,

not once did you lick the dribble
of liquor that ran across your
fingers. This is how I knew
you: Sober, strong-willed.

When I came home from Seattle,
months later, you were drinking wine
and electric-red cough syrup
I thought it was a brand new party.
Even after the night
you threatened to kill me
for smoking your last cigarette,

as the bullets fell into the snow
like awful inverted stars,

I never saw
this end. I was distracted
and jealous, because poetry
had been your first language

while I scribbled
translations on scraps
of torn beer labels.
That summer we smashed
bottles, kicked holes
in walls, chewed raw beets
and let their juices run blood
from our mouths.

We drank and we drank.

3: Buffalo or A Man I Never Met Shot You in the Back

After the bar, the slurred
fight about who ate
the sandwich, a knife
yanked from the kitchen
drawer, threats of guns—
you left. You swung the front door

wide open on to Breckenridge,
left it hanging on its hinges, cold
air flooding the house. You
stepped into the yard, where
morning snow cracked
and powdered under your boots.

Down the street people
were in their cars, hands
cupped to mouths, blowing warmth
in long breaths. Farther down
a dog barked and sun pushed
up through the gray crust
behind brick apartments.

4: Pittsburgh

You have been dead
two years. Still
sometimes when I see
a woman with short black
hair in an oversized army
coat, I think for a second,
      it's you.
But of course it's not.
A week after your funeral
I went to the Rock Room.
Kevin sat at the bar,
moving the thin black
straw between the ice
cubes in his drink.
He shrugged and said,
I always knew she'd
end up like this,
if she kept drinking.
She was just so
      out of control.

Tonight I'm home alone,
but I can hear the couple's TV
in the row house next door.
My space heater clicks.
I'm thinking about you
and that winter afternoon
it was so cold in your room
the door handle sparkled
with frost. We were drunk
off whiskey you stole
from your boyfriend
and I could almost convince
myself I was warm.

You pulled a postcard,
with a scrawled picture
of the Space Needle on the front
from beneath a stack of books.
You're the only person
who's ever written me a letter,
you said and exhaled a cloud
of warm wet breath.

The Real Warnings Are Always Too Late

RHETT ISEMAN TRULL

I want to go back to the winter I was born and warn you
that I will flood through your life like acid
and you will burn yourselves on me.
On my sixteenth birthday, I will use the candles
to set the basement aflame and run out laughing,
wearing smoke like a new dress. With a pocket knife,
I will try to root out that life you so eagerly started.
I'll dent the garage door with my head, siphon Crown Royal
from your liquor cabinet, jump from a gondola in Venice. I'll smash
my ankle with a hammer, drive through stop signs
with my eyes closed, cost you thousands
in medical bills. Forget about sleeping.
I'll dominate the prayers you keep sending up
like the last of flares from an island no one visits.
For every greeting card poem, I will write four
to hurt you. Some will be true.
Other people's lives will look perfect
as you search the house for its sharper pieces.
And when they lock me up I'll tell the walls
I'm sorry. But these warning will come like candles
after a night of pyres. I already know
how you will take one look at that new life screaming
into the world, and open your arms,
thinking, if it looks this innocent,
it cannot be so bad.

Love after Love

DEREK WALCOTT

The time will come
when, with elation
you will greet yourself arriving
at your own door, in your own mirror
and each will smile at the other's welcome,
and say, sit here. Eat.
You will love again the stranger who was your self.
Give wine. Give bread. Give back your heart
to itself, to the stranger who has loved you

all your life, whom you ignored
for another, who knows you by heart.
Take down the love letters from the bookshelf,

the photographs, the desperate notes,
peel your own image from the mirror.
Sit. Feast on your life.

The Impossible

BRUCE WEIGL

Winter's last rain and a light I don't recognize
through the trees and I come back in my mind
to the man who made me suck his cock
when I was seven, in sunlight, between boxcars.
I thought I could leave him standing there
in the years, half smile on his lips,
small hands curled into small fists,
but after he finished, he held my hand in his
as if astonished, until the houses were visible
just beyond the railyard. He held my hand
but before that he slapped me hard on the face
when I would not open my mouth for him.

I do not want to say his whole hips
slammed into me, but they did, and a black wave
washed over my brain, changing me
so I could not move among my people in the old way.
On my way home I stopped in the churchyard
to try and find a way to stay alive.
In the branches a redwing flitted, warning me.
In the rectory, Father prepared
the body and blood for mass
but God could not save me from a mouthful of cum.
That afternoon some lives turned away from the light.
He taught me how to move my tongue around.
In his hands he held my head like a lover.
Say it clearly and you make it beautiful, no matter what.

Untitled

FRANZ WRIGHT

This was the first time I knelt
and with my lips, frightened, kissed
the lit inwardly pink petaled lips.

It was like touching a bird's exposed heart
with your tongue.

Summer dawn flowing into the room parting the
curtains—the lamp dimming—breeze

rendered visible. Lightning,
                            and then soft applause
from the leaves . . .

Almost children, we lay asleep in love listening to
the rain.

We didn't ask to be born.

Untitled

GARY YOUNG

I left home when I was seventeen. Seventeen years later you and I were married, and today we have been married for seventeen years. It's a queer calculus. For seventeen years I have turned to you in the dark, and teased your nipples with my tongue. I have watched your body swell with children, and I have seen our children slip startled and wide-eyed into the world. There is a locust that rises from the ground only once every seventeen years. When the time comes, bury me deep. It's only love that's held me here this long, and even in the grave I'll still want you in my bones.

FICTION

River of Names

DOROTHY ALLISON

At a picnic at my aunt's farm, the only time the whole family ever gathered, my sister Billie and I chased chickens into the barn. Billie ran right through the open doors and out again, but I stopped, caught by a shadow moving over me. My Cousin Tommy, eight years old as I was, swung in the sunlight with his face as black as his shoes—the rope around his neck pulled up into the sunlit heights of the barn, fascinating, horrible. Wasn't he running ahead of us? Someone came up behind me. Someone began to scream. My mama took my head in her hands and turned my eyes away.

Jesse and I have been lovers for a year now. She tells me stories about her childhood, about her father going off each day to the university, her mother who made all her dresses, her grandmother who always smelled of dill bread and vanilla. I listen with my mouth open, not believing but wanting, aching for the fairy tale she thinks is everyone's life.

"What did your grandmother smell like?"

I lie to her the way I always do, a lie stolen from a book. "Like lavender," stomach churning over the memory of sour sweat and snuff.

I realize I do not really know what lavender smells like, and I am for a moment afraid she will ask something else, some question that will betray me. But Jesse slides over to hug me, to press her face against my ear, to whisper, "How wonderful to be part of such a large family."

I hug her back and close my eyes. I cannot say a word.

I was born between the older cousins and the younger, born in a pause of babies and therefore outside, always watching. Once, way before Tommy died, I was pushed out on the steps while everyone stood listening to my Cousin Barbara. Her screams went up and down in the back of the house. Cousin Cora brought buckets of bloody rags out to be burned. The other cousins all ran off to catch the sparks or poke the fire with dogwood sticks. I waited on the porch making up words to the shouts around me. I did not understand what was happening. Some of the older cousins obviously did, their strange expressions broken by stranger laughs. I had seen them helping her up the stairs while the thick blood ran down her legs. After a while the blood on the rags was thin, watery, almost pink. Cora threw them on the fire and stood motionless in the stinking smoke.

Randall went by and said there'd be a baby, a hatched egg to throw out with the rags, but there wasn't. I watched to see and there wasn't; nothing but the blood, thinning out desperately while the house slowed down and grew quiet, hours of cries growing soft and low, moaning under the smoke. My Aunt Raylene came out on the porch and almost fell on me, not seeing me, not seeing anything at all. She beat on the post until there were knuckle-sized dents in the peeling paint, beat on that post like it could feel, cursing it and herself and every child in the yard, singing up and down, "Goddamn, goddamn that girl . . . no sense . . . goddamn!"

I've these pictures my mama gave me—stained sepia prints of bare dirt yards, plank porches, and step after step of children—cousins, uncles, aunts; mysteries. The mystery is how many no one remembers. I show them to Jesse, not saying who they are, and when she laughs at the broken teeth, torn overalls, the dirt, I set my teeth at what I do not want to remember and cannot forget.

We were so many we were without number and, like tadpoles, if there was one less from time to time, who counted? My maternal great-grandmother had eleven daughters, seven sons; my grandmother, six sons, five daughters. Each one made at least six. Some made nine. Six times six, eleven times nine. They went on like multiplication tables. They died and were not missed. I come of an enormous family and I cannot tell half their stories. Somehow it was always made to seem they killed themselves: car wrecks, shotguns, dusty ropes, screaming, falling out of windows, things inside them. I am the point of a pyramid, sliding back under the weight of the ones who came after, and it does not matter that I am the lesbian, the one who will not have children.

I tell the stories and it comes out funny. I drink bourbon and make myself drawl, tell all those old funny stories. Someone always seems to ask me, which one was that? I show the pictures and she says, "Wasn't she the one in the story about the bridge?" I put the pictures away, drink more, and someone always finds them, then says, "Goddamn! How many of you were there, anyway?"

I don't answer.

Jesse used to say, "You've got such a fascination with violence. You've got so many terrible stories."

She said it with her smooth mouth, that chin that nobody ever slapped, and I love that chin, but when Jesse said that, my hands shook and I wanted nothing so much as to tell her terrible stories.

So I made a list. I told her: that one went insane—got her little brother with a tire iron; the three of them slit their arms, not the wrists but the bigger veins up near the elbow; she, now she strangled the boy she was sleeping with and got sent away; that one drank lye and died laughing soundlessly. In one year I lost eight cousins. It was the year everybody ran away. Four disappeared and were never found. One fell in the river and was drowned. One was run down hitchhiking north. One was shot running through the woods, while Grace, the last one, tried to walk from Greenville to Greer for some reason nobody knew. She fell off the overpass a mile down from the Sears, Roebuck warehouse and lay there for hunger and heat and dying.

Later, sleeping, but not sleeping, I found that my hands were up under Jesse's chin. I rolled away, but I didn't cry. I almost never let myself cry.

Almost always, we were raped, my cousins and I. That was some kind of joke, too.

"What's a South Carolina virgin?"

"At's a ten-year-old can run fast."

It wasn't funny for me in my mama's bed with my stepfather; not for my Cousin Billie in the attic with my uncle; nor for Lucille in the woods with another cousin; for Danny with four strangers in a parking lot; or for Pammy, who made the papers. Cora read it out loud: "Repeatedly by persons unknown." They stayed unknown since Pammy never spoke again. Perforations, lacerations, contusions, and bruises. I heard all the words, big words, little words, words too terrible to understand. DEAD BY AN ACT OF MAN. With the prick still in them, the broom handle, the tree branch, the grease gun . . . objects, things not to be believed . . . whiskey bottles, can openers, grass shears, glass, metal, vegetables . . . not to be believed, not to be believed.

Jesse says, "You've got a gift for words. "

"Don't talk," I beg her, "don't talk." And this once, she just holds me, blessedly silent.

I dig out the pictures, stare into the faces. Which one was I? Survivors do hate themselves, I know, over the core of fierce self-love, never understanding, always asking, "Why me and not her, not him?" There is such mystery in it, and I have hated myself as much as I have loved others, hated the simple fact of my own survival. Having survived, am I supposed to say something, do something, be something?

I loved my Cousin Butch. He had this big old head, pale thin hair and enormous, watery eyes. All the cousins did, though Butch's head was the largest, his hair the palest. I was the dark-headed one. All the rest of the family seemed pale carbons of each other in shades of blond, though later on everybody's hair went brown or red, and I didn't stand out so. Butch and I stood out—because I was so dark and fast, and he because of that big head and the crazy things he did. Butch used to climb on the back of my Uncle Lucius's truck, open the gas tank and hang his head over, breathe deeply, strangle, gag, vomit, and breathe again. It went so deep, it tingled in your toes. I climbed up after him and tried it myself, but I was too young to hang on long, and I fell heavily to the ground, dizzy and giggling. Butch could hang on, put his hand down into the tank and pull up a cupped palm of gas, breathe deep and laugh. He would climb down roughly, swinging down from the door handle, laughing, staggering, and stinking of gasoline. Someone caught him at it. Someone threw a match. "I'll teach you."

Just like that, gone before you understand.

I wake up in the night screaming, "No, no, I won't!" Dirty water rises in the back of my throat, the liquid language of my own terror and rage. "Hold me. Hold me." Jesse rolls over on me; her hands grip my hipbones tightly.

"I love you. I love you. I'm here," she repeats. I stare up into her dark eyes, puzzled, afraid. I draw a breath in deeply, smile my bland smile. "Did I fool you?" I laugh, rolling away from her. Jesse punches me playfully, and I catch her hand in the air.

"My love," she whispers, and cups her body against my hip, closes her eyes. I bring my hand up in front of my face and watch the knuckles, the nails as they tremble, tremble. I watch for a long time while she sleeps, warm and still against me.

James went blind. One of the uncles got him in the face with home-brewed alcohol.

Lucille climbed out the front window of Aunt Raylene's house and jumped. They said she jumped. No one said why.

My Uncle Matthew used to beat my Aunt Raylene. The twins, Mark and Luke, swore to stop him, pulled him out in the yard one time, throwing him between them like a loose bag of grain. Uncle Matthew screamed like a pig coming up for slaughter. I got both my sisters in the toolshed for safety, but I hung back to watch. Little Bo came running out of the house, off the porch, feet first into his daddy's arms. Uncle Matthew started swinging him like a scythe, going after the bigger boys, Bo's head thudding their shoulders, their hips. Afterward, Bo crawled around in the dirt, the blood running out of his ears and his tongue hanging out of his mouth, while Mark and Luke finally got their daddy down. It was a long time before I realized that they never told anybody else what had happened to Bo.

Randall tried to teach Lucille and me to wrestle. "Put your hands up." His legs were wide apart, his torso bobbing up and down, his head moving constantly. Then his hand flashed at my face. I threw myself back into the dirt, lay still. He turned to Lucille, not noticing that I didn't get up. He punched at her, laughing. She wrapped her hands around her head, curled over so her knees were up against her throat.

"No, no!" he yelled. "Move like her." He turned to me. "Move." He kicked at me. I rocked into a ball, froze.

"No, no!" He kicked me. I grunted, didn't move. He turned to Lucille.

"You." Her teeth were chattering but she held herself still, wrapped up tighter than bacon slices.

"You move!" he shouted. Lucille just hugged her head tighter and started to sob.

"Son of a bitch," Randall grumbled, "you two will never be any good."

He walked away. Very slowly we stood up, embarrassed, looked at each other. We knew.

If you fight back, they kill you.

My sister was seven. She was screaming. My stepfather picked her up by her left arm, swung her forward and back. It gave. The arm went around loosely. She just kept screaming. I didn't know you could break it like that.

I was running up the hall. He was right behind me. "Mama! Mama!" His left hand—he was left-handed—closed around my throat, pushed me against the wall, and then he lifted me that way. I kicked, but I couldn't reach him. He was yelling, but there was so much noise in my ears I couldn't hear him.

"Please, Daddy. Please, Daddy. I'll do anything, I promise. Daddy, anything you want. Please, Daddy."

I couldn't have said that. I couldn't talk around that fist at my throat, couldn't breathe. I woke up when I hit the floor. I looked up at him.

"If I live long enough, I'll fucking kill you."

He picked me up by my throat again.

"What's wrong with her?"

"Why's she always following you around?"

Nobody really wanted answers.

A full bottle of vodka will kill you when you're nine and the bottle is a quart. It was a third cousin proved that. We learned what that and other things could do. Every year there was something new.

You're growing up. My big girl.

There was codeine in the cabinet, paregoric for the baby's teeth, whiskey, beer, and wine in the house. Jeanne brought home MDA, PCP, acid; Randall, grass, speed, and mescaline. It all worked to dull things down, to pass the time.

Stealing was a way to pass the time. Things we needed, things we didn't, for the nerve of it, the anger, the need. You're growing up, we told each other. But sooner or later, we all got caught. Then it was When Are You Going to Learn?

Caught, nightmares happened. "Razorback desperate" was the conclusion of the man down at the county farm where Mark and Luke were sent at fifteen. They both got their heads shaved, their earlobes sliced.

What's the matter, kid? Can't you take it?

Caught at sixteen, June was sent to Jessup County Girls' Home, where the baby was adopted out and she slashed her wrists on the bedsprings.

Lou got caught at seventeen and held in the station downtown, raped on the floor of the holding tank.

Are you a boy or are you a girl?

On your knees, kid, can you take it?

Caught at eighteen and sent to prison, Jack came back seven years later blank-faced, understanding nothing. He married a quiet girl from out of town, had three babies in four years.

Then Jack came home one night from the textile mill, carrying one of those big handles off the high-speed spindle machine. He used it to beat them all to death and went back to work in the morning.

Cousin Melvina married at fourteen, had three kids in two and a half years, and welfare took them all away. She ran off with a carnival mechanic, had three more babies before he left her for a motorcycle acrobat. Welfare took those, too. But the next baby was hydrocephalic, a little waterhead they left with her, and the three that followed, even the one she used to hate so—the one she had after she fell off the porch and couldn't remember whose child it was.

"How many children do you have?" I asked her.

"You mean the ones I have, or the ones I had? Four," she told me, "or eleven."

My aunt, the one I was named for, tried to take off for Oklahoma. That was after she'd lost the youngest girl and they told her Bo would never be "right." She packed up biscuits, cold chicken, and Coca-Cola; a lot of loose clothes; Cora and her new baby, Cy; and the four youngest girls. They set off from Greenville in the afternoon, hoping to make

Oklahoma by the weekend, but they only got as far as Augusta. The bridge there went out under them.

"An Act of God," my uncle said.

My aunt and Cora crawled out downriver, and two of the girls turned up in the weeds, screaming loud enough to be found in the dark. But one of the girls never came up out of that dark water, and Nancy, who had been holding Cy, was found still wrapped around the baby, in the water, under the car.

"An Act of God," my aunt said. "God's got one damn sick sense of humor."

My sister had her baby in a bad year. Before he was born we had talked about it. "Are you afraid?" I asked.

"He'll be fine," she'd replied, not understanding, speaking instead to the other fear. "Don't we have a tradition of bastards?"

He was fine, a classically ugly healthy little boy with that shock of white hair that marked so many of us. But afterward, it was that bad year with my sister down with pleurisy, then cystitis, and no work, no money, having to move back home with my cold-eyed stepfather. I would come home to see her, from the woman I could not admit I'd been with, and take my infinitely fragile nephew and hold him, rocking him, rocking myself.

One night I came home to screaming—the baby, my sister, no one else there. She was standing by the crib, bent over, screaming red-faced. "Shut up! Shut up!" With each word her fist slammed the mattress fanning the baby's ear.

"Don't!" I grabbed her, pulling her back, doing it as gently as I could so I wouldn't break the stitches from her operation. She had her other arm clamped across her abdomen and couldn't fight me at all. She just kept shrieking.

"That little bastard just screams and screams. That little bastard. I'll kill him."

Then the words seeped in and she looked at me while her son kept crying and kicking his feet. By his head the mattress still showed the impact of her fist.

"Oh no," she moaned, "I wasn't going to be like that. I always promised myself." She started to cry, holding her belly and sobbing. "We an't no different. We an't no different."

Jesse wraps her arm around my stomach, presses her belly into my back. I relax against her. "You sure you can't have children?" she asks. "I sure would like to see what your kids would turn out to be like."

I stiffen, say, "I can't have children. I've never wanted children."

"Still," she says, "you're so good with children, so gentle."

I think of all the times my hands have curled into fists, when I have just barely held on. I open my mouth, close it, can't speak. What could I say now? All the times I have not spoken before, all the things I just could not tell her, the shame, the self-hatred, the fear; all of that hangs between us now—a wall I cannot tear down.

I would like to turn around and talk to her, tell her . . . "I've got a dust river in my head, a river of names endlessly repeating. That dirty water rises in me, all those children screaming out their lives in my memory, and I become someone else, someone I have tried so hard not to be." But I don't say anything, and I know, as surely as I know I will never have a child, that by not speaking I am condemning us, that I cannot go on loving you and hating you for your fairytale life, for not asking about what you have no reason to imagine, for that soft-chinned innocence I love.

Jesse puts her hands behind my neck, smiles and says "You tell the funniest stories."

I put my hands behind her back, feeling the ridges of my knuckles pulsing.

"Yeah," I tell her. "But I lie."

Anything for Johnny

ERIC BOYD

It felt like being born. I was granted early parole. I packed everything I had saved and said goodbye to everybody I had known there. The entire day many people became my friends, people I had never spoken to before.

I gave away most of my clothes, my extra pillow, some pens, a pair of good shoes I took from the dumpster while I was working, some books I didn't like, nudie pictures, and my radio. I kept a shaving razor, my notebooks, letters from Lucy, a heart I had made from an orange rind, some books I liked, a highlighter from the old county morgue, and the glasses I had gotten from the clinic.

My name wasn't called for release until nearly ten o'clock—the latest a person can be released—and I strutted toward the door like a disco dancer, my laundry bag of stuff flung over my shoulder. The cellblock guard gave me my yellow inmate information card. I took it, left the cellblock, and met a guard who escorted me onto an elevator. We went down to the outtake processing area. I gave the guard my yellow card. He gave it to someone else, who drew a black line through my photograph and name. I was told to go to the changing booth. My clothes were waiting. The jail food wasn't very good; my suit nearly swallowed me, I had lost over sixty pounds. But I looked all right. My glasses were on while I was in the waiting tank. I looked very good; a Jamaican guy with long dreads and baggy jeans asked me if I was a movie star. I said no, I was not. He said I looked like someone. I said I wish I was that guy, not me; that guy probably wasn't in jail. The Jamaican laughed, and then turned to look at some hookers that were bailed out by whoever. One of them joked that they'd have to do overtime tonight. "Slide down the black fire pole." The other girls laughed. None of them were very pretty. "Johnny Depp!" the Jamaican exclaimed. He said I looked like Johnny Depp.

I had ten dollars left on my commissary funds. Nobody mentioned how I could get that back and I didn't feel like bringing it up, either. Nine months. I just wanted to sign whatever I had to sign, wait for the door to be unlocked, and go. In the lobby, people were waiting for everyone being released. Some of them were waiting for people who weren't even getting out, arguing with guards who didn't know them, didn't care about them, and (they thought) didn't get paid enough to deal with them. I didn't recognize anybody in the lobby. I should have called someone, I thought, instead of assuming someone would be there. I was told of my release earlier in the day, around noon. It was almost eleven at night. Nobody would be waiting for me, they didn't even know if I'd be getting out that day. I had no cash, and the jail's pay phones shut off at eight anyway. I walked outside and it was very cold. The past few days had been surprisingly warm for February, with temperatures in the sixties, and sunny. They were beautiful days.

But the good weather had passed. It was cold and windy. I wanted to walk to my parent's house, where I'd be staying now, but it was just too cold and too windy and I was too tired. In the summer, there was a beautiful display of tall flowers in a concrete circle at the front of the jail. Now, in the winter, it was brown and dead. I sat on the concrete and watched the sky for a while. It was there. That was difficult for me to believe at first. It was still there. The sky. I looked at three flagpoles by the curb, swaying slightly in the hard wind. The American flag, the state flag, and the jail's flag. I looked down at my laundry bag and remembered that I had a shaving razor in it. I wanted to cut my armband off, but decided to wait until later. Brandishing a razorblade in front of a county penitentiary would not be wise.

I saw the Jamaican talking to one of the hookers, the only one who didn't have anyone waiting for her. I thought she was very ugly. I preferred the nudie pictures I had inside. The Jamaican offered her a ride. She said that'd be great, she was worried she'd have to wait for a guard getting off work to give her a lift. They was worse than jitneys, she said, and she'd probably have to blow him. They was so rough, always coming down your throat and laughin' when ya gag. They could be nice, though, she said. Sometimes, after, they would buy her a cheeseburger from McDonald's. The Jamaican grinned and pulled out a cell phone. He said he'd call his friend to give her a ride *whereeeever* she needed to go. She said she didn't have to go far, the YMCA was close. I walked over to the Jamaican and asked if I could borrow his phone. He said that was fine! Anything for Johnny Depp. I thanked him, and called Lucy. She sounded upset, and asked why I hadn't called anyone. I didn't have an answer. She got off of the phone quickly.

The Jamaican's friend arrived in a blue sports car. The hooker got in first; the Jamaican followed, but tripped over his baggy jeans and fell on the street. A car in the opposite lane swerved to get around him and honked. The Jamaican got up, dusted off his jeans, waved to me, and went into the backseat with the hooker. The car sped off playing very bad music. I wished I had brought my radio with me. The classical station was supposed to have two full hours of Copeland. That would have been nice to listen to, I thought.

The jail had a parking garage next to it. The garage had a trolley station. I used to watch, from my cell, the trolley traveling through the station in the morning and late afternoon. I walked to the garage to wait for Lucy. I told her that was where I'd wait. Standing with the parked cars, people drove by me, looking at me and my laundry bag, knowing exactly where I had come from. I didn't really care. Every time a car would go by me it would slow down and the people inside would stare. I looked at my reflection in the window of one of the parked vehicles. Fuck those people, I thought. I looked like a person again. I looked like I wasn't in jail, aside from the armband, which was hidden under my suit jacket. I was a person who wasn't in jail. I looked like that and I was that and I was shocked by that. I looked toward the jail. I could see my cell. The lights were off.

My mother's car pulled up by the parking garage; she was inside, alone, looking around for me. I came outside and got into the car. I put my bag on the backseat. My mother told me Lucy would meet us somewhere, that she was going to get ready to see me. I didn't say anything. My mother said I looked different, like a different person. I took my glasses off. I reached back into my bag and pulled the shaving razor out. I broke the plastic head off from the handle, bent the blade out and forward. My mother watched me, seeming shocked. Cutting the armband off wasn't easy. I had to go back and forth, like a saw, nicking my wrist a few times. When I was done, I threw the armband under the car seat. I turned the radio on. Copeland was still playing. It was nice.

We drove through the city, going home. It started raining and the wind was blowing, rocking the car as we went along. The rocking made me sleepy. Eyes half-closed, every streetlamp was very bright, yellow. More yellow than my information card was. Brighter, deeper. And every car, motorcycle, bike was very fast. Anybody walking on the sidewalks or the streets blurred by. Everything blurred by. It felt like being born.

The Solutions to Brian's Problem

BONNIE JO CAMPBELL

Solution #1

Connie said she was going out to the store to buy formula and diapers. While she's gone, load up the truck with the surround-sound home-entertainment system and your excellent collection of power tools, put the baby boy in the car seat, and drive away from this home you built with your own hands. Expect that after you leave, she will break all the windows in this living room, including the big picture window, as well as the big mirror over the fireplace, which you've already replaced twice. The furnace will run and run. Then she will go to your mother's looking for you, and when she does not find you, she will curse at your mother and possibly attempt to burn your mother's house down. Connie has long admired the old three-story farmhouse for its west-facing dining room with window seats and the cupola with a view for miles around. You and Connie have discussed living there some day.

Solution #2

Wait until Connie comes back from the "store," distract her with the baby, and then cut her meth with Drano, so that when she shoots it up, she dies.

Solution #3

Put the baby boy to bed in his crib and sit on the living room couch until Connie comes home. Before she has a chance to lie about where she's been, grab her hair and knock her head hard into the fireplace that you built from granite blocks that came from the old chimney of the house your great-grandfather built when your family first came to this country from Finland—blocks you gathered from the old foundation in the woods. Don't look at the wedding photos on the mantle. Don't look at Connie's wide wedding-day smile, or the way her head tilts back in an ecstasy that seems to have nothing to do with drugs. Don't let the blood stop you from hitting her one final time to make sure you have cracked her skull. Put her meth and her bag of syringes and blood-smeared needles in her hand so the cops find them when they arrive. You will tell them it was an accident, that you were arguing and the argument escalated because she threatened to shoot meth into your baby.

Solution #4

Just go. Head south where it's warm. After a few hours, pull over at a truck stop and call your mother to warn her to call the cops if she sees Connie. After that, pretend not to have a wife and baby boy. When put to the test, Connie might well rise to the occasion of motherhood. Contact the union about getting a job with another local. Resist taking any photographs along with you, especially the photographs of your baby at every age. Wipe your mind clear of memories, especially the memory of your wife first telling you she was pregnant and how that pregnancy and her promise to stay clean made everything seem possible. Do not remember how the two of you kept holding hands that night, how you couldn't stop reaching for each other, even in your sleep. She lost that baby, and the next one, and although you suspected the reason, you kept on trying.

Solution #5

Blow your head off with the twelve-gauge you keep behind the seat of your truck. Load the shotgun with shells, put the butt against the floor, rest your chin on the barrel, and pull the trigger. Let your wife find your bloody, headless corpse in the living room; let her scrape your brain from these walls. Maybe that will shock her into straightening up her act. Let her figure out how to pay the mortgage and the power bill.

Solution #6

Call a help line, talk to a counselor, explain that last week your wife stabbed you in the chest while you were sleeping, that she punches you, too, giving you black eyes that you have to explain to the guys at work. Explain that you're in danger of losing your job, your house, your baby. Tell her Connie has sold your mountain bike and some of your excellent power tools already, that you have been locking the remainder in your truck, which you park a few blocks away from the house now. Try to be patient when the counselor seems awkward in her responses, when she inadvertently expresses surprise at the nature of your distress, especially when you admit that Connie's only five foot three. Expect the counselor to be even less supportive when you say, hell yes, you hit her back. Tell the counselor that it's the little things, too, that at least once a week Connie rearranges things in the house, not only the furniture, but your financial files and the food, all of which last week she moved to the basement, including the milk and meat, which you then had to throw away. Then realize that the counselor probably has caller ID. Hope that the counselor doesn't call Social Services, because a baby needs his momma. Assure the counselor that Connie is a good momma, that she's good with the baby, that the baby is in no danger.

Solution #7

Make dinner for yourself and your wife with the hamburger in the fridge. Sloppy joes, maybe, or goulash with the stewed tomatoes your mother canned, your mother who, like the rest of your family, thinks your wife is just moody. You haven't told them the truth, because it's too much to explain, and it's too much to explain that, yes, you knew she had this history when you married her, when she got pregnant, but you thought you could kick it together, you thought that love could mend all broken things—wasn't that the whole business of love? Mix up some bottles of formula for later tonight, when you will be sitting in the living room feeding the baby, watching the door of the bathroom, behind which your wife will be searching for a place in her vein that has not hardened or collapsed. When she finally comes out, brush her hair back from her face, and try to get her to eat something.

Popular Mechanics

RAYMOND CARVER

Early that day the weather turned and the snow was melting into dirty water. Streaks of it ran down from the little shoulder-high window that faced the backyard. Cars slushed by on the street outside, where it was getting dark. But it was getting dark on the inside too.

He was in the bedroom pushing clothes into a suitcase when she came to the door.

I'm glad you're leaving! I'm glad you're leaving! she said. Do you hear?

He kept on putting his things into the suitcase.

Son of a bitch! I'm so glad you're leaving! She began to cry. You can't even look me in the face, can you?

Then she noticed the baby's picture on the bed and picked it up.

He looked at her and she wiped her eyes and stared at him before turning and going back to the living room.

Bring that back, he said.

Just get your things and get out, she said.

He did not answer. He fastened the suitcase, put on his coat, looked around the bedroom before turning off the light. Then he went out to the living room.

She stood in the doorway of the little kitchen, holding the baby.

I want the baby, he said.

Are you crazy?

No, but I want the baby. I'll get someone to come by for his things.

You're not touching this baby, she said.

The baby had begun to cry and she uncovered the blanket from around his head.

Oh, oh, she said, looking at the baby.

He moved toward her.

For God's sake! she said. She took a step back into the kitchen.

I want the baby.

Get out of here!

She turned and tried to hold the baby over in a corner behind the stove.

But he came up. He reached across the stove and tightened his hands on the baby.

Let go of him, he said.

Get away, get away! she cried.

The baby was red-faced and screaming. In the scuffle they knocked down a flowerpot that hung behind the stove.

He crowded her into the wall then, trying to break her grip. He held on to the baby and pushed with all his weight.

Let go of him, he said.

Don't, she said. You're hurting the baby, she said.

I'm not hurting the baby, he said.

The kitchen window gave no light. In the near-dark he worked on her fisted fingers with one hand and with the other hand he gripped the screaming baby up under an arm near the shoulder.

She felt her fingers being forced open. She felt the baby going from her.

No! she screamed just as her hands came loose.

She would have it, this baby. She grabbed for the baby's other arm. She caught the baby around the wrist and leaned back.

But he would not let go. He felt the baby slipping out of his hands and he pulled back very hard.

In this manner, the issue was decided.

from *Swimming Sweet Arrow*

MAUREEN GIBBON

Here is what they never tell you about being a girl. The lucky few will crack the nut after a time or two, but the rest of us will screw for a long time before we get it right. A long time. I screwed for four years before I came. You tell that to any guy, he'll shit. They get it from the start, and go on getting it and getting it. It takes a girl longer to figure out how to get hers, because if she isn't one of the lucky few who spill it on a cock, she's got to get it in a way that doesn't hurt the boy's feelings. Try that when you're fucking in the woods or a car, or when everyone tells you that you're only screwing because you want love. You don't even know you're supposed to come.

I first screwed a boy when I was thirteen, but I didn't come until three boyfriends later, with Del. He made me come when we were sixty-nining on a dirty bunk in a cabin we broke into, out in Mennonite Town. It was all the licking and sucking that did it. When those contractions started, I didn't know what they were. That's how ignorant I was about my own body. My mom never said a word about any of it, and the clinic in Ontelaunee where I got my birth control pills made you learn about your fallopian tubes and your ovaries, but as for the rest, as for pleasure, you were on your own. They didn't even teach you the names for your labia and clitoris—nothing that wasn't connected with reproducing.

It was a shock to me that the inside of me could feel so good and so loose, and I had to get Del's cock out of my mouth so I could make the noise that came out of my body. I think I cried out from being scared as much as from the feeling.

"It's like that toy with the rings," I told Del when I got my breath. I knew he didn't understand what I meant, and that almost made me cry. I was thinking of that toy where different colored rings of different sizes rest on the top of each other, all on a wooden dowel. Take away the peg and the rings begin to fall. But it is good to let them tumble, roll away, the red going one place, the blue somewhere else.

I tried again. "It's like rain," I said. "It's like you make my body rain."

He listened to me and he let me kiss his mouth over and over. His face was wet with me—chin, nose, cheeks—and I kissed away as much of it as I could. I liked the way it tasted, sweet and salty, not bitter at all.

"Vangie moisture," he said. "I read about girls coming before."

"Where?"

"*Skin* magazine. No one ever came with me before though."

He moved down so he could lie with his head on my belly and play with me. He put a finger up inside me. "You got all tight. Your pussy got all tight."

"Oh yeah?"

When he moved away from me, I thought we were going to start screwing, because he still hadn't come. But we didn't. Instead, he got the flashlight he'd used when we'd broken the lock on the cabin, and he shined the thing between my legs. He pulled at me, holding the flashlight in one hand, moving my lips apart with the other. His fingers were gentle, but they kept tugging. I knew he was studying me, and I had to close my eyes from nervousness. My whole body felt hot even though the air in the cabin was cool.

"Pussy looks complicated, but it's not," Del said then. "It's about as complicated as an eyelid."

It took me a second to understand what he meant, but then I got the picture in my mind of the inner corner of the eyelid with its little bud, and the way the two little lips on my vagina came up to meet over my clitoris. I'd seen it how many times in the mirror I propped between my spread legs, there on my apartment floor.

Del put his flashlight away then. This time when he got between my legs, he pushed my knees up to my chest and licked me in one long lick, bottom to top.

"I'm going to know every inch of you," he told me.

I didn't say anything. There wasn't anything to say. But that's when I fell in love with Del. If it seems like a strange reason to fall in love with someone, you're wrong. Think how good it feels when the other person's mouth is on you there, how loved you feel. If the other person will not do that for you, what else won't they do?

Chess Over Royal Street, a love story

JESSICA KINNISON

Headlights. A parade. Float and float and float down Royal Street. Wave and wave and wave from the room above the ice machine. Saying something. What? *Iko Iko* plays from the Mercedes Benz parked out front. A record spinning. Turned one hundred times a day.

Upstairs bodies and eyes. The eyes and the bodies. The nothing in the darkness. A few hours till early morning. The dark room and the turning of the pages. An absent hand on the back and the slow, silent breathing. The fitting of the two bodies together in that bed on Royal Street.

Downstairs the pre-dawn piano player is in the corner practicing. The wrong notes. A buzzing. The fruit flies on the windows. The singing tile floor and the blue painted stars on every other tile. The lost beads and the glitter in the baseboards.

The first customers and the news. A gunshot. A power outage. A warehouse fire. A train whistle by the river. A boiled egg for a quarter. Chess on the sidewalk out front with room for whole milk.

A nod. A gesture. A bark of recognition for the street and its morning routine. The traffic light covered in braches, changing quietly from red to orange to green.

Miniature oak stools and secrets. The coffee and the ice in the deep freezer. The coffee and the viewing case. The baklava and the brownies. The carrot cake. The fruits in the hanging net. The boiled eggs in the cerulean bowl—four for a dollar.

The owner of a café. Two broken marriages and a gunshot in the 7th Ward. A bullet in water. The water in the body. Means nothing at all. To anyone. Not like the tune *Iko Iko*. Not like Mercedes Benz. Not like the hot coffee and shattered ice. Not as much as piano music.

The 3 PM rain and the banana leaves. The chessboard and the boots, together under the table. Egg sandwiches and motor oil coffee. Sour cream and Half and Half.

Kids on bikes. Kids on stilts. Kids on unicycles. Kids on shoulders. Kids with licenses, with lovers, with face tattoos, with babies, with glitter wings. Ankle boots and nail polish. Gray knee-highs and a hat with a red feather.

Spilt coffee and chess players. The leashes and the dogs. The newspaper and the water bowls. Bulging toes and wet boots. Banana leaf water chutes. The Angola Prison Group sings *Rise and Fly* over the loudspeakers. "Well, if it weren't for the captin, oh lordy, and his jaggity horse, MMMHHMMM. I'd be down in New Orleans, oh Lordy, before the sun go down. MMMHMMMM. Before the sun go down." Response. Call and response. The piano player taps, barely touching the keys.

Bikes lock up. Black bars on the windows lock in. Chess games end. Pall Malls on the cracked sidewalk. Jim Beam in the bottom of the white cup.

Cats sprawled on porches, in gutters, in doorways, in entrances, in exits. The coffee. The bathroom with the names and the hearts. The X-ed out names and the blacked-in hearts. The crud in the drain.

Upstairs, Levi's jeans on the floor. Mapping the body, rooting out the sore spots. Pills for the pressure. Mississippi John Hurt.

The body in a boat full of fire. A good push clear to the Gulf. Float and float and float until the old light goes out and the river gives light to the body. Reclaiming. Swallowing whole.

Trains pass. A barge, too.

And it ain't nobody's business if the plantains burn soft, and the poached eggs fluff hard. If the coffee and the whole milk curdle and blister like skin. If the feet on the stairs and the clanking of silverware sound like piano keys.

If they get louder every day until human navel and ceramic plates collide with shoulders and napkins. Face down and arched up. Hunched over and mouth open. Tongue and epiglottis. Tongue and earlobe. Tongue and hipbone. No more tongue. No more navel. No more until you coax an egg out of that bowl.

The Boy

JOYCE CAROL OATES

There was this boy named Kit, all semester he pestered me with love, called out Hey good-lookin on the street, after class he'd hang around eyeing me, Hey teach you're a peach, smart aleck giggly staring, wet brown eyes, smooth downy skin, didn't look fourteen but he said he was seventeen which might have been true. I said, All right damn you, I drove us out to this place I knew in the woods, a motel meant to be a lodge, fake logs with fake knotholes, I brought a six-pack of beer along, the room smelled of damp and old bedclothes, somebody's deodorant or maybe Air-Wick, bedspread that hadn't been changed in a long time. It's my strategy to praise, actually I mean everything I say, God I wanted him to feel good, there was a lot of fooling around, getting high, quick wisecracks you roar your head off at but can't remember five minutes later, we were both getting excited, Hey let's dance, we got high and fell across the bed tangling and tickling. I opened his pants and took hold of him but he was soft, breathing fast and shallow, was he afraid? but why? of *me*? hey why? I blew in his ear and got him giggling, I teased and said, Okay kid now's your chance, Mommy ain't anywhere near, kissed and tickled and rubbed against him, God I was hot, down the hall somebody played a radio loud and then a door slammed and you couldn't hear it, now I was flying high and spinning going fast around a turn in the mountains, Oooooo, hair streaming out behind me like it hasn't done in fifteen years, I was crying no I was laughing, wanted to get him hard damn it, big and inside me like a man, then I'd tell him how great he was, how fantastic, it would make me happy too, not just strung out, part-time shitty teaching jobs that I had to drive twenty-three miles one way to get to, thirty miles the other, and pouches under my eyes and a twisty look that scares the nice shy kids. But he never did get hard, it felt like something little that's been skinned, naked and velvety like a baby rabbit, he was squirming like I'd hurt him or he was afraid I might hurt him, finally he said, I guess I don't love you, I guess I want to go home, but I didn't even hear it, I was thinking Oh fuck it the beer's going to be warm, I closed my eyes seeing the road tilt and spin and something about the sky, filmy little clouds that knock your heart out they're so beautiful, Hey let's dance, kid, I said giggling, let's knock the shit out of this room, he was laughing, maybe he was crying and his nose was running, I just lay there thinking, All right, kid, all right you bastards, this is it.

from *The Things They Carried*

TIM O'BRIEN

In a true war story, if there's a moral at all, it's like the thread that makes the cloth. You can't tease it out. You can't extract the meaning without unraveling the deeper meaning. And in the end, really, there's nothing much to say about a true war story, except maybe "Oh."

True war stories do not generalize. They do not indulge in abstraction or analysis.

For example: War is hell. As a moral declaration the old truism seems perfectly true, and yet because it abstracts, because it generalizes, I can't believe it with my stomach. Nothing turns inside.

It comes down to gut instinct. A true war story, if truly told, makes the stomach believe.

This one does it for me. I've told it before—many times, many versions—but here's what actually happened.

We crossed that river and marched west into the mountains. On the third day, Curt Lemon stepped on a booby-trapped 105 round. He was playing catch with Rat Kiley, laughing, and then he was dead. The trees were thick; it took nearly an hour to cut an LZ for the dustoff.

Later, higher in the mountains, we came across a baby VC water buffalo. What it was doing there I don't know—no farms or paddies—but we chased it down and got a rope around it and led it along to a deserted village where we set up for the night. After supper Rat Kiley went over and stroked its nose.

He opened up a can of C rations, pork and beans, but the baby buffalo wasn't interested.

Rat shrugged. He stepped back and shot it through the right front knee. The animal did not make a sound. It went down hard, then got up again, and Rat took careful aim and shot off an ear. He shot it in the hindquarters and in the little hump at its back. He shot it twice in the flanks. It wasn't to kill; it was to hurt. He put the rifle muzzle up against the mouth and shot the mouth away. Nobody said much. The whole platoon stood there watching, feeling all kinds of things, but there wasn't a great deal of pity for the baby water buffalo. Curt Lemon was dead. Rat Kiley had lost his best friend in the world. Later in the week he would write a long personal letter to the guy's sister, who would not write back, but for now it was a question of pain. He shot off the tail. He shot away chunks of meat below the ribs. All around us there was the smell of smoke and filth and deep greenery, and the evening was humid and very hot. Rat went to automatic. He shot randomly, almost casually, quick little spurts in the belly and butt. Then he reloaded, squatted down, and shot it in the left front knee. Again the animal fell hard and tried to get up, but this time it couldn't quite make it. It wobbled and went down sideways. Rat shot it in the nose. He bent forward and whispered something, as if talking to a pet, then he shot it in the throat. All the while the baby buffalo was silent, or almost silent, just a light bubbling sound where the nose had been. It lay very still. Nothing moved except the eyes, which were enormous, the pupils shiny black and dumb.

Rat Kiley was crying. He tried to say something, but then cradled his rifle and went off by himself.

The rest of us stood in a ragged circle around the baby buffalo. For a time no one spoke. We had witnessed something essential, something brand-new and profound, a piece of the world so startling there was not yet a name for it.

Somebody kicked the baby buffalo.

It was still alive, though just barely, just in the eyes.

"Amazing," Dave Jensen said. "My whole life, I never seen anything like it."

"Never?"

"Not hardly. Not once."

Kiowa and Mitchell Sanders picked up the baby buffalo. They hauled it across the open square, hoisted it up, and dumped it in the village well.

Afterward, we sat waiting for Rat to get himself together.

"Amazing," Dave Jensen kept saying. "A new wrinkle. I never seen it before."

Mitchell Sanders took out his yo-yo. "Well, that's Nam," he said. "Garden of Evil. Over here, man, every sin's real fresh and original."

How do you generalize?

War is hell, but that's not the half of it, because war is also mystery and terror and adventure and courage and discovery and holiness and pity and despair and longing and love. War is nasty; war is fun. War is thrilling; war is drudgery. War makes you a man; war makes you dead.

The truths are contradictory. It can be argued, for instance, that war is grotesque. But in truth war is also beauty. For all its horror, you can't help but gape at the awful majesty of combat. You stare out at tracer rounds unwinding through the dark like brilliant red ribbons. You crouch in ambush as a cool, impassive moon rises over the night-time paddies. You admire the fluid symmetries of troops on the move, the harmonies of sound and shape and proportion, the great sheets of metal-fire streaming down from a gunship, the illumination rounds, the white phosphorus, the purply orange glow of napalm, the rocket's red glare. It's not pretty, exactly. It's astonishing. It fills the eye. It commands you. You hate it, yes, but your eyes do not. Like a killer forest fire, like cancer under a microscope, any battle or bombing raid or artillery barrage has the aesthetic purity of absolute moral indifference—a powerful, implacable beauty—and a true war story will tell the truth about this, though the truth is ugly.

To generalize about war is like generalizing about peace. Almost everything is true. Almost nothing is true. At its core, perhaps, war is just another name for death, and yet any soldier will tell you, if he tells the truth, that proximity to death brings with it a corresponding proximity to life. After a firefight, there is always the immense pleasure of aliveness. The trees are alive. The grass, the soil—everything. All around you things are purely living, and you among them, and the aliveness makes you tremble. You feel an intense, out-of-the-skin awareness of your living self—your truest self, the human being you want to be and then become by the force of wanting it. In the midst of evil you want to be a good man. You want decency. You want justice and courtesy and human concord, things you never knew you wanted. There is a kind of largeness to it, a kind of godliness. Though it's odd, you're never more alive than when you're almost dead. You recognize what's valuable. Freshly, as if for the first time, you love what's best in yourself and in the world, all that might be lost. At the hour of dusk you sit at your foxhole and look out on a wide river turning pinkish red, and at the mountains beyond, and although in the morning you must cross the river and go into the mountains and do terrible things and maybe die, even so, you find yourself studying the fine colors on the river, you feel wonder and awe at the setting of the sun, and you are filled with a hard, aching love for how the world could be and always should be, but now is not.

Mitchell Sanders was right. For the common soldier, at least, war has the feel—the spiritual texture—of a great ghostly fog, thick and permanent. There is no clarity. Everything swirls. The old rules are no longer binding, the old truths no longer true. Right spills over into wrong. Order blends into chaos, love into hate, ugliness into beauty, law into anarchy, civility into savagery. The vapors suck you in. You can't tell where you are, or why you're there, and the only certainty is overwhelming ambiguity.

In war you lose your sense of the definite, hence your sense of truth itself, and therefore it's safe to say that in a true war story nothing is ever absolutely true.

Often in a true war story there is not even a point, or else the point doesn't hit you until twenty years later, in your sleep, and you wake up and shake your wife and start telling the story to her, except when you get to the end you've forgotten the point again. And then for a long time you lie there watching the story happen in your head. You listen to your wife's breathing. The war's over. You close your eyes. You smile and think, Christ, what's the *point*?

This one wakes me up.

In the mountains that day, I watched Lemon turn sideways. He laughed and said something to Rat Kiley. Then he took a peculiar half step, moving from shade into bright sunlight, and the booby-trapped 105 round blew him into a tree. The parts were just hanging there, so Dave Jensen and I were ordered to shinny up and peel him off. I remember the white bone of an arm. I remember pieces of skin and something wet and yellow that must've been the intestines. The gore was horrible, and stays with me. But what wakes me up twenty years later is Dave Jensen singing "Lemon Tree" as we threw down the parts.

You can tell a true war story by the questions you ask. Somebody tells a story, let's say, and afterward you ask, "Is it true?" and if the answer matters, you've got your answer.

For example, we've all heard this one. Four guys go down a trail. A grenade sails out. One guy jumps on it and takes the blast and saves his three buddies.

Is it true?

The answer matters.

You'd feel cheated if it never happened. Without the grounding reality, it's just a trite bit of puffery, pure Hollywood, untrue in the way all such stories are untrue. Yet even if it did happen—and maybe it did, anything's possible—even then you know it can't be true, because a true war story does not depend upon that kind of truth. Absolute occurrence is irrelevant. A thing may happen and be a total lie; another thing may not happen and be truer than the truth. For example: Four guys go down a trail. A grenade sails out. One guy jumps on it and takes the blast, but it's a killer grenade and everybody dies anyway. Before they die, though, one of the dead guys says, "The fuck you do *that* for?" and the jumper says, "Story of my life, man," and the other guy starts to smile but he's dead. That's a true story that never happened.

Twenty years later, I can still see the sunlight on Lemon's face. I can see him turning, looking back at Rat Kiley, then he laughed and took that curious half step from shade into sunlight, his face suddenly brown and shining, and when his foot touched down, in that instant, he must've thought it was the sunlight that was killing him. It was not the sunlight. It was a rigged 105 round. But if I could ever get the story right, how the sun seemed to gather around him and pick him up and lift him high into a tree, if I could somehow re-create the fatal whiteness of that light, the quick glare, the obvious cause and effect, then you would believe the last thing Curt Lemon believed, which for him must've been the final truth.

Now and then, when I tell this story, someone will come up to me afterward and say she liked it. It's always a woman. Usually it's an older woman of kindly temperament and humane politics. She'll explain that as a rule she hates war stories; she can't understand why people want to wallow in all the blood and gore. But this one she liked. The poor baby buffalo, it made her sad. Sometimes, even, there are little tears. What I should do, she'll say, is put it all behind me. Find new stories to tell.

I won't say it but I'll think it. I'll picture Rat Kiley's face, his grief, and I'll think, *You dumb cooze.* Because she wasn't listening. It *wasn't* a war story. It was a *love* story.

But you can't say that. All you can do is tell it one more time, patiently, adding and subtracting, making up a few things to get at the real truth. No Mitchell Sanders, you tell her. No Lemon, no Rat Kiley. No trail junction. No baby buffalo. No vines or moss or white blossoms. Beginning to end, you tell her, it's all made up. Every goddamn detail—the mountains and the river and especially that poor dumb baby buffalo. None of it happened. *None* of it. And even if it did happen, it didn't happen in the mountains, it happened in this little village on the Batangan Peninsula, and it was raining like crazy, and one night a guy named Stink Harris woke up screaming with a leech on his tongue. You can tell a true war story if you just keep on telling it.

And in the end, of course, a true war story is never about war. It's about sunlight. It's about the special way that dawn spreads out on a river when you know you must cross the river and march into the mountains and do things you are afraid to do. It's about love and memory. It's about sorrow. It's about sisters who never write back and people who never listen.

from *Drinking Coffee Elsewhere*

ZZ PACKER

Heidi and I signed on to work at the Saybrook dining hall as dishwashers. The job consisted of dumping food from plates and trays into a vat of rushing water. It seemed straightforward, but then I learned better. You wouldn't believe what people could do with food until you worked in a dish room. Lettuce and crackers and soup would be bullied into a pulp in the bowl of some bored anorexic; ziti would be mixed with honey and granola; trays would appear heaped with mashed-potato snow women with melted chocolate ice cream for hair. Frat boys arrived at the dish-room window, en masse. They liked to fill glasses with food, then seal them, airtight, onto their trays. If you tried to prize them off, milk, Worcestershire sauce, peas, chunks of bread vomited onto your dish-room uniform.

When this happened one day in the middle of the lunch rush, for what seemed like the hundredth time, I tipped the tray toward one of the frat boys, popping the glasses off so that the mess spurted onto his Shetland sweater.

He looked down at his sweater. "Lesbo bitch!"

"No," I said, "that would be your mother."

Heidi, next to me, clenched my arm in support, but I remained motionless, waiting to see what the frat boy would do. He glared at me for a minute, then walked away.

"Let's take a smoke break," Heidi said.

I didn't smoke, but Heidi had begun to, because she thought it would help her lose weight. As I hefted a stack of glasses through the steamer, she lit up.

"Soft packs remind me of you," she said. "Just when you've smoked them all and you think there's none left, there's always one more, hiding in that little crushed corner." Before I could respond she said, "Oh, God. Not another mouse. You know whose job that is."

By the end of the rush, the floor mats got full and slippery with food. This was when mice tended to appear, scurrying over our shoes; more often than not, a mouse got caught in the grating that covered the drains in the floor. Sometimes the mouse was already dead by the time we noticed it. This one was alive.

"No way," I said. "This time you're going to help. Get some gloves and a trash bag."

"That's all I'm getting. I'm not getting that mouse out of there."

"Put on the gloves," I ordered. She winced, but put them on. "Reach down," I said. "At an angle, so you get at its middle. Otherwise, if you try to get it by its tail, the tail will break off."

"This is filthy, eh."

"That's why we're here," I said. "To clean up filth. Eh."

She reached down, but would not touch the mouse. I put my hand around her arm and pushed it till her hand made contact. The cries from the mouse were soft, songlike. "Oh, my God," she said. "Oh, my God, ohmigod." She wrestled it out of the grating and turned her head away.

"Don't you let it go," I said.

"Where's the food bag? It'll smother itself if I drop it in the food bag. Quick," she said, her head still turned away, her eyes closed. "Lead me to it."

"No. We are not going to smother this mouse. We've got to break its neck."

"You're one heartless bitch."

I wondered how to explain that if death is unavoidable it should be quick and painless. My mother had died slowly. At the hospital, they'd said it was kidney failure, but I knew that, in the end, it was my father. He made her scared to live in her own home, until she was finally driven away from it in an ambulance.

"Breaking its neck will save it the pain of smothering," I said. "Breaking its neck is more humane. Take the trash bag and cover it so you won't get any blood on you, then crush."

The loud jets of the steamer had shut off automatically and the dish room grew quiet. Heidi breathed in deeply, then crushed the mouse. She shuddered, disgusted. "Now what?"

"What do you mean, 'now what?' Throw the little bastard in the trash."

At our third session, I told Dr. Raeburn I didn't mind if he smoked. He sat on the sill of his open window, smoking behind a jungle screen of office plants.

We spent the first ten minutes discussing the *Iliad*, and whether or not the text actually states that Achilles had been dipped in the River Styx. He said it did, and I said it didn't. After we'd finished with the *Iliad*, and with my new job in what he called "the scullery," he asked more questions about my parents. I told him nothing. It was none of his business. Instead, I talked about Heidi. I told him about that day in Commons, Heidi's plan to go on a date with Mr. Dick, and the invitation we'd been given to the gay party.

"You seem preoccupied by this soirée." He arched his eyebrows at the word "soirée."

"Wouldn't you be?"

"Dina," he said slowly, in a way that made my name seem like a song title, "have you ever had a romantic interest?"

"You want to know if I've ever had a boyfriend?" I said. "Just go ahead and ask if I've ever fucked anybody."

This appeared to surprise him. "I think that you are having a crisis of identity," he said.

"Oh, is that what this is?"

His profession had taught him not to roll his eyes. Instead, his exasperation revealed itself with a tiny pursing of his lips, as though he'd just tasted something awful and were trying very hard not to offend the cook.

"It doesn't have to be, as you say, someone you've fucked, it doesn't have to be a boyfriend," he said.

"Well, what are you trying to say? If it's not a boy, then you're saying it's a girl—"

"Calm down. It could be a crush, Dina." He lit one cigarette off another. "A crush on a male teacher, a crush on a dog, for heaven's sake. An interest. Not necessarily a relationship."

It was sacrifice time. If I could spend the next half hour talking about some boy, then I'd have given him what he wanted.

So I told him about the boy with the nice shoes.

I was sixteen and had spent the last few coins in my pocket on bus fare to buy groceries. I didn't like going to the Super Fresh two blocks away from my house, plunking government food stamps into the hands of the cashiers.

"There she go reading," one of them once said, even though I was only carrying a book. "Don't your eyes get tired?"

On Greenmount Avenue you could read schoolbooks—that was understandable. The government and your teachers forced you to read them. But anything else was antisocial. It meant you'd rather submit to the words of some white dude than shoot the breeze with your neighbors.

I hated those cashiers, and I hated them seeing me with food stamps, so I took the bus and shopped elsewhere. That day, I got off the bus at Govans, and though the neighborhood was black like my own—hair salon after hair salon of airbrushed signs promising arabesque hair styles and inch-long fingernails—the houses were neat and orderly, nothing at all like Greenmount, where every other house had at least one shattered window. The store was well swept, and people quietly checked long grocery lists—no screaming kids, no loud cashier-customer altercations. I got the groceries and left the store.

I decided to walk back. It was a fall day, and I walked for blocks. Then I sensed someone following me. I walked more quickly, my arms around the sack, the leafy lettuce tickling my nose. I didn't want to hold the sack so close that it would break the eggs or squash the hamburger buns, but it was slipping, and as I looked behind, a boy my age, maybe older, rushed toward me.

"Let me help you," he said.

"That's all right." I set the bag on the sidewalk. Maybe I saw his face, maybe it was handsome enough, but what I noticed first, splayed on either side of the bag, were his shoes. They were nice shoes, real leather, a stitched design like a widow's peak on each one, or like birds' wings, and for the first time in my life I understood what people meant when they said "wing-tip shoes."

"I watched you carry them groceries out that store, then you look around, like you're lost, but like you liked being lost, then you walk down the sidewalk for blocks and blocks. Rearranging that bag, it almost gone to slip, then hefting it back up again."

"Uh-huh," I said.

"And then I passed my own house and was still following you. And then your bag really look like it was gone crash and everything. So I just thought I'd help." He sucked in his bottom lip, as if to keep it from making a smile. "What's your name?" When I told him, he said, "Dina, my name is Cecil." Then he said, "'D' comes right after 'C.'"

"Yes," I said, "it does, doesn't it."

Then, half question, half statement, he said, "I could carry your groceries for you? And walk you home?"

I stopped the story there. Dr. Raeburn kept looking at me. "Then what happened?"

I couldn't tell him the rest: that I had not wanted the boy to walk me home, that I didn't want someone with such nice shoes to see where I lived.

Dr. Raeburn would only have pitied me if I'd told him that I ran down the sidewalk after I told the boy no, that I fell, the bag slipped, and the eggs cracked, their yolks running all over the lettuce. Clear amniotic fluid coated the can of cinnamon rolls. I left the bag there on the sidewalk, the groceries spilled out randomly like cards loosed from a deck. When I returned home, I told my mother that I'd lost the food stamps.

"Lost?" she said. I'd expected her to get angry, I'd wanted her to get angry, but she hadn't. "Lost?" she repeated. Why had I been so clumsy and nervous around a harmless boy? I could have brought the groceries home and washed off the egg yolk, but, instead, I'd just left them there. "Come on," mama said, snuffing her tears, pulling my arm, trying to get me to join her and start yanking cushions off the couch. "We'll find enough change here. We got to get something for dinner before your father gets back."

We'd already searched the couch for money the previous week, and I knew there'd be nothing now, but I began to push my fingers into the couch's boniest corners, pretending that it was only a matter of time before I'd find some change or a lost watch or an earring. Something pawnable, perhaps.

"What happened next?" Dr. Raeburn asked again. "Did you let the boy walk you home?"

"My house was far, so we went to his house instead." Though I was sure Dr. Raeburn knew that I was making this part up, I continued. "We made out on his sofa. He kissed me."

Dr. Raeburn lit his next cigarette like a detective. Cool, suspicious. "How did it feel?"

"You know," I said. "Like a kiss feels. It felt nice. The kiss felt very, very nice."

Raeburn smiled gently, though he seemed unconvinced. When he called time on our session his cigarette had become one long pole of ash. I left his office, walking quickly down the corridor, afraid to look back. It would be like him to trot after me, his navy blazer flapping, just to get the truth out of me. *You never kissed anyone.* The words slid from my brain, and knotted in my stomach.

from *Black and Blue*

ANNA QUINDLEN

The first time my husband hit me I was nineteen years old. One sentence and I'm lost. One sentence and I can hear his voice in my head, that butterscotch-syrup voice that made goose bumps rise on my arms when I was young, that turned all of my skin warm and alive with a sibilant S, the drawling vowels, its shocking fricatives. It always sounded like a whisper, the way he talked, the intimacy of it, the way the words seemed to go into your guts, your head, your heart. "Geez, Bob," one of the guys would say, "you should have been a radio announcer. You should have done those voice-over things for commercials." It was like a genie, wafting purple and smoky from the lamp, Bobby's voice, or perfume when you took the glass stopper out of the bottle.

I remember going to court once when Bobby was a witness in a case. It was eleven, maybe twelve years ago, before Robert was born, before my collarbone was broken, and my nose, which hasn't healed quite right because I set it myself, looking in the bathroom mirror in the middle of the night, petals of adhesive tape fringing the frame. Bobby wanted me to come to court when he was testifying because it was a famous case at the time, although one famous case succeeds another in New York City the way one pinky-gold sunset over the sludge of the Hudson River fades and blooms, brand-new each night. A fifteen-year-old boy from Brooklyn was accused of raping a Dominican nun at knifepoint and then asking her to pray for him. His attorney said it was a lie, that the kid had had no idea that the woman in the aqua double-knit pants and the striped blouse was a nun, that the sex was consensual, though the nun was sixty-two and paste-waxing a floor in a shelter at the time. They took paste wax from the knees of the kid's pants, brought in the paste-wax manufacturer to do a chemical comparison.

The lawyer was an old guy with a storefront in a bad neighborhood,

I remember, and the kid's mother had scraped together the money to hire him because Legal Aid had sent a black court-appointed and she was convinced that her son needed a white lawyer to win his case. Half-blind, hungover, dandruff on the shoulders of his gray suit like a dusting of snow, the kid's attorney was stupid enough to call the kid as a witness and to ask why he had confessed to a crime he hadn't committed.

"There was this cop in the room," the boy said, real low, his broad forehead tipped toward the microphone, his fingers playing idly with his bottom lip, so that his words were a little muffled. "He don't ask none of the questions. He just kept hassling me, man. Like he just keeps saying, 'Tell us what you did, Tyrone. Tell us what you did.' It was like he hypnotized me, man. He just kept saying it over and over. I couldn't get away from him."

The jury believed that Tyrone Biggs had done the rape, and so did everybody else in New York who read the tabloids, watched the news. So did the judge, who gave him the maximum, eight to fifteen years, and called him "a boil on the body of humanity." But I knew that while Tyrone was lying about the rape he was telling the truth about that police officer, because I lived with that voice every day, had been hypnotized by it myself. I knew what it could do, how it could sound. It went down into your soul, like a confessor, like a seducer, saying, "Tell me. Tell me." Frannie, Frannie, Fran, he'd croon, whisper, sing. Sometimes Bobby even made me believe that I was guilty of something, that I was sleeping with every doctor at the hospital, that I made him slip and bang his bad knee. That I made him beat me up, that it was me who made the fist, angled the foot, brought down a hand hard. Hard.

The first time he hit me I was nineteen.

I can hear his voice now, so persuasive, so low and yet somehow so strong, making me understand once again that I'm all wrong. Frannie, Frannie, Fran, he says. That's how he begins. Frannie, Frannie, Fran. The first time I wasn't your husband yet. You were already twenty, because it was the weekend after we went to City Island for your birthday. And I didn't hit you. You know I didn't hit you. You see, Fran, this is what you do. You twist things. You always twist things.

I can hear him in my head. And I know he's right. He didn't hit me, that first time. He just held onto my upper arm so tight that the mark of his fingertips was like a tattoo, a black sun with four small moons revolving around it.

It was summer, and I couldn't wear a sundress for a week, or take off my clothes when my sister, Grace, was in the room we shared, the one that looked out over the air shaft to the Tarnowski's apartment on the other side. He had done it because I danced with Dee Stemple's brother and then laughed when he challenged me on it. He held me there, he said, so that I couldn't get away, because if I got away it would be the end of him, he loved me that much. The next night he pushed back the sleeve of my blouse and kissed each mark, and his tears wet the spots as though to wash the black white again, as white as the rest of my white, white skin, as though his tears would do what absolution did for venial sins, wash them clean. "Oh, Jesus," he whispered, "I am so goddamned sorry." And I cried, too. When I cried in those days it was always for his pain, not for mine.

As rich and persuasive as Bobby Benedetto's voice, that was how full and palpable was his sorrow and regret. And how huge was his rage. It was like a twister cloud; it rose suddenly from nothing into a moving thing that blew the roof off, black and strong. I smell beer, I smell bourbon, I smell sweat, I smell my own fear, ranker and stronger than all three.

from *Push*

SAPPHIRE

It's so many different ways to walk the few blocks home. Turn a corner and you see all different. Pass 116th 'n Lenox, more abandoned land, buildings falling down. How it git so ugly is people throw trash all in it. City don't pick it up; dogs doo doo. Peoples wif no bafroom piss 'n shit. Ugliness grow multiplied by ten. Keep walkin' down Lenox to one-twelve you pass projects. I never did live in projects. I live in 444 Lenox Avenue almost all my life. Where I live before that house I don't know, maybe wif my grandmother.

Wonder about Mama sometimes. Wonder about Carl more. Carl Kenwood Jones. I got session wif counselor today. Last week we try to figure out how long I been infected. People at retard place say Lil Mongo don't got it. She say that could mean Daddy get AIDS pretty fast from time he first infected to time he die? 'Cause if Lil Mongo don't got it maybe he didn't have it 1983 when she born. Then after she born he go away a long time. So maybe I get it eighty-six, eighty-seven? Counselor say, I'm on top now. I'm young, is got no disease and stuff, not no drug addict. I could live a long time, she say. I ask her what's a long time. She don't say.

I think some of the girls at Advancement House know I am . . . am *positive*. I mean wifout trying I know some of they bizness. They never was too friendly; since Mama come wif her news, they even less friendly. But who cares? I'm not tight wif these girls in the house. These bitches got problems, come in room and steal shit. I know I ain' the only one that got it, even though that's how it feels. But I'm probably the only one get it from they daddy. Counselor, Ms Weiss, say she try to find out as much about Daddy for me as she can.

How much I want to know? And for what? I tell counselor I can't talk about Daddy now. My clit swell up I think Daddy. Daddy sick me, *dis-*

gust me, but still he sex me up. I nawshus in my stomach but hot tight in my twat and I think I want it back, the smell of the bedroom, the hurt—he slap my face till it sting and my ears sing separate songs from each other, call me names, pump my pussy in out in out in out awww I come. He bite me *hard.* A hump! He slam his hips into me HARD. I scream pain he come. He slap my thighs like cowboys do horses on TV. Shiver. Orgasm in me, his body shaking, grab me, call me Fat Mama, Big Hole! You LOVE it! Say you love it! I wanna say I DON'T. I wanna say I'm a chile. But my pussy popping like grease in frying pan. He slam in me again. His dick soft. He start sucking on my tittie.

I wait for him to get off me. Lay there stare at wall till wall is a movie, *Wizard of Oz,* I can make that one play anytime. Michael Jackson, scarecrow. Then my body take me over again, like shocks after earthquake, shiver me, I come again. My body not mine, I hate it coming.

Afterward I go bafroom. I smear shit on my face. Feel good. Don't know why but it do. I never tell nobody about that before. But I would do that. If I got to insect support group what will I hear from other girls. I bite my fingernails till they look like disease, pull strips of my skin away. Get Daddy's razor out cabinet. Cut cut cut arm wrist, not trying to die, trying to plug myself back in. I am a TV set wif no picture. I am broke wif no mind. No past or present time. Only the movies of being someone else. Someone not fat, dark skin, short hair, someone not fucked. A pink virgin girl. A girl like Janet Jackson, a sexy girl don't no one get to fuck. A girl for value. A girl wif little titties whose self is luvlee just Luv-Vell-LEE!

I hate myself when I think Carl Kenwood Jones. Hate wif a capital letter. Counselor say, "Memories." How is something a memory if you never forget? But I push it to the corner of my brain.

I exhausted, I mean wipe out! What kinda chile gotta think about a daddy like I do? But I'm not a chile. I'm a mother of a chile myself!

In school we had to memorize a poem like the rappers do. And say it in front the class. Everybody do real short poems except me and Jermaine. She do a poem by lady name Pat Parker. I get up to do my poem, it's by Langston Hughes, I dedicate it to Abdul. Introduce myself to the class (even though everybody know me). I say my name is Precious Jones and this poem is for my baby son, Abdul Jamal Louis Jones. Then I let loose:

Mother to Son
Well, son, I'll tell you:
Life for me ain't been no crystal stair.
It's had tacks in it,
And splinters,
And boards torn up,
And places with no carpet on the floor—
Bare.
But all the time
I'se been a-climbin' on,
And reachin' landin's,
And turnin' corners,
And sometimes goin' in the dark
Where there ain't been no light.
So boy, don't you turn back.
Don't you set down on the steps
'Cause you finds it's kinder hard.
Don't you fall now—
For I'se still goin', honey,
I'se still climbin',
And life for me ain't been no crystal stair.

And after I finish everyone goin', Yeah! Yeah! Shoutin', Go Precious!
And clapping and clapping and clapping. I felt very good.

from *Junkette*

SARAH SHOTLAND

No more going topless in the photo booth at the Saint.

No more throwing those tequila shots in the fake fern.

No more stealing the quarters off dollar-and-a-quarter tips for the juke box. I'm a bartender for God's sakes. Don't I have any loyalty at all?

And no more playing White Wedding. I will definitely stop playing White Wedding.

That wasn't me.

❧   ❧   ❧   ❧

Mack says I got lice from the couch at the Saint, but I never even sit on that couch, the Saint is all about up-up-up on your feet, keep working that room.

But I'll put it on the list for good measure: no more getting lice at the Saint. No more!

❧   ❧   ❧   ❧

And I'm no longer trying to do the bartender after last call; he doesn't want you, bitch.

And no more flirting with the girls who have bangs.

No more dancing when they play Michael Jackson.

No more Dirty Notes, Red Headed Sluts, Rusty Nails, and no more Jägermeister.

I said it. No more Jägermeister.

And no more cover charges. I no longer pay cover charges.

What about that?

❧   ❧   ❧   ❧

No more using the payphone. In fact, no more phone calls at all. When I'm out, I'm out. You come find me.

No more bringing the spoon and the rig to the bathroom, no more pockets full of foil, no more I'm always gonna leave, always gonna get outta here, I'm gone. Just be, bitch, just be here when you're here with the damn spoon up your sleeve. Just learn to sit in your own dumb self.

❧　❧　❧　❧

No more sleeves, I'm baring my arms and showing these people what chicken flapping really looks like.

Fuck those pretty girls in the photo booth. With their skinny arms. No one knows their names, anyway. And while I'm on the topic, no more trying to fuck the pretty girls in the photo booth. They're all prudes.

No more banging on the bathroom door from the inside. I've never been locked in.

And no more coming through the backdoor. The cooks aren't worth the smile.

No more walking around the serving side of the bar to make my own Caucasians. No one likes a showoff.

No more talking about Mack like nobody knows who he is. This is his neighborhood too. Remember when you had to hold his hand to sit second on the corner. Remember that, it's his neighborhood too, and after all, he was here first.

❧　❧　❧　❧

And no more sneaking the chicken fingers in my pants pockets. They don't keep well.

No more elbows, no more hush hush, goin' around the corner, no more fake names and fake places I'm from.

No more shut my mouth with a glass pipe to make friends moments. No more bell ringing before the dj starts again, and no more djs.

No more tabs, no more lines, no more specials with my name on them—not my name anyway.

No more trips.

❧　❧　❧　❧

No more talking about horns, it's not that kind of a crowd, and no more, absolutely no more stealing the straws. They're like the spoons at the Moonlight—can't keep 'em in stock.

No more spills and no more slipping Mack's crackerjack ring on my finger when I just don't feel like flirting anymore.

No more talking. The Saint is now a mute-mouth kind of a place. Lord knows you talk too much.

No more laughing at my own jokes, and no more seat checking.

No more get you tomorrow, no more spending all the tips and needing a front from Ra in the morning. No more bringing Ra around here, everybody knows us. No more knowing us.

No more wigs.

No more sweaters—like I said, I'm done with sleeves, let them see the smeared makeup over the train tracks on my forearms. Follow the tracks to get that red. Get that red—get that red—get that red, get it? got it, good, get that like you know how, girl.

ꙮ ꙮ ꙮ ꙮ

No more talking about finding red. Everyone's absolutely exhausted by you.

No more double neats.

No more burlesque.

No more climbing on the roof, no more push-up bras. No more talking to men with skinny jeans, or cut-off pants, or paint splattered cords. I will date a man who wears slacks, goddamnit.

ꙮ ꙮ ꙮ ꙮ

No more leaving my cigarettes burning by the record player, and no more scratching the records on purpose.

No more explaining the saints, everyone here went to Catholic school anyway.

No more blinking the lights like intermission's over—no one will leave until they're good and ready.

No more corny dogs and no more quarter cigarettes, buy a pack.

No more trying to find my shoes. I'll leave without them.

No more one-two-three, knock it on the bar, halo over the head 'nother shot. No more two drinks at a time orders. No more extra lemons. No more finishing strangers' drinks when they go to the bathroom.

No more pretending to be deaf. No more dirty talk. And no more brushing my hand across anyone's bum.

⦿   ⦿   ⦿   ⦿

No more looking for another fix. No more fixing anything.

No more getting-a-fix, getting-a-fix, getting-a-fix, getting-a-fix. You're not fucking broken, bitch. Stop trying to fix it all the time.

No more no more no more. None of it. I'm altogether done.

⦿   ⦿   ⦿   ⦿

When I say it like that, altogether, sewn into stitches that stack on top of each other, it could be true. I could never do any of the no mores ever again. And then the problem becomes as simple and big as time.

The problem is: what do I do instead?

Witness

JOHN EDGAR WIDEMAN

Sitting here one night six floors up on my little balcony when I heard shots and saw them boys running. My eyes went straight to the lot beside Mason's bar and I saw something black not moving in the weeds and knew a body lying there and knew it was dead. A fifteen year old boy the papers said. Whole bunch of sirens and cops and spinning lights the night I'm talking about. I watched till after they rolled him away and then everything got quiet again as it ever gets round here so I'm sure the boy's people not out there that night. Didn't see them till next morning when I'm looking down at those weeds and a couple's coming slow on Frankstown with a girl by the hand, had to be the boy's baby sister. They pass terrible Mason's and stop right at the spot the boy died. Then they commence to swaying, bowing, hugging, waving their arms about. Forgive me, Jesus, but look like they grief dancing, like the sidewalk too cold or too hot they had to jump around not to burn up. How'd his people find the exact spot. Did they hear my old mind working to lead them, guide them along like I would if I could get up out this damn wheelchair and take them by the hand.

Disappearing

MONICA WOOD

When he starts in, I don't look anymore, I know what it looks like, what he looks like, tobacco on his teeth. I just lie in the deep sheets and shut my eyes. I make noises that make it go faster and when he's done he's as far from me as he gets. He could be dead he's so far away.

Lettie says leave then stupid but who would want me. Three hundred pounds anyway but I never check. Skin like tapioca pudding, I wouldn't show anyone. A man.

So we go to the pool at the junior high, swimming lessons. First it's blow bubbles and breathe, blow and breathe. Awful, hot nosefuls of chlorine. My eyes stinging red and patches on my skin. I look worse. We'll get caps and goggles and earplugs and body cream Lettie says. It's better.

There are girls there, what bodies. Looking at me and Lettie out the side of their eyes. Gold hair, skin like milk, chlorine or no.

They thought when I first lowered into the pool, that fat one parting the Red Sea. I didn't care. Something happened when I floated. Good said the little instructor. A little redhead in an emerald suit, no stomach, depression almost, and white wet skin. Good she said you float just great. Now we're getting somewhere. The whistle around her neck blinded my eyes. And the water under the fluorescent lights. I got scared and couldn't float again. The bottom of the pool was scarred, drops of gray shadow rippling. Without the water I would crack open my head, my dry flesh would sound like a splash on the tiles.

At home I ate a cake and a bottle of milk. No wonder you look like that he said. How can you stand yourself. You're no Cary Grant I told him and he laughed until I threw up.

When this happens I want to throw up again and again until my heart flops out wet and writhing on the kitchen floor. Then he would know I have one and it moves.

So I went back. And floated again. My arms came around and the groan of the water made the tight blondes smirk but I heard Good that's the crawl that's it in fragments from the redhead when I lifted my face. Through the earplugs I heard her skinny voice. She was happy that I was floating and moving too.

Lettie stopped the lessons and read to me things out of magazines. You have to swim a lot to lose weight. You have to stop eating too. Forget cake and ice cream. Doritos are out. I'm not doing it for that I told her but she wouldn't believe me. She couldn't imagine.

Looking down that shaft of water I know I won't fall. The water shimmers and eases up and down, the heft of me doesn't matter I float anyway.

He says it makes no difference I look the same. But I'm not the same. I can hold myself up in deep water. I can move my arms and feet and the water goes behind me, the wall comes closer. I can look down twelve feet to a cold slab of tile and not be afraid. It makes a difference I tell him. Better believe it mister.

Then this other part happens. Other men interest me. I look at them, real ones, not the ones on TV that's something else entirely. These are real. The one with the white milkweed hair who delivers the mail. The meter man from the light company, heavy thick feet in boots. A smile. Teeth. I drop something out of the cart in the supermarket to see who will pick it up. Sometimes a man. One had yellow short hair and called me ma'am. Young. Thin legs and an accent. One was older. Looked me in the eyes. Heavy, but not like me. My eyes are nice. I color the lids. In the pool it runs off in blue tears. When I come out my face is naked.

The lessons are over, I'm certified. A little certificate signed by the redhead. She says I can swim and I can. I'd do better with her body, thin calves hard as granite.

I get a lane to myself, no one shares. The blondes ignore me now that I don't splash the water, know how to lower myself silently. And when I swim I cut the water cleanly.

For one hour every day I am thin, thin as water, transparent, invisible, steam or smoke.

The redhead is gone, they put her at a different pool and I miss the glare of the whistle dangling between her emerald breasts. Lettie won't come over at all now that she is fatter than me. You're so uppity she says. All this talk about water and who do you think you are.

He says I'm looking all right, so at night it is worse but sometimes now when he starts in I say no. I haven't been invisible. Even on days when I don't say no it's all right, he's better.

One night he says it won't last, what about the freezer full of low-cal dinners and that machine in the basement. I'm not doing it for that and he doesn't believe me either. But this time there is another part. There are other men in the water I tell him. Fish he says. Fish in the sea. Good luck.

Ma you've lost says my daughter-in-law, the one who didn't want me in the wedding picture. One with the whole family, she couldn't help that. I learned how to swim I tell her. You should try it, it might help your ugly disposition.

They closed the pool for two weeks and I went crazy. Repairing the tiles. I went there anyway, drove by in the car. I drank water all day.

Then they opened again and I went every day, sometimes four times until the green paint and new stripes looked familiar as a face. At first the water was heavy as blood but I kept on until it was thinner and thinner, just enough to hold me up. That was when I stopped with the goggles and cap and plugs, things that kept the water out of me.

There was a time I went the day before a holiday and no one was there. It was echoey silence just me and the soundless empty pool and a lifeguard behind the glass. I lowered myself so slow it hurt every muscle but not a blip of water not a ripple not one sound and I was under in that other quiet, so quiet some tears got out, I saw their blue trail swirling.

The redhead is back and nods, she has seen me somewhere. I tell her I took lessons and she still doesn't remember.

This has gone too far he says I'm putting you in the hospital. He calls them at the pool and they pay no attention. He doesn't touch me and I smile into my pillow, a secret smile in my own square of the dark.

Oh my God Lettie says what the hell are you doing what the hell do you think you're doing. I'm disappearing I tell her and what can you do about it not a blessed thing.

For a long time in the middle of it people looked at me. Men. And I thought about it. Believe it, I thought. And now they don't look at me again. And it's better.

I'm almost there. Almost water.

The redhead taught me how to dive, how to tuck my head and vanish like a needle into skin, and every time it happens, my feet leaving the board, I think, this will be the time.

DRAMA

from *Why We Have a Body*

CLAIRE CHAFEE

AT RISE: *Lights up on* RENEE, *somewhere in Mexico, in a bathing suit and shirt.*

RENEE: The other day I went into the supermarket . . . and all I could see were women. Now, I go into the supermarket all the time . . . but I never noticed women. There are women everywhere . . . picking out heads of lettuce, picking out cans . . . standing behind their metal carts they stare at the frozen foods in their own little world.

And I want to go up to them . . . any one of them and say: "Excuse me, but I made love to a woman, and I could probably make love to you too, if you would like me to."

I could barely control myself not to do that.

I made eye contact with every woman in there. I would stand beside them, wait till I got their attention and look them straight in the eye. I think they thought I was psychotic.

I especially made eye contact with the check-out girl who, I swear, imbued the question, "do you want paper or plastic" with the vague feel of sex. I would have never noticed this before . . . but now I do. There is a subterranean life that runs just beneath and below the normal life, and you only see it if you fall in there . . . and you either fall in there or you get pushed in, but you really don't go there for just a little excursion . . . because there really is no way back . . . to not noticing once you start. So I really don't know why they call it sexual preference. [. . .]

☙ ☙ ☙ ☙

RENEE: *(reading from* Esquire*).* HOW TO MAKE LOVE TO A WOMAN: start with the throat. Start there.

Look at this place. Is it open? Is it closed?
Notice the Adam's apple. Place of the great fall.
The face may be the road map, but the throat will show you all
your short cuts.
Look at her lips. Now kiss them.
Here, the rules of the road apply:

If you go into a skid, steer right into it . . . and for god sakes keep
your foot off the brake.

Take all the hard righthand turns you want, but always always
signal.

Pass a hand across her belly, travel South. Slow down on the
entrance ramp.
Cross the isthmus of her down-below . . . as lost and as convinced as any Columbus. [. . .]

◎ ◎ ◎ ◎

LILI: When I was growing up,
     they taught you very young to tell them right away
     if you were a boy or if you were a girl.
     And from then on you were sent to live in two different worlds.
     Even before you were born, they ask
     this question over and over,
     And from in there you can't imagine what the problem is. And
     from then on you're sent to live in two different worlds.

(She starts to look through a file.)

     Girls did crewelwork, boys had shop.
     They got to bring home breakfast trays made out of plywood:
     things you had a use for.
     We sewed those pictures with the poked out holes. A picture of a
     rabbit done in yarn. We all did the same picture of a rabbit, or else
     you could choose a baby chick, but that was it.
     The good part about living in the world of the girl
     is it prepares you for absurdity.

Centuries from now, they are going to dig up those things and wonder: "what culture, what form of life, what pattern too intricate to discern created the need for these?" [. . .]

❧ ❧ ❧ ❧

LILI: The first lesbian I ever met was Harriet the spy. The second, Margaret Mead. I knew she didn't fit in . . . it was obvious, she had thick ankles and she took herself seriously. Around about the same time I was also aware of girl actor Jodi Foster, girl actor Tatum O'Neal . . . and that lady on the *Beverly Hillbillies* . . . Miss Hathaway. All of whom also took themselves seriously and were sturdy in one way or another. All of them investigators. I think this is because they had to learn so well from an early age to do surveillance.

I fell in love four times before the age of eight . . . and each time it was with a girl . . . and no: I did not want to be like them.

I did not want to write romantic letters from camp.

I did not want to share their skates.

What I wanted was to take them on the rug.

Of their parents' bedroom.

Exactly.

So, I had no other choice than to be a spy. [. . .]

❧ ❧ ❧ ❧

LILI: *(into recorder)* Dear Renee. I have to tell you something right now.

I may be a first for you . . . but you are my one-too-many times.

You are the thing that keeps coming back at different intervals. What's missing is the same. It's the same ache.

You want to play missing persons? You pretend you're missing and I search for your whereabouts?

So I can trail you, do surveillance? . . . dust for prints? . . . stake out your home? . . . run a credit check? . . . figure out if you're gay? So that you could be my subject . . . and I could deliver you back explained.

I have stared in people's eyes until they bloom their secrets . . . took their private puzzles on and solved them.

I have cracked the hard ones, Renee.

But secretly, I became a private investigator because I wanted, with something approaching despair, for someone to figure *me* out.

That I could just for once be the subject . . . of an investigation.

That it would be my turn to be the mystery.

It is my turn to be the fucking mystery. [. . .]

(Lights up on ELEANOR, *pointer in hand.)*

ELEANOR: Compare the brain of a perfectly normal woman, with that of a Lesbian.

The Lesbian Brain is divided into three sections,

As opposed to the sub-division into two sections of the normal brain.

MEMORY . . . LUST . . . and HAMMERING DOUBT.

(Points to a small circle below Lust.)

Because the Lesbian is born without a future, the Lesbian Brain is born with more past

to remember

and has developed a larger location

in the pre-frontal cortex, specifically for this function.

It is still not clear, however,

whether this area develops in-utero, therefore

forming a certain predilection to be a lesbian,

or whether

this extended capacity for memory develops later, simply as a by-product of years of living

without a future and more past than one can possibly manage.

It is confusing.

I sincerely try to pierce that question.

At one time I did blame myself that Lili was a lesbian . . . but she just asked me: "Why should you take all the credit?"

So I guess that finally just sunk in.

Now I live by the great words of Ophelia: "Lord we know what we are, but know not what we may be."

And as you know with science, once you start to *ask*
there are just more questions than there are answers.
However, it is safe to say that . . . since the dawn of time, we have been mostly sleeping. [. . .]

❧   ❧   ❧   ❧

ELEANOR: I suppose my girls are mad at me.
I imagine I did a number of horrible things to them growing up. Whole entire lapses of concern . . .
In fact I spent the whole time
that they would describe as their childhood
in a sort of fog.

I was in a light trance at the time. And now I honestly do not remember when I said, for instance: ",,,,,,,,,,,,,,,,,,,,,,," which turned Mary into a criminal. Or the time I asked the salesgirl for help in Bloomingdale's and completely mortified Lili, to the point where she *still* hates being naked. I take their word for it but I don't remember.

If it's true that we replace each cell entirely every seven years, and if the soul does
progress across the sky, like the planets . . .
then it's fair to say I was a different person.
Someone I no longer am. The person you have come for is no longer here.
And the little girls they were, are no longer here.
So . . . it is just a memory talking to a memory.

There maybe should be a statute of limitations on this kind of thing, but there isn't.

hunger blog

EVE ENSLER

Blog 1

i don't really like celery. tastes like disappointment. egg whites taste like baby skin. learning to graze. used to watch cows. they move their mouth around the grass. hover, hang, munch a little, rest. don't swallow too much.

Blog 2

everyone's mad at me. here's a picture of my hips. bone jutting. love those two words: bone jutting. just right for jeans. sade, sexy music, and espresso help a lot. perfect combo. slow music and caffeine annihilate hunger.

Blog 3

bad taste in my mouth. this girl jewel said i was sick in gym class. she's jealous. last night i ate cooked vegetables naked in front of the mirror. it grossed me out so much i haven't been hungry for almost 24 hrs.

Blog 4

everything sucks. had to stay home from school. too tired. dad gave me a big lecture. said i wasn't fooling anyone. tried to exercise. only got through a hundred sit-ups. watched tv. saw this program about hundreds of people in Africa forced to leave their land 'cause of war. they were drinking dirty water. everyone was so hungry and sick. my mother was crying. she said i look just like them. she made me soup. wanted to share it with the people on tv. i like soup.

Blog 5

can't stop crying. disgust myself. family forced me to eat a meal 'cause it's christmas eve. now i'm gross. putrid. foul. holidays make me so sad. we're not happy like everyone else. always feel there is something i should be doing, somewhere i should be going. don't know where that is. maybe santa claus will leave me diet pills under the tree. had christmas nightmares. dreamed my family was making me eat reindeer meat. there were sad antlers on my plate. then i was trying to run in really deep snow and it turned to jello and i was happy 'cause jello is a safe food but it turned out it was radioactive and i was going to die.

Blog 6

i believe in splenda. i like all substitutes. even miss hammer who only teaches on occasion. she never makes me feel bad. i can tell she was really skinny once 'cause she's got wrinkles like that. she asked me what i felt like when i was thin. empty, not full of bad stuff.

Blog 7

my doctor said he is going to sue me for malpractice to my own body. he was gentle the way he examined me. i got so cold and was shivering. exciting to see bone. like finally getting to water after digging for years. almost pretty.

Blog 8

was sent to an eating disorder clinic. today we planted a tree in the yard, which symbolized our bodies growing healthy. i like my roommate china a lot. she has a tattoo of a hamburger on her ass. a reminder. reimagining our bodies in art therapy. i saw myself as a belly dancer with sparkly shaking bells and things. it was good for about two hours.

then i got really depressed. beautiful is a country with gates around it. i'll never be invited.

Blog 9

the therapist just doesn't understand. it's not like i think about it, okay? it lives there. must be thin. logo stenciled across my consciousness. like a permanent demand, like a mental coffee stain. maybe the whole system will just crash and they'll have to program me with something else. shrink asks what would that be? i don't know. annoying shrink asks again. okay, okay. maybe new logo reads: must not hurt so much. must be MORE PROFOUND. must be easy. must not be about only me. must not take up all this time. must not make me feel left out. MUST NOT MAKE ME WANT TO KILL MYSELF. i think i sound angry. everyone is really quiet for a long time. then china says maybe there's no more logos or demands. maybe we just make it up as we go and so there's no pressure or point. we're just here, okay. with each other, doing stuff.

from *August: Osage County*

TRACY LETTS

Scene 5

Barbara, still wearing her nightgown, and Ivy, in the dining room. The house has taken on a ghostly cast. Elsewhere in the house: Johnna prepares dinner in the kitchen.

IVY: Is she clean?

BARBARA: Clean-ish.

IVY: So she's not clean.

BARBARA: The woman's got brain-damage, dummy. If you think I'm going to strip-search her every time she slurs a word—

IVY: You know the difference.

BARBARA: She's moderately clean.

IVY: "Moderately"?

BARBARA: You don't like "moderately"? Then let's say tolerably.

IVY: Is she clean, or not?

BARBARA: Back off. We're trying to get by here, okay?

IVY: I'm nervous.

BARBARA: Why? Oh, Christ, Ivy, not tonight.

IVY: Why not?

BARBARA: We're only just now settling into some kind of rhythm around here. Now you come in here with your little *issues*—

IVY: I have to tell her, don't I? We're leaving for New York tomorrow.

BARBARA: That's not a good idea.

IVY: "A good idea."

BARBARA: For you and Little Charles to take this thing any further.

IVY: Where is this coming from?

BARBARA: I just got to thinking about it, and I think it's a little weird, that's all.

IVY: It's not up to you.

BARBARA: Lot of fish in the sea. Surely you can rule out the one single man in the world you're related to.

IVY: I happen to love the man I'm related—

BARBARA: *Fuck love,* what a crock of shit. People can convince themselves they love a painted rock. *(Johnna brings food from the kitchen.)* Looks great. What is it?

JOHNNA: Catfish.

BARBARA: Bottom feeders, my favorite. *(Johnna retires to the kitchen. Violet enters from the second-floor hallway, heads slowly for the dining room.)*

IVY: You think I shouldn't tell her.

BARBARA: You should rethink the whole proposition. New York City is a ridiculous idea. You're almost fifty years old, Ivy, you can't go to New York, you'll break a hip. Eat your catfish.

IVY: You're infuriating.

BARBARA: I ain't the one fuckin' my cousin.

IVY: I have lived in this town, year in and year out, hoping against hope someone would come into my life—

BARBARA: Don't get all Carson McCullers on me. Now wipe that tragic look off your face and eat some catfish.

IVY: Who are you to speak to me like this? *(Violet enters the dining room.)*

BARBARA: Howdy, Mom.

VIOLET: What's howdy about it?

BARBARA: Look, catfish.

VIOLET: Catfish.

BARBARA: *(Calling off.)* Johnna! *(To Violet.)* You hungry?

VIOLET: Ivy, you should smile. Like me. *(Johnna enters.)*

BARBARA: Mom needs her dinner, please. *(Johnna exits.)*

VIOLET: I'm not hungry.

BARBARA: You haven't eaten anything today. You didn't eat anything yesterday.

VIOLET: I'm not hungry.

BARBARA: You're eating. You do what I say. Everyone do what I say.

IVY: May I ask why neither of you is dressed?

BARBARA: What is it with you?

VIOLET: Yeah.

BARBARA: We're dressed. We're not sitting here naked, are we? Or did you want us to dress up?

VIOLET: Right, 'cause you're coming over for fish.

BARBARA: Right, 'cause you're coming over for fish we're supposed to dress up. *(Johnna reenters with two plates of food.)*

JOHNNA: I'll eat in my room.

BARBARA: That's fine, thank you. *(Johnna exits with her plate of food. To Violet.)* Eat.

VIOLET: No.

BARBARA: Eat it. Mom? Eat it.

VIOLET: No.

BARBARA: Eat it, you fucker. Eat that catfish.

VIOLET: Go to hell!

BARBARA: That doesn't cut any fucking ice with me. Now eat that fucking fish.

IVY: Mom. I have something to talk to you about.

BARBARA: No, you don't.

IVY: Barbara—

BARBARA: No, you don't. Shut up. Shut the fuck up.

IVY: Please—

VIOLET: What's to talk about?

IVY: Mom—

BARBARA: Forget it. Mom? Eat that fucking fish.

VIOLET: I'm not hungry.

BARBARA: Eat it.

VIOLET: NO!

IVY: Mom, I need to—!

VIOLET: NO!

IVY: Mom!

BARBARA: EAT THE FISH, BITCH!

IVY: Mom, please!

VIOLET: Barbara . . . !

BARBARA: Okay, fuck it, do what you want.

IVY: I have to tell you something.

BARBARA: Ivy's a lesbian.

VIOLET: What?

IVY: Barbara—

VIOLET: No, you're not.

IVY: No, I'm not—

BARBARA: Yes, you are. Did you eat your fish?

IVY: Barbara, stop it!

BARBARA: Eat your fish.

IVY: Barbara!

BARBARA: Eat your fish.

VIOLET: Barbara, quiet now—

IVY: Mom, please, this is important—

BARBARA: Eatyourfisheatyourfisheatyourfish— *(Ivy hurls her plate of food, smashes it.)* What the fuck—

IVY: I have something to say!

BARBARA: Are we breaking shit? *(Barbara takes a vase from the sideboard, smashes it.)* 'Cause I can break shit— *(Violet throws her plate, smashes it.)* See, we can all break shit.

IVY: Charles and I—

BARBARA: You don't want to break shit with *me*, muthah-fuckah!

IVY: Charles and I—

BARBARA: Johnna?! Little spill in here!

IVY: Barbara, stop it! Mom, Charles and I—

BARBARA: Little Charles—

IVY: Charles and I—

BARBARA: Little Charles—

IVY: Charles and I—

BARBARA: Little Charles—

IVY: Charles and I—

BARBARA: Little Charles—

IVY: Barbara—

BARBARA: You have to say "Little Charles" or she won't know who you're talking about.

IVY: Little Charles and I . . . *(Barbara relents. Ivy will finally get to say the words.)* Little Charles and I are—

VIOLET: Little Charles and you are brother and sister. I know that.

BARBARA: Oh . . . Mom.

IVY: What? *No*, listen to me, Little Charles—

VIOLET: I've always known that. I told you, no one slips anything by me.

IVY: *Mom*—

BARBARA: Don't listen to her.

VIOLET: I knew the whole time Bev and Mattie Fae were carrying on. Charlie shoulda known too, if he wasn't smoking all that grass.

BARBARA: It's the pills talking.

VIOLET: Pills can't talk.

IVY: Wait . . .

VIOLET: Your father tore himself up over it, for thirty some-odd years, but Beverly wouldn't have been Beverly if he didn't have plenty to brood about.

IVY: Mom, what are you . . . ?

BARBARA: Oh, honey . . .

VIOLET: It's better you girls know now, though, now you're older.

Never know when someone might need a kidney. Better if everyone knows the truth.

IVY: Oh my God . . .

VIOLET: Though I can't see the benefit in Little Charles ever knowing, break his little heart. *(Tells Ivy.)* Tell me though, honey: how'd *you* find out? *(Ivy looks from Violet to Barbara . . . suddenly lurches away from the table, knocking over her chair.)*

BARBARA: Ivy?

IVY: Why did you tell me? Why in God's name did you tell me this?

VIOLET: Hey, what do *you* care?

IVY: You're monsters.

VIOLET: Come on now—

IVY: Picking the bones of the rest of us—

VIOLET: You crazy nut.

IVY: Monsters.

VIOLET: Who's the injured party here? *(Ivy staggers out of the dining room, into the living room. Barbara pursues her.)*

BARBARA: Ivy, listen—

IVY: Leave me alone!

BARBARA: Honey—

IVY: I won't let you do this to me!

BARBARA: When Mattie Fae told me, I didn't know what to do—

IVY: I won't let you change my story! *(Ivy exits. Barbara chases after her and catches her on the front porch.)*

BARBARA: Goddamn it, listen to me: I tried to protect you—

IVY: We'll go anyway. We'll still go away, and you will never see me again.

BARBARA: Don't leave me like this.

IVY: *You will never see me again.*

BARBARA: This is not my fault. I didn't tell you, *Mom* told you. It wasn't me, it was *Mom*.

IVY: There's no difference. *(Ivy exits. Barbara reenters the house. She finds Violet lighting a cigarette in the living room.)*

VIOLET: You know well's I do, we couldn't let Ivy run off with Little Charles. Just wouldn't be right. Ivy's place is right here.

BARBARA: She says she's leaving anyway.

VIOLET: Nah. She won't go. She's a sweet girl, Ivy, and I love her to death. But she isn't strong. Not like you. Or me.

BARBARA: Right. *(Beat.)* You've known about Daddy and Mattie Fae all these years.

VIOLET: Oh, sure. I never told them I knew. But your father knew. He knew I knew. He always knew I knew. But we never talked about it. I chose the higher ground.

BARBARA: Right.

VIOLET: Now if I'd had the chance, there at the end, I would've told him, "I hope this isn't about Little Charles, 'cause you know I know all about that." If I'd reached him at the motel, I would've said, "You'd be better off if you quit sulking about this ancient history. And anyway, just 'cause you feel cast down doesn't let you off the hook."

BARBARA: If you had reached him at the motel.

VIOLET: I *called* the motel, the Country Squire Motel—

BARBARA: —the Country Squire Motel, right—

VIOLET: —but it was too late, he must've already checked out. I called over there on Monday, after I got into that safety deposit box. I told you I had to wait until Monday morning for the bank to open so I could get into that safety deposit box. I should've called him sooner,

I guess, should've called the police, or Ivy, someone. But Beverly and I had an arrangement. You have to understand, for people like your father and me, who never had any money, ever, as kids, people from our generation, that money is important.

BARBARA: How'd you know where he was?

VIOLET: He left a note. Said I could call him at the Country Squire Motel. And I did, I did call him, called him on Monday.

BARBARA: After you got into your safety deposit box.

VIOLET: We had an arrangement.

BARBARA: If you could've stopped Daddy from killing himself, you wouldn't have *needed* to get into your safety deposit box.

VIOLET: Well, hindsight's twenty-twenty, isn't it.

BARBARA: Did the note say Daddy was going to kill himself? *(No response.)* Mom?

VIOLET: If I'd had my wits about me, I might've done it different. But I was, your father and me both, we were . . .

BARBARA: You were both fucked-up. *(Beat.)* You were fucked-up. *(Beat.)* You're fucked-up.

VIOLET: You had better understand this, you smug little ingrate, there is at least one reason Beverly killed himself and that's *you*. Think there's any way he would've done what he did if you were still here? No, just him and me, here in this house, in the dark, left to just ourselves, abandoned, wasted lifetimes devoted to your care and comfort. So stick that knife of judgment in me, go ahead, but make no mistake, his blood is just as much on your hands as it is on mine. *(No response. Violet enters the study. Barbara follows.)* He did this, though; this was his doing, not ours. Can you imagine anything more cruel, to make *me* responsible? And why, just to weaken me, just to make me prove my character? So no, I waited, I waited so I could get my hands on that safety deposit box, but I would have waited anyway. You want to show who's stronger, Bev? Nobody is stronger than me, goddamn it. When nothing is left, when everything is gone and disappeared, I'll be here. Who's stronger now, you son-of-a-bitch?!

BARBARA: No, you're right, Mom. You're the strong one. *(Barbara kisses her mother . . . exits the study, returns to the living room. Violet calls after her.)*

VIOLET: Barbara? *(Barbara grabs her purse, digs out rental car keys.)* Barbara? *(Barbara stands, listens to her mother.)* Barbara, please. *(Barbara exits the house.)* Please, Barbara. *Please. (Violet shuffles into the living room.)* Barbara? You in here? *(She crosses to the dining room.)* Ivy? Ivy, you here? Barb? *(She crosses to the kitchen.)* Barb? Ivy? *(She turns in a circle, disoriented, panicked. She crosses to the study.)* Bev? *(She reenters the living room, stumbles to the stereo, puts on Clapton . . . stares at the turntable as the album spins . . . attacks the record player, rakes the needle across the album. She looks around, terrified, disoriented.)* Johnna?! *(She reels to the stairway, crawls up the stairs on all fours.)* Johnna, Johnna, Johnna . . . *(She arrives on the second floor. Johnna puts her plate of food aside and turns toward the stairs. Violet, on all fours, continues up the stairs to the attic. She arrives in Johnna's room. She scrabbles into Johnna's lap. Johnna holds Violet's head, smoothes her hair, rocks her.)* And then you're gone, and Beverly, and then you're gone, and Barbara, and then you're gone, and then you're gone, and then you're gone—*(Johnna quietly sings to Violet.)*

| JOHNNA: "This is the way the world ends, this is the way the world ends, this is the way the world ends . . . " *(Blackout.)* | VIOLET: —and then you're gone, and then you're gone, and then you're gone, and then you're gone— |

End of Play.

from *How I Learned to Drive*

PAULA VOGEL

FEMALE GREEK CHORUS: *(As Mother.)* A Mother's Guide to Social Drinking:

A lady never gets sloppy—she may, however, get tipsy and a little gay.

Never drink on an empty stomach. Avail yourself of the bread basket and generous portions of butter. *Slather* the butter on your bread.

Sip your drink, slowly, let the beverage linger in your mouth—interspersed with interesting, fascinating conversation. Sip, never . . . slurp or gulp. Your glass should always be three-quarters full when his glass is empty.

Stay away from *ladies'* drinks: drinks like pink ladies, sloe gin fizzes, daiquiris, gold cadillacs, Long Island iced teas, margaritas, piña coladas, mai tais, planter's punch, white Russians, black Russians, red Russians, melon balls, blue balls, humming birds, hemorrhages and hurricanes. In short, avoid anything with sugar, or anything with an umbrella. Get your vitamin C from *fruit*. Don't order anything with Voodoo or Vixen in the title or sexual positions in the name like Dead Man Screw or the Missionary. *(She sort of titters.)*

Believe me, they are lethal . . . I think you were conceived after one of those.

Drink, instead, like a man: straight up or on the rocks, with plenty of water in between.

Oh, yes. And never mix your drinks. Stay with one all night long, like the man you came in with: bourbon, gin, or tequila till dawn, damn the torpedoes, full speed ahead! *(As the Female Greek Chorus retreats, the Male Greek Chorus approaches the table as a Waiter.)*

MALE GREEK CHORUS: *(As Waiter.)* I hope you all are having a pleasant evening. Is there something I can bring you, sir, before you order? *(Li'l Bit waits in anxious fear. Carefully, Uncle Peck says with command:)*

PECK: I'll have a plain iced tea. The lady would like a drink, I believe. *(The Male Chorus does a double take; there is a moment when Uncle Peck and he are in silent communication.)*

MALE GREEK CHORUS: *(As Waiter.)* Very good. What would the . . . lady like?

LI'L BIT: *(A bit flushed.)* Is there . . . is there any sugar in a martini?

PECK: Not that I know of.

LI'L BIT: That's what I'd like then—a dry martini. And could we maybe have some bread?

PECK: A drink fit for a woman of the world. — Please bring the lady a dry martini, be generous with the olives, straight up.

(The Male Greek Chorus anticipates a large tip.)

MALE GREEK CHORUS: *(As Waiter.)* Right away. Very good, sir. *(The Male Greek Chorus returns with an empty martini glass, which he puts in front of Li'l Bit.)*

PECK: Your glass is empty. Another martini, madam?

LI'L BIT: Yes, thank you. *(Peck signals the Male Greek Chorus, who nods.)* So why did you leave South Carolina, Uncle Peck?

PECK: I was stationed in D.C. after the war, and decided to stay. Go North, Young Man, someone might have said.

LI'L BIT: What did you do in the service anyway?

PECK: *(Suddenly taciturn.)* I . . . I did just this and that. Nothing heroic or spectacular.

LI'L BIT: But did you see fighting? Or go to Europe?

PECK: I served in the Pacific Theater. It's really nothing interesting to talk about.

LI'L BIT: It is to me. *(The Waiter has brought another empty glass.)* Oh, goody. I love the color of the swizzle sticks. What were we talking about?

PECK: Swizzle sticks.

LI'L BIT: Do you ever think of going back?

PECK: To the Marines?

LI'L BIT: No—to South Carolina.

PECK: Well, we do go back. To visit.

LI'L BIT: No, I mean to live.

PECK: Not very likely. I think it's better if my mother doesn't have a daily reminder of her disappointment.

LI'L BIT: Are these floorboards slanted?

PECK: Yes, the floor is very slanted. I think this is the original floor.

LI'L BIT: Oh good. *(The Female Greek Chorus as Mother enters swaying a little, a little past tipsy.)*

FEMALE GREEK CHORUS: *(As Mother.)* Don't leave your drink unattended when you visit the ladies' room. There is such a thing as white slavery; the modus operandi is to spike an unsuspecting young girl's drink with a "mickey" when she's left the room to powder her nose.

But if you feel you have had more than your sufficiency in liquor, do go to the ladies' room—often. Pop your head out of doors for a refreshing breath of the night air. If you must, wet your face and head with tap water. Don't be afraid to dunk your head if necessary. A wet woman is still less conspicuous than a drunk woman. *(The Female Greek Chorus stumbles a little; conspiratorially.)*

When in the course of human events it becomes necessary, go to a corner stall and insert the index and middle finger down the throat almost to the epiglottis. Divulge your stomach contents by such persuasion, and then wait a few moments before rejoining your beau waiting for you at your table.

Oh, no. Don't be shy or embarrassed. In the very best of establishments, there's always one or two debutantes crouched in the corner stalls, their beaded purses tossed willy-nilly, sounding like cats in heat, heaving up the contents of their stomachs. *(The Female Greek Chorus begins to wander off.)*

I wonder what it is they do in the men's rooms . . .

LI'L BIT: So why is your mother disappointed in you, Uncle Peck?

PECK: Every mother in Horry County has Great Expectations.

LI'L BIT: —Could I have another mar-ti-ni, please?

PECK: I think this is your last one. *(Peck signals the Waiter. The Waiter looks at Li'l Bit and shakes his head no. Peck raises his eyebrow, raises his finger to indicate one more, and then rubs his fingers together. It looks like a secret code. The Waiter sighs, shakes his head sadly, and brings over another empty martini glass. He glares at Peck.)*

LI'L BIT: The name of the county where you grew up is "Horry"? *(Li'l Bit, plastered, begins to laugh. Then she stops.)* I think your mother should be proud of you. *(Peck signals for the check.)*

PECK: Well, missy, she wanted me to do—to *be* everything my father was not. She wanted me to amount to something.

LI'L BIT: But you have! You've amounted to a lot . . .

PECK: I'm just a very ordinary man. *(The Waiter has brought the check and waits. Peck draws out a large bill and hands it to the Waiter. Li'l Bit is in the soppy stage.)*

LI'L BIT: I'll bet your mother loves you, Uncle Peck. *(Peck freezes a bit. To Male Greek Chorus as Waiter:)*

PECK: Thank you. The service was exceptional. Please keep the change.

MALE GREEK CHORUS: *(As Waiter, in a tone that could freeze.)* Thank you, sir. Will you be needing any help?

PECK: I think we can manage, thank you. *(Just then, the Female Greek Chorus as Mother lurches on stage; the Male Greek Chorus as Waiter escorts her off as she delivers:)*

FEMALE GREEK CHORUS: *(As Mother.)* Thanks to judicious planning and several trips to the ladies' loo, your mother once outdrank an entire regiment of British officers on a good-will visit to Washington! Every last man of them! Milquetoasts! How'd they ever kick Hitler's cahones, huh? No match for an American lady—I could drink every man in here under the table. *(She delivers one last crucial hint before she is gently "bounced.")* As a last resort, when going out for an evening on the town, be sure to wear a skin-tight girdle—so tight that only a surgical knife or acetylene torch can get it off you—so that if you do pass out in the arms of your escort, he'll end up with rubber burns on his fingers before he can steal your virtue—

from *Two Trains Running*

AUGUST WILSON

Act 1, Scene 2

MEMPHIS: Hey, Holloway, you know what I just found out? You know who that boy is . . . that Sterling boy? I was talking to Hendricks. . . . That's the boy robbed that bank and was out spending the money ten minutes later. You remember that? Hendricks gave him a job to help him get out and the boy worked one week and quit. See, Hendricks don't know . . . he don't know like I know. He trying to help him, but that boy don't wanna work.

HOLLOWAY: He say Hendricks laid him off. But I can't blame him if he did quit. Who wanna haul bricks on a construction site for a dollar and a quarter an hour? That ain't gonna help him. What's he gonna do with ten dollars a day?

MEMPHIS: That be ten more than he got now. His granddaddy used to work for three dollars a day. He doing good!

HOLLOWAY: I ain't talking about that. Hell, his great-grandaddy used to work for nothing, for all that matter. I'm talking about he can make two or three hundred dollars a day gambling . . . if he get lucky. If he don't, somebody else will get it. That's all you got around here is niggers with somebody else's money in their pocket. And they don't do nothing but trade it off on each other. I got it today and you got it tomorrow. Until sooner or later as sure as the sun shine . . . somebody gonna take it and give it to the white man. The money go from you to me to you and then—bingo, it's gone. You give it to the white man. Pay your rent, pay your telephone, buy your groceries, see the doctor—bingo, it's gone. Just circulate it around till it find that hole, then—bingo. Like trying to haul sand in a bucket with a hole in it. Time you get where you going the bucket empty. That's why that ten dollars a day ain't gonna do him no good. A nigger with five hundred dollars in his pocket around here is a big man. But you go out there where they at . . . you go out to Squirrel Hill, they walking around there with five thousand dollars in their pocket trying to figure out how to make it into five hundred thousand.

MEMPHIS: Ain't nothing wrong in saving your money and do like they do. These niggers just don't want to work. That boy don't want to work. He lazy.

HOLLOWAY: People kill me talking about niggers is lazy. Niggers is the most hard-working people in the world. Worked three hundred years for free. And didn't take no lunch hour. Now all of a sudden niggers is lazy. Don't know how to work. All of a sudden when they got to pay niggers, ain't no work for him to do. If it wasn't for you the white man would be poor. Every little bit he got he got standing on top of you. That's why he could reach so high. He give you three dollars a day for six months and he got him a railroad for the next hundred years. All you got is six months' worth of three dollars a day.

(RISA enters carrying a pie box.)

Now you can't even get that. Ain't no money in niggers working. Look out there on the street. If there was some money in it . . . if the white man could figure out a way to make some money by putting niggers to work . . . we'd all be working. He ain't building no more railroads. He got them. He ain't building no more highways. Somebody done already stuck the telephone poles in the ground. That's been done already. The white man ain't stacking no more niggers. You know what I'm talking about, stacking niggers, don't you? Well, here's how that go. If you ain't got nothing . . . you can go out here and get you a nigger. Then you got something, see. You got one nigger. If that one nigger get out there and plant something . . . get something out the ground . . . even if it ain't nothing but a bushel of potatoes . . . then you got one nigger and one bushel of potatoes. Then you take that bushel of potatoes and go get you another nigger. Then you got two niggers. Put them to work and you got two niggers and two bushels of potatoes. See, now you can go buy two more niggers. That's how you stack a nigger on top of a nigger. White folks got to stacking . . . and I'm talking about they stacked up some niggers! Stacked up close to fifty million niggers. If you stacked them on top of one another they make six or seven circles around the moon. It's lucky the boat didn't sink with all them niggers they had stacked up there. It take them two extra months to get here cause it ride so low in the water. They couldn't find you enough work back then. Now that they got to pay you they can't find you none. If this was different time wouldn't be nobody out there on the street. They'd all be in the cotton fields.

MEMPHIS: I still say that boy don't want to work.

CONTENTS BY THEME

Family

Gratitude

Love and Sex

Prison

Violence

BIBLIOGRAPHY AND
RECOMMENDED SOURCES

Anthologies

Barnstone, Aliki, ed. *The Shambhala Anthology of Women's Spiritual Poetry*. Boston: Shambhala, 2002.

Bauer, Mark S., ed. *A Mind Apart: Poems of Melancholy, Madness, and Addiction*. New York: Oxford University Press, 2008.

Epstein, Leah Odze, and Caren Osten Gerszberg, eds. *Drinking Diaries: Women Serve Their Stories Straight Up*. Berkeley: Seal Press, 2012.

Franklin, H. Bruce, ed. *Prison Writing in 20th-century America*. New York: Penguin, 1998.

Gorham, Sarah, and Jeffrey Skinner, eds. *Last Call: Poems on Alcohol, Addiction, and Deliverance*. Louisville: Sarabande, 1997.

Harris, Miriam, ed. *Rape, Incest, Battery: Women Writing Out the Pain*. Fort Worth: TCU Press, 2000.

Hirshfield, Jane, ed. *Women in Praise of the Sacred: 43 Centuries of Spiritual Poetry by Women*. New York: Harper, 1995.

Housedon, Roger, ed. *Risking Everything: 110 Poems of Love and Revelation*. New York: Harmony Books, 2003.

Lamb, Wally, ed. *I'll Fly Away: Further Testimonies from the Women of York Prison*. New York: Harper Perennial, 2008.

Lamb, Wally, and the Women of York Correctional Institution. *Couldn't Keep It to Myself: Testimonies from Our Imprisoned Sisters*. New York: Harper, 2003.

Levi, Robin, and Ayelet Waldman, eds. *Inside This Place, Not of It: Narratives from Women's Prisons*. San Francisco: McSweeney's, 2011.

Messit, Holly, and James Tolan, eds. *New America: Contemporary Literature for a Changing Society*. Pittsburgh: Autumn House Books, 2013.

Mitchell, Stephen, ed. *The Enlightened Heart: An Anthology of Sacred Poetry.* New York: HarperCollins, 1989.

Mulvey-Robert, Marie, ed. *Writing for Their Lives: Death Row USA.* Urbana: University of Illinois Press, 2007.

Porterfield, Kay Marie, ed. *Sleeping with Dionysus: Women, Ecstasy, and Addiction.* Freedom, Calif.: Crossing Press, 1994.

Raab, Diana M., and James Brown, eds. *Writers on the Edge: 22 Writers Speak about Addiction and Dependence.* Ann Arbor: Modern History Press, 2012.

Nonfiction

Allison, Dorothy. *Two or Three Things I Know for Sure.* New York: Penguin, 1995.

Baca, Jimmy Santiago. *A Place to Stand.* New York: Grove Press, 2001.

———. *Working in the Dark: Reflections of a Poet of the Barrio.* Santa Fe: Museum of New Mexico Press, 1992.

Bernstein, Neil. *All Alone in the World: Children of the Incarcerated.* New York: New Press, 2005.

Betts, R. Dwayne. *A Question of Freedom: A Memoir of Learning, Survival, and Coming of Age in Prison.* New York: Avery, 2009.

Bottoms, Greg. *Angelhead: My Brother's Descent Into Madness.* Chicago: University of Chicago Press, 2000.

———. *Fight Scenes.* Berkeley: Counterpoint, 2008.

Bragg, Rick. *All Over but the Shoutin'.* New York: Random House, 1997.

Burroughs, Augusten. *Dry: A Memoir.* New York: Picador, 2003.

———. *Running with Scissors: A Memoir.* New York: Picador, 2002.

Cheever, Susan. *Note Found in a Bottle: My Life as a Drinker.* New York: Simon & Schuster, 1999.

Cohen, Kerry. *Loose Girl: A Memoir of Promiscuity.* New York: Hyperion, 2008.

Elliot, Stephen. *The Adderall Diaries: A Memoir of Moods, Masochism, and Murder.* Minneapolis: Graywolf, 2009.

Flynn, Nick. *Another Bullshit Night in Suck City.* New York: Norton, 2004.

Hartman, Kenneth. *Mother California: A Story of Redemption behind Bars.* New York: Atlas, 2010.

Holden, Kate. *In My Skin: A Memoir.* New York: Arcade, 2005.

Karr, Mary. *Lit: A Memoir*. New York: HarperCollins, 2009.

Kincaid, Jamaica. *My Brother*. New York: Farrar, Straus and Giroux, 1997.

Knapp, Caroline. *Drinking: A Love Story*. New York: Dell, 1996.

Lamberton, Ken. *Beyond Desert Walls: Essays from Prison*. Tucson: University of Arizona Press, 2005.

Marlowe, Ann. *How to Stop Time: Heroin from A to Z*. New York: Basic Books, 1999.

Salzman, Mark. *True Notebooks*. New York: Knopf, 2003.

Ray, Janisse. *Ecology of a Cracker Childhood*. Minneapolis: Milkweed, 2000.

Sanders, Scott Russell. "Under the Influence." In *Secrets of the Universe*. Boston: Beacon Press, 1991.

Scoblic, Sasha. *Unwasted: My Lush Sobriety*. New York: Citadel Press, 2011.

Sheehan, Susan. *Life for Me Ain't Been No Crystal Stair: One Family's Passage through the Child Welfare System*. New York: Pantheon Books, 1993.

Shef, Nic. *Tweak: Growing up on Methamphetamines*. New York: Atheneum Books for Young Readers, 2009.

Sheff, David. *Beautiful Boy: A Father's Journey through His Son's Addiction*. New York: Mariner, 2009.

Shelton, Richard. *Crossing the Yard: Thirty Years as a Prison Volunteer*. Tucson: University of Arizona Press, 2004.

Slater, Lauren. *Lying: A Metaphorical Memoir*. New York: Random House, 2001.

Stahl, Jerry. *Permanent Midnight: A Memoir*. New York: Warner Books, 1995.

St. Germain, Sheryl. *Navigating Disaster: Sixteen Essays of Love and a Song of Despair*. Hammond, La.: Literature Press, 2012.

———. *Swamp Songs*. Salt Lake City: University of Utah Press, 2003.

Sullivan, Felicia. *The Sky Isn't Visible from Here*. Chapel Hill: Algonquin Books, 2008.

Tannenbaum, Judith. *Disguised as a Poem: My Years Teaching Poetry at San Quentin*. Boston: Northeastern University Press, 2000.

Tannenbaum, Judith, and Spoon Jackson. *By Heart: Poetry, Prison, and Two Lives*. Oakland, Calif.: New Village Press, 2010.

Upchurch, Carl. *Convicted in the Womb: One Man's Journey from Prisoner to Peacemaker*. New York: Bantam Books, 1996.

Ward, Jesmyn. *Men We Reaped: A Memoir.* New York: Bloomsbury, 2013.

Wideman, John Edgar. *Brothers and Keepers.* New York: Vintage, 1995.

———. *Hoop Roots: Playground Basketball, Love, and Race.* New York: Houghton Mifflin, 2001.

Zailckas, Koren. *Smashed: Story of a Drunken Girlhood.* New York: Penguin, 2005.

Poetry

Abani, Chris. *Sanctificium.* Port Townsend: Copper Canyon Press, 2010.

Betts, R. Dwayne. *Shahid Reads His Own Palm.* Farmington, Maine: Alice James, 2010.

Bonair-Agard, Roger. *Bury My Clothes.* Chicago: Haymarket, 2013.

Clifton, Lucille. *Good Woman: Poems and a Memoir, 1969–1980.* Rochester: BOA Editions, 1987.

Davis, Christopher. *The Tyrant of the Past and the Slave of the Future.* Lubbock: Texas Tech University Press, 1989.

Diaz, Natalie. *When My Brother Was an Aztec.* Port Townsend: Copper Canyon Press, 2012.

Hayes, Terrance. *Hip Logic.* New York: Penguin, 2002.

———. *Lighthead.* New York: Penguin, 2010.

Howe, Marie. *The Good Thief.* New York: Persea, 1988.

———. *What the Living Do.* New York: Norton, 1998.

Hughes, Langston. *Selected Poems.* New York: Alfred A. Knopf, 1926.

Jess, Tyehimba. *Leadbelly.* Amherst, Mass.: Verse Press, 2004.

Knight, Etheridge. *The Essential Etheridge Knight.* Pittsburgh: University of Pittsburgh Press, 1991.

Komunyakaa, Yusef. *Neon Vernacular: New and Selected Poems.* Hanover, N.H.: Wesleyan University Press, 1993.

Larkin, Joan. *A Long Sound.* Penobscot, Maine: Granite Press, 1986.

Merwin, W. S. *The Rain in the Trees.* New York: Knopf, 1988.

Nye, Naomi Shihab. *Words under the Words: Selected Poems.* Portland: Eighth Mountain Press, 1994.

Seibles, Tim. *Hammerlock.* Cleveland: Cleveland State University Poetry Center, 1999.

———. *Hurdy Gurdy.* Cleveland: Cleveland State University Poetry Center, 1992.

St. Germain, Sheryl. *Let It Be a Dark Roux: New and Selected Poems.* Pittsburgh: Autumn House Press, 2007.

Trull, Rhett Iseman. *The Real Warnings.* Tallahassee: Anhinga Press, 2009.

Walcott, Derek. *Collected Poems, 1948–1984.* New York: Farrar, Straus and Giroux, 1987.

Young, Gary. *Even So: New and Selected Poems.* Buffalo: White Pine Press, 2012.

Plays

Chafee, Claire. *Why We Have a Body.* New York: Dramatic Publishing, 1996.

Ensler, Eve. *I Am an Emotional Creature.* New York: Villard Books, 2010.

Letts, Tracy. *August: Osage County.* New York: Dramatists Play Service, 2009.

Shange, Ntozake. *For Colored Girls Who Have Considered Suicide When the Rainbow Was Enuf.* New York: Bantam Books, 1980.

Vogel, Paula. *How I Learned to Drive.* New York: Dramatists Play Service, 1997.

Wilson, August. *Two Trains Running.* New York: Plume Drama, 1993.

Fiction

Allison, Dorothy. *Trash: Short Stories.* Ithaca, N.Y.: Firebrand Books, 1988.

Campbell, Bonnie Jo. *American Salvage.* Detroit: Wayne State University Press, 2009.

Carver, Raymond. *What We Talk About When We Talk About Love.* New York: Knopf, 1981.

Gibbon, Maureen. *Swimming Sweet Arrow.* New York: Little Brown, 2000.

Hannah, Barry. *Captain Maximus.* New York: Knopf, 1985.

Hirson, Denis. "Arrest Me." In *Sudden Fiction International.* Ed. Robert Shapard and James Thomas. New York: Norton, 1989.

Johnson, Denis. *Jesus' Son.* New York: Farrar, Straus and Giroux, 1992.

Kincaid, Jamaica. "Girl." In *The Vintage Book of Contemporary American Short Stories.* Ed. Tobias Wolff. New York: Vintage, 1994.

Musgrave, Susan. *Cargo of Orchids*. Toronto: Alfred A. Knopf Canada, 2000.

Oates, Joyce Carol. "The Boy." *Sudden Fiction International*. Ed. Robert Shapard and James Thomas. New York: Norton, 1989.

O'Brien, Tim. *The Things They Carried*. Boston: Houghton Mifflin, 1990.

Packer, ZZ. *Drinking Coffee Elsewhere*. New York: Riverhead Books, 2003.

Quindlen, Anna. *Black and Blue*. New York: Random House, 1998.

Sapphire [Ramona Lofton]. *Push*. New York: Random House, 1996.

Shotland, Sarah. *Junkette*. Belford, N.J.: White Gorilla Press, 2014.

Wideman, John Edgar. *Briefs: Stories for the Palm of the Mind*. Raleigh, N.C.: Lulu, 2010.

Wood, Monica. "Disappearing." In *Sudden Fiction International*. Ed. Robert Shapard and James Thomas. New York: Norton, 1989.

Writing and Other Resources

Adams, Kathleen. *Journal to the Self: Twenty-two Paths to Personal Growth*. New York: Grand Central, 1990.

Alexander, Buzz. *Is William Martinez Not Our Brother? Twenty Years of the Prison Creative Arts Project*. Ann Arbor: University of Michigan Press, 2010.

Bolton, Gillie, Victoria Field, and Kate Thompson, eds. *Writing Works: A Resource Handbook for Therapeutic Writing Workshops and Activities*. London: Jessica Kingsley, 2006.

Cameron, Julia. *The Artist's Way: A Spiritual Path to Higher Creativity*. New York: Tarcher/Putnam, 1992.

Chavis, Geri Giebel. *Poetry and Story Therapy: The Healing Power of Creative Expression*. London: Jessica Kingsley, 2011.

Daniell, Beth. *A Communion of Friendship: Literacy, Spiritual Practice, and Women in Recovery*. Carbondale: Southern Illinois University Press, 2003.

DeSalvo, Louise. *Writing as a Way of Healing: How Telling Our Stories Transforms Our Lives*. Boston: Beacon Press, 1999.

Goldberg, Natalie. *Writing Down the Bones: Freeing the Writer Within*. Boston: Shambhala. 1986.

Gray, Katti. "The Run-On Sentence: Eddie Ellis on Life after Prison." *The Sun*, July 2013.

Johnson, David. "Creative Spirits: The Arts in the Treatment of Substance Abuse." In *Essays on the Creative Arts Therapies: Imaging the Birth of a Profession.* Springfield, Ill.: Charles C. Thomas, 1999.

Lamott, Anne. *Bird by Bird: Some Instructions on Writing and Life.* New York: Doubleday, 1994.

Leonard, Linda Schierse. *Witness to the Fire: Creativity and the Veil of Addiction.* Boston: Shambhala, 2011.

Levin, Jay, ed. *The Fix.* www.thefix.com.

Malchiodi, Cathy A., ed. *Handbook of Art Therapy.* New York: Guilford Press, 2012.

National Association for Poetry Therapy. Des Moines, Iowa.

Norton, Lisa Dale. *Shimmering Images: A Handy Little Guide to Writing Memoir.* New York: St. Martin's, 2008.

PEN American Center. *Handbook for Writers in Prison.* New York: PEN American Center, 2010.

Rohr, Richard. *Breathing under Water: Spirituality and the Twelve Steps.* Cincinnati: St. Anthony Messenger Press, 2011.

Rosen, Kim. *Saved by a Poem: The Transformative Power of Words.* New York: Hay House, 2009.

Simon, John Oliver, and Leslie Simon. *The Caged Collective! The Life and Death of the Folsom Prison Creative Writers' Workshop.* Berkeley: Aldebaran Review, 1978.

St. Germain, Sheryl, and Sarah Shotland. Words Without Walls. www.wordswithoutwalls.com.

Thomas, Abigail. *Thinking about Memoir.* New York: Sterling, 2008.

Williams, Rachel Marie-Crane. *Teaching the Arts behind Bars.* Boston: Northeastern University Press, 2003.

Wilson, Marie. "Art Therapy in Addictions Treatment: Creativity and Shame Reduction." In *Handbook of Art Therapy.* Ed. Cathy A. Malchiodi. New York: Guilford Press, 2012.

CONTRIBUTORS' NOTES

DOROTHY ALLISON describes herself as a working-class storyteller. Her novel *Bastard Out of Carolina* was a finalist for the 1992 National Book Award. The themes in her writing reflect her background growing up poor and female in the South. She writes affectingly about familial violence and rape.

JOHN AMEN is the author of four collections of poetry. He founded and continues to edit the *Pedestal Magazine*. He has led writing workshops in prisons, homeless shelters, and recovery centers and corresponds regularly with inmates imprisoned throughout the United States.

JEN ASHBURN served as student coordinator and teacher for the Words Without Walls (WWW) program in Pittsburgh, teaching creative writing classes in the Allegheny County Jail (ACJ) and facilitating a weekly community workshop called VoiceCATCH, designed for those released from jail who want to keep writing.

JIMMY SANTIAGO BACA's memoir, *A Place to Stand*, recounts the story of how he became a poet while in prison. Of Apache and Chicano descent, he is the founder of Cedar Tree, a literary nonprofit that provides outreach programs and writing workshops for prisoners, ex-prisoners, at-risk youth, and underserved communities.

R. DWAYNE BETTS is a spokesperson for the Campaign for Youth Justice, an organization dedicated to stopping the trial and incarceration of juveniles in the adult justice system. He is author of the memoir *A Question of Freedom: A Memoir of Learning, Survival, and Coming of Age in Prison* as well as a book of poems.

ROGER BONAIR-AGARD's most recent poetry collection, *Bury My Clothes*, was a finalist for the 2013 National Book Award for Poetry. A native of

Trinidad, he was a member of the 1997 Nuyorican Poets Cafe Poetry Slam. He is cofounder of the louderARTS project and teaches poetry at the Cook County Temporary Juvenile Detention Center in Chicago.

GREG BOTTOMS is best known for his memoirs, *Angelhead,* which chronicles his brother's schizophrenia, and *Fight Scenes,* stories from his adolescence. A collection of graphic memoirs and stories titled *Pitiful Criminals,* with illustrations by W. David Powell, is forthcoming.

ERIC BOYD is an alum of the Words Without Walls program and a winner of the 2012 PEN Prison Writing Contest. His first collection of short stories, a chapbook called *Whiskey Sour,* was released in the spring of 2012. Currently he attends MFA classes at the Writer's Foundry of St. Joseph's College in Brooklyn.

GWENDOLYN BROOKS authored numerous books of poems, including *A Street in Bronzeville* and *Annie Allen.* As Illinois Poet Laureate, she visited prisons, hospitals, drug rehabilitation centers, and schools to speak about poetry. She was the first black woman to win the Pulitzer Prize.

JAMES BROWN is the author of seven books, most recently *This River,* the sequel to his memoir, *The Los Angeles Diaries,* in which he chronicles a life marked by alcohol and drug abuse, mental illness, and the suicides of his two siblings. He maintains a website on drugs, alcohol, and literature.

BONNIE JO CAMPBELL is the author of several short fiction collections, including *Women and Other Animals* and *American Salvage,* which was a finalist for the 2009 National Book Award in Fiction. She teaches writing in the low-residency program at Pacific University.

CLAIRE CHAFEE is a playwright whose works include *Why We Have a Body, Darwin's Finches, Even among These Rocks,* and *Five Women on a Hill in Spain.* She writes about sexual identity, feminism, and lends her voice to 3Girls Theatre Company, which aims to bring more women's voices to the stage.

CHRISTOPHER DAVIS has published three poetry collections: *The Tyrant of the Past and the Slave of the Future, The Patriot,* and *A History of the Only War.* He has written about the murder of a younger brother as well as the effect of AIDS on modern gay culture.

TOI DERRICOTTE is the author of five verse collections, most recently *The Undertaker's Daughter,* and the memoir *The Black Notebooks.* She is cofounder of Cave Canem: A Home for Black Poetry and on the Academy of American Poets' board of chancellors and the Words Without Walls board.

NATALIE DIAZ is the author of the poetry collection *When My Brother Was an Aztec.* She directs a language revitalization program and works with the last Elder speakers of the Mojave language at Fort Mojave.

MARK DOTY is the author of eight books of poetry, four books of creative nonfiction, and a handbook for writers. His writing has been much informed by the AIDS epidemic. He is the only American poet to win the T. S. Eliot Prize in the UK.

EVE ENSLER is an award-winning playwright, activist, and performer. She is best known for *The Vagina Monologues* and V-Day, a movement to stop violence against women and girls. V-Day campaigns around the world host benefit performances of *The Vagina Monologues, Any One of Us: Words from Prison,* and other plays.

NICK FLYNN is the author of seven books, most recently *The Reenactments,* the final book in his memoir trilogy. The first book in the trilogy, *Another Bullshit Night in Suck City,* traces the reunion with his father at the Pine Street Inn, a homeless shelter in Boston, where Flynn worked and where his father showed up as a "guest."

MAUREEN GIBBON is the author of two novels, *Swimming Sweet Arrow* and *Thief,* and the poetry collection *Magdalena.* She is a graduate of Barnard College and the Iowa Writers' Workshop. She writes unflinchingly about sexuality, violence, work, and drug use.

STEPHON HAYES was a Words Without Walls student in 2012. His poetry reflects not only his frustration with his life experiences, having been a repeat offender, but also explores hope and redemption. Hayes was the co-winner of the Words Without Walls 2012 Sandra Gould Ford Prize.

TERRANCE HAYES is the author of the poetry collections *Lighthead, Wind in a Box, Hip Logic,* and *Muscular Music. Lighthead* won the 2010 National Book Award. A member of the Words Without Walls board, he has come into jails to share his work and interact with those incarcerated.

MARIE HOWE is the New York State Poet Laureate. She is the author of *The Kingdom of Ordinary Time*, *What the Living Do*, and *The Good Thief* as well as coeditor of *In the Company of My Solitude: American Writing from the AIDS Pandemic*.

TYEHIMBA JESS is the author of *leadbelly*, a poetry collection that explores the life of blues musician Huddie "Lead Belly" Ledbetter. Jess was Chicago's Poetry Ambassador to Accra, Ghana. He is also the author of *African American Pride: Celebrating Our Achievements, Contributions, and Enduring Legacy*.

ALLISON JOSEPH's most recent poetry collection is *My Father's Kites: Poems*. She is director of the Young Writers Workshop at Southern Illinois University Carbondale, which she founded in 1999, a four-day summer program for high school students. She is also a founding editor of *Crab Orchard Review*.

NATALIE KENVIN is the author of *Bruise Theory*, chosen by poet Carolyn Forché as a finalist in the 1993 AWP Award Series. Kenvin writes on themes of emotional illness, mother-daughter relationships, love, and physical abuse, as well as the strength it takes to endure.

JESSICA KINNISON taught creative writing at the Allegheny County Jail as part of the WWW program. She now teaches creative writing in the Wellness University at Orleans Parish Prison as part of the Humanities: Orleans Parish Education Project (H:OPE) and at the Loyola University New Orleans Writing Institute.

ETHERIDGE KNIGHT began writing while at the Indiana State Prison. His first poetry collection, *Poems from Prison*, was published one year before he was released from prison. In 1970 he edited *Black Voices from Prison*. Knight rose from a life of poverty, crime, and drug addiction to become a prolific poet.

KEN LAMBERTON began his writing career in a creative writing workshop while he was in prison and quickly began publishing essays and articles. After his release, he completed an MFA in creative writing. He is the author of several books of nonfiction, including *Beyond Desert Walls: Essays from Prison*.

JOAN LARKIN's poetry collections include *Housework, Cold River,* and *My Body: New and Selected Poems.* She cofounded the independent press Out & Out Books and has coedited groundbreaking poetry anthologies such as *Gay and Lesbian Poetry in Our Time* and *Amazon Poetry.*

TRACY LETTS is an actor and playwright best known for his Pulitzer Prize–winning play *August: Osage County,* which was released as a feature film in 2013. His other plays include *Bug* and *Killer Joe.* Letts's plays are often about people struggling with moral and spiritual questions.

TERRA LYNN was a Words Without Walls student for two years. She wrote about her abusive marriage, suicide attempts, and mental health problems. Terra was a co-winner of the WWW 2012 Sandra Gould Ford Prize.

ANN MARLOWE is the author of three books, including the memoir *How to Stop Time: Heroin from A to Z,* about her own addiction to heroin. She is a journalist who covers Afghanistan and Libya for *World Affairs Journal, Wall Street Journal, New York Post,* and other publications.

HEATHER MCNAUGHER is the author of *System of Hideouts* and *Panic & Joy.* She has taught at the ACJ as part of the WWW program. Her work has appeared in *The Gay & Lesbian Review* and *Bellevue Literary Review,* a journal focused on illness, health, and healing.

W. S. MERWIN's poetry and prose focus on issues of social and environmental justice. He has won two Pulitzer Prizes for his books *The Carrier of Ladders* and *The Shadow of Sirius.* A practicing Buddhist, he has lived since the late 1970s on an old pineapple plantation in Hawaii, which he has painstakingly restored to its original rainforest state.

NAOMI SHIHAB NYE is the author of many poetry volumes as well as fiction and poetry for children and young adults. An Arab American, she gives voice to her experience through poems about heritage and peace. She has traveled to the Middle East and Asia for the U.S. Information Agency three times, promoting international goodwill through the arts.

JOYCE CAROL OATES most often explores the darker aspects of the human psyche through fictional characters who demonstrate a spiritual, intellectual, and sexual dysfunction. In addition to her over eighty books of fiction, Oates has also written a memoir, *A Widow's Tale*, chronicling her own experiences with severe depression.

TIM O'BRIEN is author of the best-selling novel *The Things They Carried* as well as several other novels, including *If I Die in a Combat Zone, Box Me Up and Ship Me Home*. He served in the U.S. Army in Vietnam, and much of his writing is inspired by his time in Vietnam.

SHARON OLDS's poetry collections include *Satan Says, The Dead and the Living,* and *The Unswept Room*. She teaches in the Graduate Creative Writing Program at New York University and helped found NYU workshop programs for veterans of the Afghanistan and Iraq wars and residents of Goldwater Hospital on Roosevelt Island.

GREGORY ORR is the author of ten collections of poetry, most recently *How Beautiful the Beloved,* as well as memoirs and books of essays. In poetry and prose, much of Orr's work focuses on life-changing events, including the unexpected death of his mother and his father's drug addiction.

ZZ PACKER is the author of the national best-seller *Drinking Coffee Elsewhere,* a collection of short stories. Her work often explores race, gender, and working-class life. She is currently at work on a novel about Buffalo Soldiers, blacks who left the South after the Civil War and traveled west.

ANNA QUINDLEN is the author of a dozen books, including the novel *Black and Blue,* which explores domestic violence. As a journalist, she is best known for her reporting on issues affecting women's lives, including the right to choose, women in politics, and the trials of modern motherhood.

SARAH RIES published her first book of poetry, *Come In, We're Open,* in 2010. She lives in Buffalo, New York, where her parents own the Woodlawn Diner, the inspiration for her book. She runs community workshops and readings from the diner.

SCOTT RUSSELL SANDERS is the author of twenty books, including *A Conservationist Manifesto* and *A Private History of Awe*. He has written about his father's alcoholism and his love for his father in early essays. Most of his recent work has focused on environmental issues and the importance of cultivating a connection with the natural world.

SAPPHIRE (Ramona Lofton) is the author of several books of poetry and prose, including *Push*, which was released as the film *Precious* in 2009. She has long been a supporter of the New York Writers Coalition, one of the largest community-based writing groups in the country. Her writing often explores incest and sexual violence, sexuality, and poverty.

TIM SEIBLES is the author of several poetry collections, his latest being *Fast Animal*. He has been a workshop leader for Cave Canem and the Hurston/ Wright Foundation, organizations dedicated to developing black writers. He has worked with WWW in the ACJ and is known for his sensuous, celebratory poems.

CHRISTINE STROUD works as the associate editor for Autumn House Press. Her poetry collection, *The Buried Return*, deals with themes of substance abuse, violence, and gender.

RHETT ISEMAN TRULL's first book of poetry, *The Real Warnings*, received the 2008 Anhinga Prize for Poetry. Trull writes of the brutal paradoxes of love and of loving damaged ones. She and her husband, Jeff Trull, publish *Cave Wall*, a literary journal of poetry.

MERSIHA TUZLIC took WWW creative writing classes in the ACJ, was a resident of Sojourner House in 2013 and 2014, and participated in two creative writing classes there. She won the WWW Sandra Gould Ford prize for her writing in 2014.

PAULA VOGEL is a Pulitzer Prize–winning playwright and women's rights advocate whose plays include *The Baltimore Waltz, And Baby Makes Seven*, and *How I Learned to Drive*, which explores the strained sexual relationship between an uncle and niece, fueled by manipulation, alcohol, and psychological violence.

DEREK WALCOTT won the 1992 Nobel Prize in Literature. A poet and playwright from Saint Lucia in the West Indies, he identifies himself primarily as a Caribbean writer. Much of his writing is inspired by his desire to make sense of the legacy of deep colonial damage.

JESMYN WARD has written two novels and a memoir titled *Men We Reaped*. Her novel *Salvage the Bones* won the 2011 National Book Award for Fiction. Her fiction tells stories of poor black siblings growing up on the Gulf

Coast, and her memoir explores the lives of her brother and four other young black men who lost their lives in her hometown.

BRUCE WEIGL is author of over a dozen books of poetry and a memoir, *The Circle of Hanh*. A Vietnam War veteran and practicing Buddhist, he founded a student veterans group at Lorain Community College. Weigl writes, "The paradox of my life as a writer is that the war ruined my life and in return gave me my voice."

JOHN EDGAR WIDEMAN is the author of thirteen books, most recently *Briefs: Stories for the Palm of the Mind*. His nonfiction book *Brothers and Keepers* is inspired by the life of his brother, who is serving a life sentence for murder. He is a two-time winner of the International PEN/Faulkner Award.

AUGUST WILSON was an award-winning playwright from Pittsburgh, best remembered for his ten plays known as *The Pittsburgh Cycle*, each play covering one decade of the twentieth century. He cofounded the community-based Black Horizon Theater and the Kuntu Writers Workshop in Pittsburgh.

MONICA WOOD is the author of the novels *Any Bitter Thing*, *Secret Language*, and *My Only Story* and the memoir *When We Were the Kennedys*. She oversees a creative writing program for women at the Maine Correctional Center.

FRANZ WRIGHT is author of the Pulitzer Prize–winning poetry collection *Walking to Martha's Vineyard* and numerous other volumes of poetry. He has taught creative writing in universities and worked in mental health clinics. He writes often about his own experiences with depression, drugs, and alcohol.

GARY YOUNG is the author of several collections of poetry, most recently *Even So: New and Selected Poems*. He is the editor and publisher of Greenhouse Review Press. His recent books employ the prose-poem format exclusively and are meditations on the everyday experience. Young has written that he believes every poem is a prayer.

ACKNOWLEDGMENTS AND CREDITS

We want to thank the team who generously assisted in creating this anthology: Jonny Blevins, Dakota Garilli, Erin Hutton, and Kinsley Stocum. Erin Hutton deserves special thanks for her work obtaining permissions as well as overall organizational assistance. Thanks also to those who offered important support in other ways: Jack Pischke at the Allegheny County Jail; Cheryl Coney and Sharon Jones at Sojourner House; Kerry Vance at the State Correctional Institution in Pittsburgh; the Words Without Walls board of directors; and the many dedicated WWW teachers over the years: Jen Ashburn, Brigette Bernagozzi, Jonathan Blevins, Adrienne Block, Matt Bohn, Leah Brennan, John Caputo, Laura Castonguay, Tony Ciotoli, Claudette Dagorn, Alicia Dean, Andy Decker, Laura Drumm, Rob Farrell, Dakota Garilli, Richard Gegick, D. Gilson, Ben Gwin, Sarah Hamm, Whitney Hayes, Libba Hockley, Jessica Kinnison, Alysa Landry, Cody Leutgens, Siobhan Lyons, Libba Nichols, Hayley Notter, Katrina Otuonye, Vincent Rendoni, Ian Riggins, Ryan Rydzewski, Lindsey Scherloum, Jessica Server, Marla Sink-Druzgal, Alison Taverna, Nicholette Telech, Kelly Lynn Thomas, Maryann Ullmann, Lorena Williams, Tess Wilson, and Jamie Wyatt.

Henry and Laurie Mansell Reich's generous support has been critical in the creation of this anthology, for the creation of the Mansell Fellowship for a graduate student to teach in the WWW program, and for the continuing health of the WWW program. We also want to thank Fred and Melanie Brown and Tom and Margaret Whitford for their support of WWW. We appreciate the ongoing contributions of Chatham University, which provided a large part of the funding for permissions for this anthology as well as invaluable assistance in the grant-writing necessary to keep Words Without Walls alive, and to the Pittsburgh Foundation, whose assistance has allowed us to buy books for those who need them and invite contributors to this anthology to enter our jails and read from their work.

⦵ ⦵ ⦵ ⦵

Dorothy Allison, "River of Names," from *Trash: Short Stories*, published by Firebrand Books in 1988. Reprinted by permission of the author.

John Amen, "23," from *Writers on the Edge: 22 Writers Speak about Addiction and Dependency* (Modern History Press, 2010). Reprinted by permission of the author.

Jen Ashburn, "Bed Sheets," first published in *The Poet's Billow*, and "Schubert's Unfinished Symphony." Used by permission of the author.

Jimmy Santiago Baca, "Coming into Language," from *A Place to Stand*, copyright © 2001 by Jimmy Santiago Baca. Used by permission of Grove/Atlantic, Inc. Any third-party use of this material, outside of this publication, is prohibited.

Reginald Dwayne Betts, "Ghazal" ["Men bleed without insight . . . "] and "Red Onion State Prison," from *Shahid Reads His Own Palm*, copyright © 2010 by Reginald Dwayne Betts. Reprinted with the permission of the Permissions Company, Inc., on behalf of Alice James Books, www .alicejamesbooks.org

Reginald Dwayne Betts, "Thirty Minutes," from *A Question of Freedom: A Memoir of Learning, Survival, and Coming of Age in Prison*, copyright © 2009 by Reginald Dwayne Betts. Used by permission of Avery Publishing, an imprint of Penguin Group (USA), LLC.

Roger Bonair-Agard, "Ode to the Man Who Grabbed My Arm in the Bar" and "Ode to the Man Who Leaned Out the Truck to Call Me Nigger," from *Bury My Clothes*, published by Haymarket Books in 2013.

Greg Bottoms, "Fight," from *Fight Scenes*, published by Counterpoint Press in 2008.

Eric Boyd, "Anything for Johnny." Used by permission of the author.

Says, copyright © 1980 by Sharon Olds. Reprinted by permission of the University of Pittsburgh Press.

Gregory Orr, "If There's a God . . . " from *The Caged Owl: New and Selected Poems*, copyright © 2002 by Gregory Orr. Reprinted with permission of the Permissions Company, Inc., on behalf of Copper Canyon Press, www.coppercanyonpress.org.

ZZ Packer, from *Drinking Coffee Elsewhere*, copyright © 2003 by ZZ Packer. Used by permission of Riverhead Books, an imprint of Penguin Group (USA), LLC.

Anna Quindlen, from *Black and Blue: A Novel*, copyright © 1998 by Anna Quindlen. Used by permission of Random House, an imprint and division of Random House, LLC. All rights reserved.

Sara Ries, "Dad's at the Diner," from *Come In, We're Open*, published by the National Federation of State Poetry Societies in 2010.

Scott Russell Sanders, "Under the Influence," copyright © 1989 by Scott Russell Sanders; first published in *Harper's;* from the author's *Secrets of the Universe* (Beacon, 1991); reprinted by permission of the author.

Sapphire, from *Push*, copyright © 1996 by Sapphire/Ramona Lofton. Used by permission of Alfred A. Knopf, an imprint of the Knopf Doubleday Publishing Group, a division of Random House, LLC. All rights reserved.

Tim Seibles, "For Brothers Everywhere" and "Natasha in a Mellow Mood," from *Hurdy-Gurdy*, copyright © 1992 by Tim Seibles. Reprinted with the permission of the Permissions Company, Inc., on behalf of the Cleveland State University Poetry Center.

Sarah Shotland, "An Incomplete List of Things I'm No Longer Doing at the Saint," from *Junkette*, published by White Gorilla Press in 2014.

Sheryl St. Germain, "Addiction" and "Eating," from *Let It Be a Dark Roux: New and Selected Poems*, copyright © 2007 by Sheryl St. Germain. Reprinted by permission of Autumn House Press. "Young Night," from *Rape, Incest, Battery: Women Writing Out the Pain*, published by Texas Christian University Press in 2000.

ABOUT THE EDITORS

SHERYL ST. GERMAIN has facilitated countless readings and community projects in the past twenty-five years, including the Dallas Poets Happy Hour Reading series and the Dallas Poets Network; creative writing workshops for troubled teens and victims of domestic violence in Texas; creative writing workshops for the women of the Mitchellville Correctional Institution in Iowa; and the Words Without Walls program in Pittsburgh. She has taught creative writing at the University of Texas at Dallas, the University of Louisiana at Lafayette, Knox College, and Iowa State University. For the past nine years she has been director of the MFA program in Creative Writing at Chatham University. Of her ten published poetry and prose books, the most recent is *Navigating Disaster: Sixteen Essays of Love and a Poem of Despair.*

SARAH SHOTLAND earned her MFA in fiction and screenwriting at Chatham University and is the author of the novel *Junkette*. Her plays have been produced in Chicago, Dallas, New Orleans, and Austin as well as internationally in Madrid and Chongqing, People's Republic of China. As a teaching artist, she has worked for over fifteen years in and outside of academic classrooms, teaching theater and creative writing in jails, rehabilitation facilities, professional theaters, after-school programs, retirement communities, and veterans' centers. She is the program coordinator of Words Without Walls at Chatham University.

WORDS WITHOUT WALLS (WWW) is a collaborative venture among the Chatham University MFA program, the Allegheny County Jail, the State Correctional Institution of Pittsburgh, and Sojourner House (a drug and treatment facility for mothers and their children). With the help of MFA graduate students, alumni and some faculty, the program teaches sixteen creative writing courses a year to these vulnerable populations and brings them in contact with inspirational published writers. WWW publishes the best writing from the classes in yearly chapbooks, offers a prize for the best writings, and facilitates public readings for those who are released from the jail, prison, or rehabilitation facility. The program also offers a weekly creative writing workshop in Pittsburgh as follow-up for those who are interested post release.